HOLY

TO

YAHVEH

By

Terrye Goldblum Seedman

June 25, 1997
Dear Uncle Stanley and aunt Florence,
May Yahveh, the God of Israel bless
you with a deeper understanding
of His Eternal plan and infinite love
for all people - especially to His chosen
people - the Jewish race of whom we are
privileged to be heirs. In His love,
Terrye

Published by:
Longwood Communications
397 Kingslake Drive
DeBary, FL 32713
(904) 774-1991

Further permission has been extended to the author by The Lockman Foundation for the following:

1. All quotations appear in italics. Words in the NASB text that are already italicized are not differentiated.

2. The Hebrew name *YAHveh* replaces "the LORD" as it appears in the NASB. The original name *YAHshua* replaces "Jesus" and the term *Messiah* replaces "Christ." In many of the New Testament verses cited, *YAHveh's* sacred name replaces the title "God" and "the Lord."

3. Upper and lower case caps (SMALL CAPS) are used for special emphasis the author wishes certain parts of a quotation to have.

4. Clarifying words added to the text appear in brackets and in Roman type. No other indication of these (i.e., "emphasis added") is included with the reference when the quote is from the NASB.

5. When the NASB text is already capitalized, this has been maintained. In instances of the author's desire to add emphasis to such text, bold type is used.

Verses marked NKJV are taken from the *New King James Version*, Thomas Nelson Inc., 1982.

Verses marked AMP are taken from *The Amplified Bible*, Zondervan Publishing House, 1965.

Verses marked NIV are taken from *The New International Version*, The Zondervan Corporation, 1985.

Verses marked KJV are taken from the *Authorized King James Version*.

The Goldblum Seedman Corporation
P.O. Box 1371
Salinas, CA 93902

Table of Contents

CONTENTS

CONTENTS

About the Cover

The cover design originally was given by inspiration to the author upon conception of this book. Each symbol conveys an important theme in *Holy to YAHveh*. The purpose of both the book and its cover is to bring a remnant to a place of reverential awe of the Almighty as they are drawn closer to His glorious presence, learning to bring Him the praise and honor due His holy name.

The meaning of each symbol or object will be clarified within the book. The crown bearing the Hebrew inscription has a dual symbolism. It represents the *sacred diadem* (Ex 39:30) initially worn by the Levitical priests; it also is an invisible seal worn by those who have been drawn close to *YAHveh* through the blood of the Lamb, *YAHshua* the Messiah. The diadem worn on the forehead of the priest was inscribed with the words *Kodesh La YAHveh,* or "*Holy to YAHveh.*" The second meaning of the crown is the *"crown of glory"* (1Pe 5:4) that awaits a redeemed remnant of Jews and Gentiles who have been consecrated as a holy priesthood to serve in His soon-coming messianic kingdom.

The golden ark of the covenant with the cherubim has been described in the Holy Scriptures as the symbolic earthly throne of the Holy One of Israel who dwelled in the midst of His people. The ark is *"called by the NAME, the Name of YAHveh Almighty, who is enthroned above the cherubim that are on the ark"* (2Sa 6:2). In it were housed the Ten Commandments and other symbolic elements. The Hebrew letters on the front of the ark are *Yod Hey Vav Hey*—read from right to left spelling the sacred name *YAHveh.* The golden atonement cover on top of the ark under the cherubim's wings is known as the mercy seat. The ark, *YAHveh's* throne, rested in the Most Holy Place of the sanctuary. His throne room, the Holy of Holies, was accessible only one day each year on *Yom Kippur* (the Day of Atonement), and then only by the high priest. This priest had the awesome responsibility and privilege to appear before *YAHveh's* presence, bringing the blood of the sacrificial animal to make atonement for his sins and the sins of all the people of Israel.

The ultimate and final sacrifice was made through the Lamb of *YAHveh*—*YAHshua* the Messiah. He came to dwell among His people Israel and shed His blood as the Passover Lamb and *Yom Kippur* sacrifice. His life's blood was poured out on earth and eternally covers the mercy seat of the heavenly ark, thus mercifully opening the way for both Jews and Gentiles to be reconciled to a holy God and to one another.

Through the atoning blood of *YAHshua*, a remnent has been redeemed to be a priesthood who is *Holy to YAHveh*. This remnent has the privileged access moment by moment into *YAHveh's* life changing presence.

Beautiful reproductions of this original cover design are available in 18 x 24 inch frameable posters. For further information see SUPPLEMENTARY ITEMS at the end of this book.

About the Author

The Scripture says, *"And you will seek Me and find Me, when you search for Me with all your heart"* (Jer 29:13), and *"... He is the Rewarder of those who earnestly and diligently seek Him ..."* (Heb 11:6 AMP).

Terrye Goldblum Seedman, since her earliest remembrance, has had an unquenchable thirst and an insatiable hunger to know intimately the God of her forefathers: Abraham, Isaac, and Jacob. After graduating with honors from UCLA she embarked on a prolonged and compelling search for eternal truth. Through many dramatic trials and great opposition, Terrye met her Messiah and became a completed Jew through faith in Him.

The author devoted the past fifteen years to intense scriptural study, prayer, and intimacy with her Savior. During these years, Terrye has found that many vital aspects of the holy Hebraic root of the Scriptures have been obscured and hidden under the doctrines and traditions of religion. In wholehearted devotion and passionate love for the Almighty and His immutable truths, she has dedicated her life to teach others to love Him with all their heart, mind, soul, and strength. Through this motivating desire she has taught in numerous religious and church settings including television, radio interviews, and seminars. She has successfully led many on to the uncompromised path of holiness and true spiritual revival.

Terrye and her Jewish husband Ron, and their sons Joshua and Joel, are leaders of the Promised Blessing Ministry and the Goldblum Seedman Corporation, which are dedicated to reconciling Jewish and Gentile people through *YAHshua* the Messiah for the glory of *YAHveh's memorial-name.*

Dedication

It is with reverential awe that I humbly
dedicate this book to
YAHveh, the Holy One of Israel
whose *memorial-name* will be magnified
to a place of prominence
within the hearts of a righteous remnant;
and to
YAHveh's only Son, YAHshua, the Messiah
Who willingly poured out His atoning life's blood
for all people
—the Jew first, then to the Gentile—
that *together* they would share
in the promise of eternal life.

Acknowledgments

First and foremost, all honor and praise go to *YAHveh*, for revealing to me the truth of my Messiah and the holy Hebraic root of the messianic faith. I thank Him for His mercy in manifesting His holy character and revealing the importance of His divine *memorial-name*. In all humility I thank my heavenly Father for the unfathomable privilege of being the vessel through whom this life-changing book was written. Thank you *YAHveh*, for what is impossible with man is possible with You.

I thank my loving husband Ron, who's been willing to sacrifice his comforts, time, and energies. Thank you for your unconditional love and for being a noble servant who has taken up immeasurable slack in our family, releasing me to do the work required for the last three years. You've been a true helper and encourager; together we'll rejoice in the fruit of our labors. Additional appreciation is due because of your devoted advisory role in creating the book's cover.

To my precious sons Joshua and Joel, you bring heaven's delights to my heart. Thank you for your patience and lovingkindness as you willingly gave up your mother's time and attentions to this holy work. Special thanks to Joshua, my first-born, for his heavenly piano playing which uplifts me with glorious refreshment. And thank you dear Joel; you are truly my bringer of joy and fortifier of my faith. I'm so grateful for the tenderness of your soft, sweet heart which has mightily blessed your mom.

Deepest gratitude to the Botelho family—Greg, Teri, Stephen and Katie. Thank you Greg for being a beloved brother and a steadfast pillar of support for me in this glorious, yet difficult journey. Precious Teri, the one whom *YAHveh* chose to be by my side much as a mid-wife bringing forth a new born. You're a devoted assistant, allowing me to accomplish that which *YAHveh* ordained. Your loving help, prayers, and selfless service in His kingdom have poured out great blessings upon *Holy to YAHveh*. Stephen, your prayers have availed much; and thank you Katie for your willingness to share your mother as we all work together for *YAHveh's* glory.

David Corpus, *"a man after YAHveh's own heart,"* thank you for your prayerful support and continued encouragement. Your contributions to the art work and Hebrew letters of the book's cover are also deeply appreciated.

Helen Kocker; for years you've been a caring spiritual sister. Thank you for being the one whom *YAHveh* used to exhort me to write this book.

Don Mathews; deepest gratitude is due to you as a spiritual father, watching over our family as a loving daddy watches over his children. Your presence in our lives has been a gift from our heavenly Father.

My appreciation to the Moitoso family—Roger, Barbara, Neena, Natalie, Nyssa, and Nicholas. Each of you has brought joy and practical as well as spiritual support. Thank you, Barbara, for always being there to lift my spirits, and Roger for working on the cover as well as the seals for the twelve tribes of Israel.

To Mark and Shelly Ryburn—thank you Mark for being available as the on-call physician to keep the computer doing its job to facilitate my writing. Your loyalty and invaluable support also as a co-laborer and prayer warrior has helped keep me afloat during difficult times. Added appreciation for all you have done in helping to create a very special Internet Web site for *Holy to YAHveh*. And thank you Shelly for being patient the many times Mark had to make "emergency house calls."

Thank you Anne Vanoli, for your prayerful support and dedicated assistance in typing the first draft of the manuscript. Thank you for your beautiful music that has continually blessed us, filling our hearts and mouths with joyful praise. Chris, you're a beacon lighting our lives with the presence of *YAHshua*.

Thanks and appreciation are due to many others who've been on the periphery praying fervently for *YAHveh's* purposes through this book—Jane Anthony, Jessie and Cecilia Bravo, Cort and Candy Elliott, Marian Fritz, Alfred and Vickie Gavina, Zarayah Israel, Kathy Morasco, Robert and Femia Perez, Manuel and Mary Lou Robledo and Leslie Tankersley.

Added thanksgiving is definitely in order to my publisher, Murray Fisher, and his wife Donna. Dear Murray, you've been a treasure chest of blessing. Your gentleness accompanied with experience and wisdom have been invaluable in making this book a reality. Thank you for your patience and wise counsel.

Overflowing gratitude goes to Pike Lambeth and The Lockman Foundation for granting permission to restore the original holy *memorial-names* of *YAHveh* and *YAHshua* the Messiah to references quoted from the *New American Standard Bible*. May the Holy One of Israel abundantly bless you with the promised blessings of Genesis 12:3.

Wayne Buchanan, my editor; what joy overflows my heart because of the great privilege of interacting with such a precious man. Our dialoging for the past months of editing has been as one going from glory to glory as you critiqued, advised, and edited.

Thank you also, Dana Shafer, for the wonderful assistance and biblical insight you added to your father's editing process. I'm looking forward to your work as primary editor for the workbook to accompany and supplement *Holy to YAHveh.*

To Geoff Sprague goes deep appreciation for your patience as you skillfully labored to create the professional refinements and intricate color illustrations which beautifully perfected this book's cover for *YAHveh's* glory.

Jeff Brown, thank you for helping to refine the seals of the twelve tribes of Israel. Your expertise has truly created a beautiful and dynamic web site on the Internet.

Pastor Jeffrey Lemucchi, thank you for allowing your inspirational letter to the rabbi to be printed as an example of reconciliation for others to humbly follow.

Kurt Kessel, thank you for your patience and diligence in doing a beautiful job typesetting this book.

To all of those mentioned above, I pray that the storehouses of heaven pour out unfathomable blessings upon you and your families because of your faithfulness. Truly the promise of Genesis 12:3 for *YAHveh's* blessings to be upon those who bless the Jews are part of your eternal inheritance.

— *Terrye Goldblum Seedman*

A Preliminary Explanation
The Use of the Holy Names *YAHveh* and *YAHshua*

YAHveh (YHVH) is the original *memorial-name* of the eternal living God. Traditional biblical scholarship acknowledges this.

The title, *LORD*, used in most translations of the Bible is the accepted substitute for the original Old Testament name, pronounced "*YAHveh.*" This Hebrew word is commonly known as the *Tetragrammaton*, a word derived from the Greek which means "four letters."

In the New Testament, the name, *YAHveh*, has been substituted with the titles, *Lord* and *God*. These are translated from the Greek words κύριος *(kurios)*, "Lord," and Θεός *(theos)*, "God."

With permission from the Lockman Foundation, the author has restored the *memorial-name YAHveh*, to its original place within passages quoted in this book from the Old Testament, the *New American Standard Bible* (NASB). In the New Testament verses where *YAHveh's* name replaces the title "God" or "the Lord," this is the author's best approximation. This issue has been obscured due to the Greek translations neglecting the importance and use of the divine names.

It is the author's humble intent to reveal, exalt, and restore the original and sacred names of *YAHveh* and *YAHshua* to their rightful place of preeminence within the holy Scriptures and the hearts of a holy remnant.

The vital issue regarding the use of the divine names hopefully will be clarified throughout *Holy to YAHveh*.

Preface

In November 1993, after several years of public speaking and teaching about *the Holy One of Israel*, the Messiah, and the Hebrew roots of Christianity, a dear friend said, "Terrye, you should write this vital message in a book."

I questioned the Almighty whether or not I was to be the vessel through whom such a book should be written. He, who is the Living God, mercifully answered and within my beseeching heart I heard a gentle voice say, "Isaiah, chapter 8."

Wondering whether I had heard my own vain imaginations or truly heard His voice, I opened the Scriptures and began to read. Instantly, the words spoken to Isaiah came to life and literally leaped off the page, answering my heart's deep yearning and questioning. It read: *"Then YAHVEH said to me, 'Take for yourself a large tablet and write on it in ordinary letters ...'"* (v. 1).

I heard and immediately began to obey. My dedication to this awesome commission has taken me on a three-year difficult, yet glorious journey into His divine presence. This book is the fruit of my obedience and intense fellowship with the Holy One, and the offspring of His faithfulness. He, Who is *"... the Glory of Israel ..."* (1Sa 15:29) and the *"... LIGHT OF REVELATION TO THE GENTILES, ..."* (Lk 2:32) is exalted and magnified on these pages.

Holy to YAHveh honors His chosen people, the twelve tribes of Israel, who are forever engraved upon His loving heart and the palms of His mighty hands. In sincere respect for His first-born beloved people, the seals of Israel are placed at the heading of each major part of this book.

It is the author's greatest hope and intention that the Almighty will complete His purpose to have a people who are *Holy to YAHveh*, a righteous remnant who will pour out their lives for the praise, honor, and glory due His holy *memorial-name*. May you, the reader, have eyes to see the splendor of His majesty, a receptive heart to beat with His, and an open mind to grasp His eternal purposes for all mankind—for the Jew and the Gentile alike.

Through the prophet Jeremiah, the Almighty speaks to our hearts today:

Thus says YAHVEH,

"Let not a wise man boast of his wisdom,

and let not the mighty man boast of his might

let not a rich man boast of his riches;

but let him who boasts boast of this,

THAT HE UNDERSTANDS AND KNOWS ME,

THAT I AM YAHVEH

who exercises lovingkindness, justice,

and righteousness on earth;

for I delight in these things," declares YAHVEH.

(Jer 9:23–24)

Introduction
The Wooing of a Righteous Remnant

The Mighty One, the God of Abraham, Isaac, and Jacob, is wooing a remnant, both Jews and Gentiles, to be reconciled to Him and one another—a righteous remnant who will know and worship Him in spirit and in truth. *Holy to YAHveh* is written to and for the wholehearted seeker of the Most High and His immutable truths. It is not recommended for casual reading.

It is the prayer of the author that the Spirit of Truth will take the reader on a pilgrimage onward and upward on the *Highway of Holiness* (Isa 35:8). May His Spirit open the seals of many vital Scriptures that have been hidden in the *scroll* of ancient biblical truths.

For many centuries these truths have been covered in obscurity by the doctrines of men and their historical religious traditions. The topic of the divine *memorial-names* of *YAHveh*, the Almighty, and *YAHshua*, the Messiah, will be a primary golden thread woven through the fabric of this book, creating a vivid portrait of the Holy One of Israel and the Messiah of mankind. The Hebraic root of the Messiah and messianic faith will be interwoven throughout this tapestry.

The goal of this book is that a divinely chosen remnant may be humbled and circumcised in heart, as the plumb line of biblical truths is held next to the crooked walls of certain doctrines and religious traditions. As errors or deceptions are revealed, this plumb line will become as a flint knife of circumcision in the hand of the Almighty.

Only a remnant circumcised in heart can rightly approach the Shekinah glory (divine presence) of the Most High. Many will grieve with broken and contrite hearts, as they clearly see how far religious systems with their self-centered ways have veered from *YAHveh's* precepts and holy commandments.

According to the ancient prophets, the Almighty's righteous judgment will soon fall upon those who veer from His truth. The Hebrew apostle Peter said, *"And so we have the prophetic word made more sure, to which you do well to pay attention as to a lamp shining in a dark place ..."* (2Pe 1:19). It is the author's deepest desire that this book, along with the enabling guidance of the Spirit of Truth, will help illuminate the words of the prophets.

Over the last two thousand years, various religious systems have greatly neglected the Old Testament Scriptures. Due to the absence of the bright light of the prophets' words and the limited knowledge of the Hebrew root of the Messiah, many Jews and Gentiles alike have made their spiritual pilgrimages on a confusing and dimly lit path. Their pathway has been overshadowed by religious traditions rather than the sure light of the Creator's full counsel and countenance. Messiah sacrificed His precious blood to redeem and consecrate a remnant as a priesthood made *Holy to YAHveh*. He is calling out Jews from every tribe of Israel and Gentiles from every nation and religious background. This chosen remnant will be as *"one new man,"* (Eph 2:15) redeemed and united through the atoning blood of the Hebrew Messiah. In willing response to the heart cry of the Mighty One of Israel (Isa 1:24), this humble remnant will leave the doomed world system with its false religious traditions to ascend His holy mountain.

There He will spread out a net of protection over those who love and worship Him *"in spirit and truth"* (Jn 4:23-24). There in His presence, His people will find a place of safety and refuge from the coming trials and ultimate divine judgments that will fall upon the earth.

The Hebrew prophets' words are now being fulfilled regarding the regathering of the Jewish people from the Gentile nations back to Israel, their divinely given homeland. The word describing this regathering and immigration is *AliYAH*, which is a Jewish expression meaning "to go up, to ascend." There is a parallel regathering in the spiritual realm as His Spirit (the *Ruach HaKodesh*) is wooing a remnant to make spiritual *AliYAH*, to return to the pure worship of *YAHveh*, and ascend into His glorious presence, as in days of old.

Through the words of His prophets and the heartbeat of this book, His Spirit is beseeching a remnant to make spiritual *AliYAH* saying:

"Come let us go up to the mountain of YAHVEH,
And to the house of the God of Jacob,
That He may teach us about His ways
And that we may walk in His paths." ...
THOUGH ALL THE PEOPLES WALK
EACH IN THE NAME OF HIS GOD,
AS FOR US, WE WILL WALK
IN THE NAME OF YAHVEH OUR GOD FOREVER AND EVER.
(Mic 4:2, 5)

PART ONE

Dedicated to the Tribes of Reuben and Simeon

Reuben   Simeon

Revive us, and we will CALL UPON THY NAME.

(Ps 80:18)

Surely the righteous will GIVE THANKS TO THY NAME;

the upright will dwell in Thy presence.

(Ps 140:13)

Chapter 1
The Unsealing of the Ancient Scroll

*Hear this ... I PROCLAIM TO YOU NEW THINGS FROM THIS TIME,
EVEN HIDDEN THINGS WHICH YOU HAVE NOT KNOWN. ... And
before today you have not heard them, ...* (Isa 48:1, 6-7)

In a very short time, ... the [spiritually] *deaf will HEAR THE
WORDS OF THE SCROLL* [the holy Scriptures], *and out of
gloom and darkness the eyes of the blind will see. Once
more the humble will rejoice ... and the needy will rejoice
in the Holy One of Israel. "... they will KEEP MY NAME HOLY
... they will acknowledge the holiness of the Holy One of
Jacob, and will STAND IN AWE OF THE GOD OF ISRAEL. Those
who are wayward in spirit will gain understanding; those
who complain will accept instruction."* (Isa 29:17-24 NIV —
emphasis added)

The prophet Daniel was shown visions concerning the
future. YAHveh said to him:
*"And there will be a time of distress such as never
occurred since there was a nation until that time; and at
that time your people, everyone who is found written in
the book, will be rescued. And many of those who sleep in
the dust of the ground will awake, these to everlasting
life, but the others to disgrace and everlasting contempt.
And those who have insight will shine brightly like the
brightness of the expanse of heaven, and those who lead
the many to righteousness, like the stars forever and ever.
But as for you, Daniel, CONCEAL THESE WORDS AND SEAL UP THE
BOOK UNTIL THE END OF TIME; many will go back and forth,
and knowledge will increase* [seeking to understand the
hidden truths of the holy Scriptures]. *... Many will be
purged, purified and refined; but the wicked will act
wickedly, and none of the wicked will understand, but
THOSE WHO HAVE INSIGHT WILL UNDERSTAND."* (Da 12:1-4, 10)

The prophet Zechariah was shown *"A FLYING SCROLL; its
length is twenty cubits and its width ten cubits* [30 feet long by 15
feet wide]*"* (Zec 5:2). This scroll contained the truths,

commandments and righteous decrees of the Holy One of Israel as spoken through the words of His prophets and scribes. These words and visions had been sealed and hidden from man's understanding until the time of the end.

The Almighty had shown Zechariah the scroll opening as the seals were broken in order for its contained mysteries to be revealed in the last days. Through His mercy, *the unsealed scroll would be magnified to such huge dimensions that no man could miss or plead ignorant of its contents.*

The scroll, with writing on both sides, was to fly *"over the face of the whole land"* (Zec 5:3). The plumb line of truth in this scroll, *YAHveh's* holy Scriptures, would become a standard which will judge all who transgress His righteous commandments and holy decrees.

At the close of this age, "gloom and darkness" will cover the earth; Isaiah prophesied that the scroll would be opened during these dark, end days (Isa 29:18-24). As the seals are broken, the words of the prophets will become as a bright light illuminating the path which Isaiah spoke of as a *"highway ... called the* HIGHWAY OF HOLINESS ..." (Isa 35:8).

The Almighty is calling out a redeemed remnant to make pilgrimage on this narrow path as they flee the world and the religious systems slated for destruction. He is ushering a chosen remnant to advance on this *Highway of Holiness* into the eternal refuge of His glorious presence.

The Holy One has decreed that the seals be broken on the scroll. He desires the spiritually blind to see Him in the fullness of all He is, and the spiritually deaf to have opened ears to hear Him say, *"This is the way, walk in it, ..."* (Isa 30:21). *YAHveh* is summoning and preparing a righteous remnant to ascend His holy mountain and worship Him in spirit and in truth.

As the scroll is unsealed and magnified and its truths enter our hearts, the humble will see how far mankind and religious systems have veered from *YAHveh's* plumb line of truth. There will be great mercy and promised blessings poured out upon a repentant and contrite remnant who see and heed the commands of the Almighty.

Divine *mercy* will soon become divine *judgment.* The Mighty One is going to judge all who transgress His righteous commandments regardless of what religious label, title, or badge they wear or profess.

The eternal King will separate His chosen remnant from

the world, its religious systems, and everything which has compromised His plumb line of immutable truths. He is separating and preparing a priesthood to be *Holy to YAHveh.*

Chapter 2
What Is His Name?

The time is at hand when the almighty Creator shall return and restore all things. As He approaches the earth, the light of His countenance is piercing the shroud of darkness and deception that has covered it. Multitudes lie in this darkness and they WILL perish for lack of knowledge (Hos 4:6). Yet in His sovereignty, He desires no man to perish and ALL to be saved.

The prophet Joel proclaims: *"whoever calls on* THE NAME *of* THE LORD *will be delivered, ..."* (Joel 2:32).

Proverbs asks a vital question which is foundational to this book: *"Who has ascended into heaven and descended? ... Who has established all the ends of the earth?* WHAT IS HIS NAME OR HIS SON'S NAME? SURELY YOU KNOW!" (Pr 30:4). Do you know? Is the Creator's name *God* or *LORD*? Perhaps *Jehovah*?

Most world religions have an object of worship that they call *Lord* or *God*; however, these are titles, not proper names. The noun *god* or *God* can be described as anything that is worshiped by men as a deity, and *lord* or *Lord* as one who has power and authority from headship or leadership. The dictionary defines *God* as "... any of various beings conceived of as supernatural, immortal and having special powers over the lives and affairs of people and the course of nature; deity, especially a male deity."[1] Multitudes from innumerable religions call their deity(s) by the common title *God*. The name of the pagan god, Baal, in the Old Testament, means "lord."[2] This is the origin of the word *Baalzebub* (*Beelzebub*) or "Lord of the flies."[3] We must ask then, who is *their* "God" and "Lord"?

The more important question is, *"What is the Name of YOUR God—the one you call Lord?"* The Creator of heaven and earth has an incomparable and sacred name which He will not share with other gods—for He will give His Glory to no other (see

---

[1] *Webster's New World Dictionary*, college ed., s.v. "God."

[2] "Baal means 'lord' or 'owner' and was often used as a general term for god." Footnote to Hos 2:13. *Ryrie Study Bible* — NASB (Chicago: Moody Press, 1995), p. 1377.

[3] "Beelzebub. The prince of demons (Mt 12:24); the Greek form of the Hebrew name Baal-Zebub ('lord of flies'), ..." Footnote on Mt 10:25. *The NIV Study Bible* (Grand Rapids: The Zondervan Corporation, 1985), p. 1457.

Isa 42:8). His name throughout the Scriptures is called *holy* and *exalted*. In the Old Testament, the names of pagan gods are spelled out (e.g., Molech, Dagon, Ashtoreth, Baal, Marduk and others) yet His divine and most holy name has been substituted, with rare exceptions, with the generic title *LORD*.

It is important to emphasize that the common title *God* (Θεός, *theos* in Greek) has its roots in paganism. This title has been shared among the various heathen deities throughout history.

Since the second century the Hebrew word, *Elohim*, which means "the Mighty One" has been translated as *God* throughout most versions of Scripture.

Due to the focus of this book and the desire for simplicity in its presentation, the central issue will be the Mighty One's original *memorial-name* as proclaimed to Moses for Israel and all generations of Jews and Gentiles to come.

"This Is My Name Forever"

He declares in His Word: *"For nothing is hidden that shall not become evident, nor anything secret that shall not be known and come to light"* (Lk 8:17). Let us search the holy Scriptures and petition the Holy One to reveal to us that which has been hidden with regard to His most holy name, and the truth and power which His name embodies.

Two reference points help to clarify the use of His divine name, *YAHveh*, as proclaimed to Moses at the burning bush.

In regard to the divine name *YHWH*, commonly referred to as the *Tetragrammaton*, the translators adopted the device used in most English versions of rendering that name as "LORD" in capital letters to distinguish it from *Adonai*, another Hebrew word rendered "Lord," for which small letters are used.[4]

Here we see the intervention of man's devices in substituting the common title of "LORD" in place of His sacred name, *YHVH* or *YHWH*, seen below in Hebrew characters:

יהוה

---

[4] Ibid., p. xii.

Read right to left, this is phonetically spelled: *Yod Hey Vav Hey*. This explanation is to be found in the Preface of most English Bibles.

Second, a footnote on Deuteronomy 28:58 expresses with perplexity: "One of the oddities of history and revelation is the loss of the proper pronunciation of the Hebrew *YHWH*, the most intimate and personal name of God in the OT [Old Testament]." (emphasis added)[5]

Many dictionaries render *YAHveh* or *YAHweh* as the accurate spelling and pronunciation of the original name of the Almighty. The Hebrew letter "vav" is represented in English by the letters "V" or "W." However, Jewish scholarship leans towards the "V" as the ancient and correct representation of the letter "vav." "Overwhelming scholarly opinion holds that YHVH [*Yod Hey Vav Hey*] was in Moses' time pronounced Yahveh." (emphasis added)[6]

Because the most conservative scholarship of the ancient Hebrew Scriptures supports the use of *YHVH*, this author will be reinserting His original name, *YAHveh*, in place of the substituted *LORD* in all Scripture verses quoted in this book.

In Exodus 3, Moses, the deliverer of Israel, is timid yet obedient in his call to go to Pharaoh to deliver the Jews from bondage. Before going to Pharaoh, Moses asks:

"Behold, I am going to the sons of Israel, and I shall say to them, 'The God of your fathers has sent me to you.' Now they may say to me, 'WHAT IS HIS NAME?' What shall I say to them?" And God said to Moses, 'I AM WHO I AM;'[7] ... I AM has sent me to you." And God, furthermore, said to Moses, "Thus you shall say to the sons of Israel, 'YAHveh, the God of your fathers, the God of Abraham, the God of Isaac, and the God of Jacob, has sent me to you.' THIS IS MY NAME FOREVER, AND THIS IS MY MEMORIAL-NAME TO ALL GENERATIONS." (Ex 3:13-15)

Did He intend for His Name to be forgotten? The Scripture says: *"let YAHveh be found true, though every man be found a liar ..."* (Ro 3:4). YAHveh is the same yesterday and today and forever.

---

[5] Ibid., p. 279.

[6] *THE TORAH, A Modern Commentary* (New York: Union of American Hebrew Congregation, 1981), p. 426.

[7] *HAYAH*, the Hebrew root verb meaning "I AM," is also the root of the divine name, *YAHveh*.

His Name Was Hidden

יהוה

The most holy name, consisting of the Hebrew letters **Yod Hey Vav Hey**, appears approximately 7000 times in the Old Testament. It is commonly referred to as the *Tetragrammaton*, a Greek word meaning "four letters," but originally by the Hebrew, *hashem ha-meforash*, which means "the ineffable name."

Is the title, *LORD*, an acceptable substitute for His original and ancient name *YAHveh*, or is this in fact an invention of man? The Scriptures speak: *"There is a way which seems right to a man, But its end is the way of death"* (Pr 14:12).

What has happened is the death of a vital truth! *The name of the Mighty One of Israel has been buried in obscurity by tradition.*

At some point in history, Jewish leaders concluded that *YAHveh's* name was too holy to be spoken by common man. The priests were concerned that the name of the God of Israel would be irreverently used, especially by Gentiles. Desiring to protect the holy name, the convention was instituted which permitted only the high priest of Israel to pronounce His holy name *one day a year* on *Yom Kippur*. This soon became a tradition based on the commandment not to misuse or take *YAHveh's* name in vain (Ex 20:7; Lev. 19:12, 24:10-16, 23).

From here, the Jewish Orthodoxy and subsequent Gentile translators transgressed His mandate for all mankind to remember, proclaim, and revere His holy name (Ex 3:15). Israel's history is laced with grave consequences due to their substituting and forgetting *YAHveh's* name. The hiding of His *memorial-name* under substitute titles brought the diminishing of His abiding presence and glory, causing a diluted, compromised form of religious worship to develop down to the present time.

His name was hidden under the substituted title *Adonai* in Hebrew and *Kurios* in Greek, both of which are translated "LORD" in English. Many Orthodox Jews have used the title *Hashem*—meaning, "The Name"—out of reverence for His unspoken holy name.

Scribal Errors

The dictionary supports the fact that *Jehovah* **is not a biblical name** and has no warrant or authentic place in the Scriptures. The form *Jehovah* did not exist as a Hebrew word. ... The Hebrew alphabet consists only of characters for consonants; vowels are indicated as dots or "points" written in characteristic positions above or below the consonants. The Hebrew name for God, the consonants of which are transliterated Y<small>HWH</small>, was considered so sacred that it was never pronounced and its proper vowel points were never written. In some texts the vowel points for a completely different word, *Adonai,* "lord," ... was to be spoken whenever the reader came upon the word Y<small>HWH</small>. Y<small>HWH</small> was never intended to be pronounced with the vowels of *Adonai,* but *Christian scholars of the Renaissance made exactly that mistake,* and the forms Iehovah (*using the classical Latin equivalents of the Hebrew letters*) and Jehovah (*substituting in English, J for consonantal I*) came into common use.[8]

The third commandment, which forbids the taking of the name of God in vain, was interpreted in ancient days also as forbidding the utterance of the proper name of God, which was written by the Tetragrammaton YHVH. Once a year, on the Day of Atonement, the high priest pronounced the Tetragrammaton or the *shem ha-meforash* ("ineffable name"). At all other times it was, and is, read by Jews as *Adonay,* translated by "Lord," or as *Elohim,* translated by "God." ... The transliteration, *Jehovah,* is the result of pronouncing YHVH with the vowels of *Adonay,* ... and is, therefore, no indication of the proper Hebrew pronunciation. ...The transliteration, *Jehovah,* is generally ascribed to Peter Galatin, the confessor of Pope Leo X, but it occurs as early as the thirteenth century in the writings of Raymond Martin (c. 1270). The pronunciation *Jehovah* began to be popularly used by Christian scholars in the early part of the sixteenth century.[9]

---

[8] *Webster's New Riverside University Dictionary,* 2d. ed., s.v. "Jehovah."
[9] *Collier's Encyclopedia, Vol. 13* (New York: Macmillian Educational Company, A Division of Macmillian, Inc., 1989), p. 534.

Thus, the vowels of **Adonai** and/or **Elohim** mixed with YHVH, rendered in error, **YeHoVaH,** or *Jehovah.* "The people who introduced this name were medieval Christian Hebrew scholars; Jews never acknowledged such a name. The defense of this Christian hybrid is the same as the defense of the Jewish avoidance of pronouncing the name—tradition!"[10]

It must be emphasized that the English letter "J," as we know it, does not exist in Hebrew. "J, the tenth letter of the English alphabet, is one of the *few relatively modern additions* to the Semitic-Greek-Etruscan-Latin line of development that gave rise to the alphabet."[11] In fact, J was the *last letter* to be added to our alphabet. In the translation of Scripture, the letter "Y" in Hebrew was commonly replaced by the English letter "J" in the late Middle Ages. This method explains the innumerable changes in Scripture such as the name *Eliyahu* becoming Elijah and *Halleluyah* becoming Hallelujah.

Once again the Almighty wants us to ask ourselves, "What is His name?" Are we part of a heritage of believers who have continually from generation to generation remembered His name? *YAHveh* speaks to us through the prophet Ezekiel:

> "So will I make MY HOLY NAME known in the midst of my people Israel [and all Gentiles joined with her]; and I will not let them POLLUTE [dissolve][12] MY NAME any more: and the heathen shall know that I AM [YAHveh], the Holy One in Israel." (Eze 39:7 KJV — emphasis added)

Unholy Substitutes

As we continue, let us keep in mind that *LORD* in the Old Testament, is the commonly accepted substitute for *YHVH* or *YAHveh.* It is important to note that the title "Lord" with a capital "L" but lower case "ord" in the Old Testament is to be translated "master." However, in many New Testament translations where the Old Testament is quoted, "LORD" (substituted for *YAHveh*) was replaced by New Testament translators with "Lord" or "God,"

---

[10] *New Open Bible Study Edition* — NASB (Nashville: Thomas Nelson, Inc., 1990), p. 70.

[11] *Multimedia Encyclopedia, Ver. 1.* (I.J. Gelb and R.M. Whiting, Grolier Inc., 1992), s.v. "alphabet."

[12] *Strong's Concordance*, s.v. #2490 — *pollute*, "to dissolve."

further losing the obvious connection to the divine name, *YHVH*.

The name, *YAHveh* (translated *LORD*) throughout the Old Testament appears 6823 times. In the New Testament, His memorial-name should have appeared, *at least* in the form of its Old Testament substitute, "LORD." Grievously however, it has been deleted in many translations even when directly quoting from the Old Testament—the *New American Standard Bible* is one of the exceptions. In the New Testament, the NASB capitalizes all quotes from the Old Testament and therefore maintains the capitalization of the word "LORD."

In the *New International Version*, we read in Acts 2:21: "'... everyone who calls on the name of the **Lord** shall be saved'" (emphasis added). Here the apostle Peter is quoting from the book of Joel: "*And everyone who calls on the name of the LORD [YAHveh] will be saved ...*" (Joel 2:32 NIV — emphasis added).

Another example is in the *King James Version*. Messiah Himself is quoted as saying: "*... It is written, Man shall not live on bread alone, but by every word that proceedeth out of the mouth of **God**"* (Mt 4:4 KJV — emphasis added).

Yet the *Torah*[13] from which He quoted reads: "*man doth not live by bread only, but by every word that proceedeth out of the mouth of the LORD [YAHVEH] ...*" (Dt 8:3 KJV — emphasis added).

Controversy regarding the original language of the New Testament Scriptures (Hebrew, Aramaic, or Greek) is irrelevant. It is unthinkable that the Jewish apostles when writing the New Testament would have substituted *YAHveh's* holy name with the Greek title *Theos* (God) or *Kurios* (Lord).

This confusion was an inevitable by-product of the early Gentile translators. Many were oblivious or indifferent to the vital importance of remembering and maintaining *YAHveh's* holy name. But the Spirit of Truth will set you free from such confusion as He continues to unseal the scroll of His eternal Word.

---

[13] The *Torah* is the sacred writings of Moses and constitutes the central foundation of Jewish religion since the giving of the Ten Commandments on Mt Sinai. Literally, the word *Torah* means "teaching." It is often referred to as the *Law*, from the Greek word νόμος (*nomos*). *Torah*, the first five books of Moses, is also referred to as the Pentateuch.

Honor His Name

The Jewish priests were correct regarding the requirements of purity and holiness in order to speak His name. They simply felt His name was too holy to utter; however, there was provided through the Old Covenant the sacrificial blood system for Israel which continually atoned for their sins, in order that they, as a redeemed people could speak His name with honor.

YAHveh never intended for His name to be lost to a common title shared by other gods. He declares through His prophet Isaiah: *"I AM YAHVEH; THAT IS MY NAME; I will not give My glory to another, ..."* (Isa 42:8). *"... for YAHveh, whose name is Jealous, is a jealous God* [He is jealous for his holy *memorial-name!*]*"* (Ex 34:14). In Exodus 20:24 we have a beautiful promise to those who revere His name: *"'... IN EVERY PLACE WHERE I CAUSE MY NAME TO BE REMEMBERED, I will come to you and bless you.'"*

Through the New Covenant, all people can speak and honor His name through the atoning blood of the Lamb—the Messiah of Israel. As His redeemed priesthood, we can speak His name with purified hearts and lips, and He will come to us personally and bless us.

In fact, in Deuteronomy 6:13 and 10:8 and 20 we read that the priests were commanded to take their vows and to bless Israel in *YAHveh's* name. Because He is jealous for His name, He desires a purified and separated remnant—redeemed by the blood of the Messiah—to proclaim and bring praise and glory to His holy name.

Name above All Names

As the Old Testament Scriptures lead to and magnify the New Testament, so does *YAHveh's* name lead to and magnify His Son's name. The importance and sanctity of *"the name which is above every name, ..."* (Php 2:9) is the major golden thread woven throughout the tapestry of the Bible as well as this book. The most vital issue regarding the Son's name will be explained later in great detail; however, a brief explanation here is necessary inasmuch as His original Hebrew name will be reinserted where it was originally written in the holy Scriptures.

The Original Hebrew Name of the Son Is *YAHshua*

In the English Bibles, the name of our Savior is rendered *Jesus.* This is an English/Latin transliteration from the Greek Ἰησοῦς (*Iesous*), not the original Hebrew name of the Son. The name *Iesous* is a Greek word fashioned after the name "Joshua," a corruption of the Hebrew *YAHshua.* The Greek name, *Jesus,* was not the name proclaimed to the Jewish virgin by the angel before Messiah's birth. The Hebrew Messiah was named and called *YAHshua,* a very Hebrew name befitting the Jew of all Jews, the Messiah of Israel.

During His sojourn on earth, the Savior never heard himself referred to as Jesus. The rendering of *YAHshua's* name as "Jesus," is man's attempt to approximate a form of His Hebrew name in Greek. *YAHshua* means "YAH"—*YAHveh*—is "SHUA"—Hebrew for "salvation" or "YAHveh saves."

YAHshua Means "YAH Is Salvation"

The Father, *YAHveh,* and the Son, *YAHshua* are one both in essence and in name. The very fact that *YAHshua* said, *"I have come in MY FATHER'S NAME, and you do not receive Me; ..."* (Jn 5:43) is a perfect example of Israel's erroneous tradition which said only the high priest could speak *YAHveh's* name. Through spiritual blindness and self-righteous indignation, the religious leaders viewed *YAHshua* as a mere carpenter's son; not even a Levite priest, speaking the name of *YAHveh,* proclaiming that He and *YAHveh* are one. To the traditional Jewish leadership, to even mention *YAHveh's* name was blasphemy.

Through the process of reading this book, may the Spirit of Truth fill your heart and mouth with praises to His holy name. May your heart be united with the great King David in proclaiming with reverential joy: *"Teach me Thy way, O YAHveh; I will walk in Thy truth; unite my heart to FEAR THY NAME. I will give thanks to Thee ... with all my heart, and will GLORIFY THY NAME FOREVER"* (Ps 86:11-12).

In biblical times, names were a vital embodiment of the nature and character of the person or deity. Thus, the name of the Mighty One of Israel is the very manifestation and embodiment of His character:

"God spoke further to Moses and said to him, 'I AM YAHVEH; and I appeared to Abraham, Isaac, and Jacob, as God Almighty [EL SHADDAI], BUT BY MY NAME, YAHVEH, I DID NOT MAKE MYSELF KNOWN TO THEM. ... I have remembered My covenant. Say, therefore, to the sons of Israel, "I AM YAHVEH, and I will bring you out ... I will deliver you ... I will also redeem you with an outstretched arm and with great judgments. Then I will take you for My people, and I will be your God; and you shall know that I am YAHVEH your God, ... And I will bring you to the land which I swore to give to Abraham, Isaac, and Jacob, I will give it to you for a possession; I AM YAHVEH."'" (Ex 6:2-8)

The "I AM" of Exodus 3:14 comes from the Hebrew verb, *hayah*, meaning "to be" or "he will be." *HaYAH* is the causative root of His name, *YAHveh*. His name is the embodiment of His character. His character and name are the manifestation of His sovereign promise to redeem His people from the hand of their enemies and to righteously judge all the enemies of Israel. *YAHveh's* name implies that He is the covenant-keeping God. He will redeem Israel and all Gentiles joined with her through Messiah's sanctifying blood.

My People Shall Know My Name

We are going on a little archaeological dig which will strengthen you in this truth. No scorching sun and heat; no sand in your eyes; no sweat on your brow; no shovel in your hand; no back breaking labor. A real artifact regarding His holy name is to be found in the Psalms—in the *New King James Version*—which uses the original letter "Y" instead of the substitute letter "J": *"Sing to God, sing praises to HIS NAME; extol Him who rides on the clouds, by HIS NAME YAH, and rejoice before Him"* (Ps 68:4 NKJV — emphasis added).

YAH is a poetic contraction of *YAHveh*. The *New King James Version* has three other verses that use *YAH* in its original form. *"...'For YAH, the LORD, is my strength ...'"* (Isa 12:2); *"Trust in the LORD forever, for in YAH, the LORD, is everlasting strength. ..."* (Isa 26:4); *"'I shall not see YAH, the LORD in the land of the living; ...'"* (Isa 38:11).

His voice declares to us through Isaiah: *"Therefore My people shall KNOW MY NAME; therefore in that day I am the one who is speaking, 'Here I am'"* (Isa 52:6).

Let us go back to the original question posed in Proverbs 30:4: *"What is His name or His Son's name? Surely you know!"* As we come to Him as little children, we can answer with childlike faith and excitement, "I know, I know. His name is *YAHveh!*"

Now for the less childlike and more reserved in demeanor who might be thinking, "So what? I've heard *that name* before. What's the difference? I know of whom I'm speaking and to whom I'm praying when I call Him *Lord* or *God*." To you I say, "Hold on!" We have just begun to unearth treasures of truth that will make a golden pathway into a more glorious and intimate relationship with the Almighty, as He, by His Spirit, builds this foundation *"... precept upon precept, Line upon line, ..."* (Isa 28:10 NKJV); be patient! Do not despise small beginnings. After all, we do not want any cracks in this foundation, lest the whole structure be built on shaky ground.

Hallelu*YAH* (Praise Be To *YAH*)

Hoping we can all with one accord, to one degree or another, say *HalleluYAH;* we can move on to this universal and well-known word. This most exalted form of praise has been spoken, written, prayed and sung by Jews and Christians alike for thousands of years. Hallelu*YAH* is simply: *Hallelu*—"praise be to," *YAH*— "*YAHveh*, the one true living God." Praise be to *YAH—HalleluYAH!*

The proclamation of *YAHveh's* name elicits from the worshiper the highest form of praise, glory, and honor due to the almighty King. His name speaks of His salvation for Israel and all Gentiles joined with her. His name proclaims His infinite mercy, compassion, goodness, protection, and deliverance for those who love Him and revere His name.

His name also declares His holiness and resulting vengeance against Israel's enemies and His judgments and wrath upon all who mock His name and transgress His righteous commandments. Those who wholeheartedly exclaim, "*HalleluYAH*," bring glory to the name of *YAHveh* and give praise to all that His name embodies. *"There is none like Thee, O YAHVEH;* THOU ART GREAT, AND GREAT IS THY NAME IN MIGHT. *Who would not fear Thee, O King of the nations? Indeed it is Thy due! ..."* (Jer 10:6-7).

Many of King David's psalms, as well as those written by the other psalmists, were aimed at the magnification and exaltation of *YAHveh's* holy *memorial-name*.

"Ascribe to YAHVEH the glory due to HIS NAME; worship

YAHVEH in holy array" (Ps 29:2). — *"Let them* PRAISE THE NAME OF *YAHVEH, For* HIS NAME ALONE IS EXALTED; *..."* (Ps 148:13). — *"O* MAGNIFY *YAHVEH with me, And let us* EXALT HIS NAME *together"* (Ps 34:3). — *"Oh give thanks to YAHVEH,* CALL UPON HIS NAME; ... GLORY IN HIS HOLY NAME; *Let the heart of those who seek YAHVEH be glad."* (Ps 105:1-3)

The holy Scripture, *YAH's* written, eternal Word, concludes the ages with a resounding of heavenly *HalleluYAHs:*

> *"I heard, as it were, a loud voice of a great multitude in heaven, saying, 'Hallelu**YAH**! Salvation and glory and power belong to our God ...' And a second time they said, 'Hallelu**YAH**! ... And the twenty-four elders and the four living creatures fell down and worshiped YAHVEH who sits on the throne saying, 'Amen. Hallelu**YAH**!' ... And I heard, as it were, the voice of a great multitude and as the sound of many waters and as the sound of mighty peals of thunder, saying, 'Hallelu**YAH**! For YAHVEH our God, the Almighty, reigns.'"* (Rev 19:1-6)

The ultimate Hallelu**YAH** chorus is going to close this age and welcome all the redeemed of all ages into the eternal kingdom— of **Who? What is His name?** Surely you know it is *YAHveh! "and He will reign ... forever; and His kingdom will have no end"* (Lk 1:33).

Does He love His name? Yes. He and His name are *inseparable.* Do YOU love His name? Let us all who love the holy name of *YAHveh* proclaim together this psalm. It is the first psalm of the *Hallel.*[14] For centuries it has been joyfully recited by the Jewish people for the holy festivals of Passover (*Pesach*), Pentecost (*Shavuot*) and Tabernacles (*Sukkot*). Quite possibly this psalm, among the others of the *Hallel* was reverently sung from the mouth of Messiah and His twelve disciples at the *Passover Seder* (the Last Supper — Mt 26:30).

---

[14] "A song of praise. The name derives from the Hebrew 'Praise Thou.' The singing of psalms of praise was a special duty of the Levites (2 Chron. 7:6; Ezra 3:11). The 'Egyptian' Hallel (Pss. 113-118) was recited in homes as part of the Passover celebration (compare Ps. 114:1; Matt. 26:30).... . The 'Great Hallel' was recited in the Temple as the Passover lambs were being slain and at Pentecost, Tabernacles, and Dedication." *Holman Bible Dictionary,* s. v., "Hallel."

PRAISE YAHVEH! [HALLELUYAH!]
Praise, O Servants of YAHveh.
PRAISE THE NAME OF YAHVEH.
BLESSED BE THE NAME OF YAHVEH.
From this time forth and forever.
From the rising of the sun to it setting
THE NAME OF YAHVEH IS TO BE PRAISED.
PRAISE YAHVEH! [HALLELUYAH!]

(Ps 113:1-3, 9)

Chapter 3
The Heartbeat of *YAHveh*

How much intimacy do you desire to have with your Creator? You can remain where you are by calling Him *God* or *Lord;* or you can draw closer to Him and hear His voice speak His name, *YAHveh,* to your heart, proclaiming as He did to Moses: *"This is my name forever, the name by which I am to be remembered from generation to generation"* (Ex 3:15 NIV). He wants to be our God and for us to be His people—to have a closeness and intimacy that surpasses the acquaintance level we so often have with Him.

Would you call your spouse, your best friend, your brother, or your sister, "Madam," "Mister," "Sir," "Lord," or perhaps "Master"? Probably not. Such titles would create a distance between you and that loved one. So it is between you and *YAHveh* when you don't address Him by His most holy name. He longs to draw you so close that even His heartbeat is audible to you.

YAHveh has redeemed us out of Satan's bondage to be His people, His treasured possession through the blood of His Son, *YAHshua.* He wants us to know Him intimately so the time we spend in His presence will bear eternal fruit.

He calls to you through His love letter—His matchless Word—emphasizing with passion to a people who have ears to hear Him say: "My name is *YAHveh.* Draw near to Me; hear My name, speak My name, praise My name, honor My name; then I will most certainly come and bless you" (author's paraphrase).

As an ambassador of the Almighty, I urge you to hear His plea. He is beseeching you, His beloved, to call Him by His name. He desires such closeness and intimacy that His name, *YAHveh,* flowing from your lips, will bring forth the outpouring of His promised blessings and glory upon you.

As He pours out that fragrant oil of His love through His name, let us sing along with Solomon:

"Your oils have a pleasing fragrance, YOUR NAME IS LIKE PURIFIED OIL; Therefore the maidens love you. Draw me after you and let us run together! The king has brought me into his chambers. ..." (SS 1:3-4)

Oh how our God, *YAHveh,* longs for a people who are intimate with Him; a people who willingly leave the distractions of this world to go into His chambers to love and worship Him—a honeymoon with no end! But because of *YAHveh's* infinite love, we have the requirement of obedience to His words, His commandments. We have been redeemed as His "*treasured possession*" (Dt 26:18), His "*royal PRIESTHOOD, ... A PEOPLE FOR YAHVEH'S OWN POSSESSION, ...*" (1Pe 2:9).

So many who call Him "Lord and Savior" have been seduced or distracted by the cares of this world and religious agendas, like an adulterous wife who never wholeheartedly loved her husband. Yet out of His compassion and forgiveness, His love is extended through the words of Hosea, speaking first to Israel and now to us:

> "*Therefore, behold, I will allure her, Bring her into the wilderness, And speak kindly to her. ... And it will come about in that day,' declares YAHVEH, 'That you will call Me Ishi* [my Husband] *and will no longer call me Baali* [my Master, Lord, or my Baal]. *For I will remove the names of the Baals from her mouth, So that they will be mentioned by their names no more. ... And I will betroth you to Me forever; ... and I will betroth you to Me in faithfulness. THEN YOU WILL KNOW YAHVEH.*'" (Hos 2:14-20)

The Forgetting of His Name

The Almighty admonishes His people: "*Whatever I command you, you shall be careful to do; YOU SHALL NOT ADD TO NOR TAKE AWAY FROM IT*" (Dt 12:32).

In Proverbs, in keeping with the initial question posed in this book: "What is His name and the name of His Son?" we see this warning: "*Do NOT ADD TO HIS WORDS, Lest He reprove you, and you be proved a liar*" (Pr 30:6). And Jeremiah warns:

> "*To whom shall I speak and give warning, That they may hear? Behold, their ears are closed, And they cannot listen. Behold the word of YAHVEH has become a reproach to them; They have no delight in it.*" (Jer 6:10)

I realize this chapter is a combination of mother's milk followed by castor oil; however, against the backdrop of His love, He wants us to know His displeasure and grief over the forgetting of His name. Jeremiah the prophet cries out:

> "*Can any hide himself in secret places that I shall not see him?' sayeth YAHVEH. ... How long shall this be in the heart of the prophets that prophesy lies? yea, they are*

prophets of the deceit of their own heart; Which think to cause my people to FORGET MY NAME by their dreams which they tell every man to his neighbour, as THEIR FATHERS HAVE FORGOTTEN MY NAME for Baal [Lord]." (Jer 23:24-27 KJV — emphasis added)

According to a footnote for Hosea 2:13, *"Baal* means 'lord' or 'owner' and was often used as a general term for 'God.'"[1] All of us have worshiped the Father and the Son by the common title, *Lord,* but this does NOT imply that we as believers have been worshiping pagan idols; rather, He is *revealing His name and removing titles* which would hinder the intimacy He so longs to have with us.

Eli*YAH*—My *ELOHIM* (God) Is *YAH*

The prophet Elijah was sent to Israel during the time of his nation's great apostasy. Israel had rebelled and intermingled with the surrounding Gentile nations. Consequentially, the pure worship of *YAHveh* was compromised and tainted. Israel mixed the holy worship of *YAHveh* with the profane worship of the pagan god, Baal (see 1Ki 18).[2]

Elijah was sent to turn the people back to the pure worship of *YAHveh* and the use of His *memorial-name.* The very name, Elijah, in Hebrew, is *EliYAHu* which means "my God is *YAH.*"[3]

John the Baptist came in the spirit and power of *EliYAHu* (Elijah) to once again turn Israel back to *YAH* (Lk 1:17 and Mt 11:14). After John's death, Messiah proclaimed: *"... 'Elijah [EliYAHu] is coming and will restore all things; ...'"* (Mt 17:11).

Malachi wrote: *"Behold, I am going to send you Elijah [EliYAHu] the prophet before the coming of the great and terrible day of YAHVEH"* (Mal 4:5).

We are approaching the day when *YAHveh* will return and pour out His righteous judgments on those who have veered from

---

[1] *The Ryrie Study Bible* (Chicago: Moody Press, 1978), p. 1377.

[2] "At first the name Baal (The Lord) was used by the Jews for their God without discrimination, but as the struggle for the two religions developed, the name Baal was given up in Judaism as thing of shame ..." *The Zondervan Pictorial Bible Dictionary* (Grand Rapids: Zondervan Publishing House, 1967), p. 87.

[3] It was common practice among the Jews to use the root "YAH" in names. For example, biblical names ending in "iah" in English were *Continued on next page*

His plumb line of truth. In His mercy, He again sends the spirit of *EliYAHu* who is calling:

> *"... 'MAKE READY THE WAY OF YAHVEH, MAKE HIS PATHS STRAIGHT. ... AND THE CROOKED* [including man's religious systems] *SHALL BECOME STRAIGHT, AND THE ROUGH ROADS SMOOTH; AND ALL FLESH SHALL SEE THE SALVATION OF GOD.'"* (Lk 3:4-6)

The *EliYAHu* spirit is beckoning a holy remnant to wholeheartedly embrace *YAHveh* and stop wavering between religion and righteousness. *EliYAHu* says: *"... 'How long will you hesitate between two opinions? If YAHVEH is God, follow Him;' ..."* (1Ki 18:21).

Over the centuries, multitudes of believers have been the recipients of many doctrines and traditions of men. We simply did not know this hidden vital truth as it has been buried under the religious doctrines with which we have been involved. However, there is hope! *"Therefore having overlooked the times of ignorance, YAHveh is now declaring to men that all everywhere should repent"* (Ac 17:30).

"Thy Name to All Generations"

It is important to understand why, after all these centuries, His true holy name is again being revealed. As His Spirit blows the dust from this jewel-like artifact, we read:

> *"But Thou, O YAHVEH, dost abide forever; And THY NAME TO*

Continued from previous page transliterated from "yah" in Hebrew. Many Hebrew prophets had names bearing the name of *YAHveh*:

Nehemiah	*NehemYAH*	"*YAHveh* has comforted"
Isaiah	*YeshaYAHu*	"Salvation is of *YAHveh*"
Jeremiah	*YirmeYAHu*	"*YAHveh* establishes"
Ezekiel	*YAHezkel*	"*YAHveh* God strengthens"
Daniel	*DaniYAHel*	"*YAHveh* God judges"
Joel	*YAHel*	"*YAHveh* is God"
Obadiah	*ObadYAH*	"Worshiper or servant of *YAHveh*"
Micah	*MichaYAHu*	"Who is like *YAHveh*?"
Zephaniah	*TsephanYAH*	"*YAHveh* has hidden"
Zechariah	*ZekarYAH*	"*YAHveh* remembers"
Malachi	*MalakYAH*	"Messenger of *YAHveh*"

ALL GENERATIONS. *Thou wilt arise and have compassion on Zion; For it is time to be gracious to her,* FOR THE APPOINTED TIME HAS COME. ... *So the nations will* FEAR THE NAME OF YAHVEH. ... *For YAHVEH has built up Zion; He has appeared in His glory.* ... *This will be written for the* GENERATION TO COME; THAT A PEOPLE YET TO BE CREATED MAY PRAISE YAHVEH. ... THAT MEN MAY TELL OF THE NAME OF YAHVEH IN ZION, *And His praise in Jerusalem; When the peoples* [Gentiles] *are gathered together, And the kingdoms,* TO SERVE YAHVEH." (Ps 102:12-22)

We ARE that "generation to come." *YAHveh's* name shall now go forth from the lips of multitudes of Gentiles who worship the God of Israel through faith in *YAHshua*, the Messiah. Then, a remnant of Jews will once again turn back to *YAHveh* calling upon His name and His Son's name. This will hasten the day of the Messiah's return and the establishment of His kingdom inasmuch as He declared to Israel: *"you shall not see Me until you say, 'BLESSED IS HE [YAHSHUA] WHO COMES IN THE NAME OF YAHVEH!'"* (Mt 23:39).

At the close of the age of the Gentiles (Lk 21:24), we see the prophecy of Jeremiah being fulfilled in our midst.

"'... it will no longer be said, "As YAHVEH lives, who brought up the sons of Israel out of the land of Egypt," but, "As YAHVEH lives, who brought up the sons of Israel from the land of the north and from all the countries where He had banished them." ...'" (Jer 16:14-15)

Jewish people, even from Russia and the four corners of the earth, are being gathered by *YAHveh's* outstretched arm to their homeland, Israel (Ex 6:6). Thus, the very meaning of His name, *YAHveh*, will ultimately be declared and fulfilled as the Redeemer and Holy One of Israel.

As He proclaimed to Pharaoh through Moses: *"for this cause I have allowed you to remain, in order to show you My power, and in order to PROCLAIM MY NAME through all the earth"* (Ex 9:16).

This same *YAHveh*, who declared to Pharaoh, also speaks vehemently to the Prince of this world (Satan): *"... 'Let My people go, that they may serve Me'"* (Ex 9:1).

The heart cry of the Almighty has never changed; it continues resounding in the ears of those who hear His voice. Come out of this world, be *Holy to YAHveh*, and worship Him in spirit and in truth.

Let the redeemed remnant joyously respond with Isaiah:

"Thou, O YAHVEH, art our Father, Our Redeemer FROM OF OLD IS THY NAME" (Isa 63:16). A righteous band with a joyful heart like King David's will respond with his words: *"I was glad when they said to me, 'Let us go to the house of YAHVEH.' ... To which the tribes go up, even the tribes of YAHVEH ... To give thanks to THE NAME OF YAHVEH"* (Ps 122:1, 4).

"My Name Will Be Great"

The pride and arrogance of mankind will be brought low; but the pure and humble will be lifted up for the praise and honor of *YAHveh* in the holiness of His name. The Hebrew prophets loved and reverenced *YAHveh's* incomparable name proclaiming by His Spirit:

"'For from the rising of the sun, even to its setting, MY NAME WILL BE GREAT among the nations, and in every place incense [prayers] is going to be offered TO MY NAME, ... FOR MY NAME will be GREAT AMONG THE NATIONS,' says YAHVEH of hosts" (Mal 1:11). — *"For then I will give to the peoples purified lips, That all of them may CALL ON THE NAME OF YAHVEH, To serve Him shoulder to shoulder"* (Zep 3:9). — *"And YAHVEH will be king over all the earth; in that day YAHVEH will be THE ONLY ONE, and HIS NAME THE ONLY ONE"* (Zec 14:9).

And John, writing from Patmos, says: *"And they sang the song of Moses, the bond-servant of YAHVEH, and the song of the Lamb, saying, ... 'WHO WILL NOT FEAR, O YAHVEH, AND GLORIFY THY NAME? ...'"* (Rev 15:3-4).

HalleluYAH! He is preparing a righteous people, a blameless body, a spotless bride. This *one new man* (Eph 2:15) is to be a holy remnant composed of redeemed Jews and Gentiles who will honor and glorify *His name*, now and throughout eternity. This sanctified remnant has the spiritual privilege to wear the priestly garments befitting *YAHveh's* holy presence. The priestly turban (see Ex 28:36-38) representing the mind of *YAHshua* covers their foreheads with a gold plaque, marking them as *YAHveh's* treasured possession. On this golden diadem, He inscribes with His finger these words: *"KODESH to YAHveh."* *Kodesh* is the Hebrew word meaning "separate and holy."

Even now His mighty finger is poised, ready to write His name on the foreheads of a righteous remnant. His intent is to

42

separate you and mark you as *Holy to YAHveh*. At the very end of the Scriptures, we find this inscription written on the foreheads of the eternal priesthood: *"the throne of YAHveh and of the Lamb shall be in it, and His bond-servants shall serve Him; and THEY SHALL SEE HIS FACE, AND HIS NAME SHALL BE ON THEIR FOREHEADS"* (Rev 22:3-4).

As the early chapters of this book bearing *YAHveh's* name conclude, my prayer is that the words of *YAHveh* will flow through you as that river of life described in Revelation: *"And he showed me a river of the water of life, clear as crystal, coming from the throne of YAHVEH and of the Lamb, in the middle of its street ..."* (Rev 22:1-2).

May this river of life flow from His heart to yours—a river such as Ezekiel described (chap. 47)—so deep and filled with *YAHveh's* Spirit that multitudes of people will find eternal life wherever that river flows. As its crystal clear, cleansing waters gush from His throne outward upon and through you, may the glorious, matchless name of *YAHveh* encompass your body, soul, spirit, and mind; and cause new life (revival) to spring forth.

Thus far we are ankle high, so let go of your worldly cares and religious baggage and get into His great *River of Life*. Come on in. **The water is divine!**

PART TWO

Dedicated to the Tribes of Gad and Asher

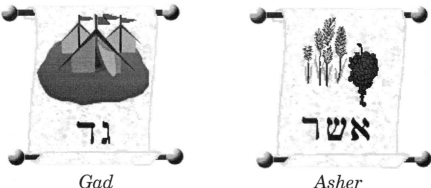

Gad   Asher

Thus He showed me, and behold, the Lord [Master]

WAS STANDING BY A VERTICAL WALL WITH A PLUMB LINE IN HIS HAND.

And YAHVEH said to me, "What do you see … ?"

And I said, "A plumb line." Then YAHVEH said,

"Behold I am about to put a plumb line in the midst of My people

…

I will spare them no longer."

(Am 7:7-8)

Chapter 4

Zerubbabel's Plumb Line

The Holy One of Israel is bringing forth His eternal "plumb line" of truth. He wants His children to see how crooked their ways have become as they personally and corporately have veered from and compromised His truths.

The Master Architect has a divine blueprint for His eternal temple. An unfathomable high price was paid to procure the building materials. His death and atoning blood purchased stones, living stones—Jews and Gentiles—built on the foundation of the Hebrew apostles and prophets with the Jewish Messiah Himself, as the *Chief Cornerstone, "in whom the whole building, being fitted together is growing into a holy temple in YAHVEH ... into a dwelling of YAHVEH in the Spirit"* (Eph 2:21-22).

YAHveh prophesied through Isaiah, *"See, I lay a stone in Zion, a tested stone, a precious cornerstone for a sure foundation; ... And I will make justice the measuring line, And RIGHTEOUSNESS THE PLUMB LINE; ..."* (Isa 28:16-17 NIV — emphasis added)

A plumb line is a vertical measuring line with a weight at the end. When dropped parallel to the wall of a structure, it determines whether the wall is straight or crooked. YAHveh, the great architect and builder, is standing with His divine blueprints and checking His house for foundational and structural accuracy.

The Master Architect spared nothing for the building of His earthly temple through His servant, King Solomon. Solomon's temple was to be a dwelling place befitting the eternal God's name, presence and glory. Everything for this temple was precisely carried out as the Architect had ordained. Foundation, beams, walls, every square inch was custom made for the Holy One's dwelling place. From Solomon's experience we have a key note of wisdom: *"Unless YAHVEH builds the house, They labor in vain who build it; ..."* (Ps 127:1).

Haggai and Zechariah are speaking prophetically to a latter day people about a house to be filled with greater glory than Solomon's temple. In the book of Zechariah, Zerubbabel is instructed to oversee the rebuilding of the temple which lay in ruins.

"NOT BY MIGHT NOR BY POWER, BUT BY MY SPIRIT," SAYS YAHVEH OF HOSTS. ... "The hands of Zerubbabel have laid the

foundation of this house, and his hands will finish it. Then you will know that YAHVEH of hosts has sent me to you. For who has despised the day of small things? ... these [the remnant] ... WILL BE GLAD WHEN THEY SEE THE PLUMB LINE IN THE HAND OF ZERUBBABEL— ..." (Zec 4:6-10)

As the Gentile age is concluding, Messiah is sending forth His ancient plumb line of truth to facilitate His eternal building program. His words speak to us in detail about His house. This is what YAHveh almighty says:

"Is it time for you yourselves to dwell in your paneled houses while this house [of mine] lies desolate?" Now therefore, thus says YAHVEH of hosts, "CONSIDER YOUR WAYS! You have SOWN MUCH, but HARVEST LITTLE ... CONSIDER YOUR WAYS! ... rebuild the temple, that I may be pleased with it and be glorified," says YAHVEH. "You LOOK FOR MUCH, but behold IT COMES TO LITTLE; when you bring it home, I blow it away. Why?" declares YAHVEH of hosts. "Because of My house which lies desolate, while each of you runs to his own house. Therefore, because of you the sky has withheld its dew, and the earth has withheld its produce. And I called for a drought ..." (Hag 1:4-11)

In Haggai's day, the drought was physical; in our day, there is a growing spiritual drought. *"Do consider from this day onward, ... from the day when the temple of YAHVEH was founded, consider ... the vine ... and the olive tree ... has not borne fruit ..."* (Hag 2:18-19).

This Scripture applies to Israel at the time they were to rebuild the temple. Today, it directs our hearts to the conditions regarding the building up of His temple of holy, living stones.

The Spirit of Truth is speaking to our generation, saying that while we have labored to build our churches, synagogues, religious programs, homes, and personal wealth, we have neglected His holy house. God's plumb line, which He uses to evaluate the faulty foundations we have built, is revealing crooked places.

Many Jews and Gentiles alike have become disappointed and disillusioned in their faith—expecting much from their forms of religion, yet receiving little. Genuine evidence of YAHveh's power has been greatly lacking. It should be as abundant as the rains that cause the ground to produce its bountiful crops.

YAHveh is asking, "Why so little, after all that has been said and done? Why have the multitudes received so little compared with the spiritually abundant life they have hoped for and were promised?"

America is filled with spiritual meeting places. There is no shortage of Bibles or even professing believers; however, neither Judaism or Christianity (with its varied and segmented groups) are not, by and large, producing devoted, holy worshipers who walk in utmost reverence for the Almighty. Instead, many sit in congregations as frustrated, confused "pew warmers." They are withering in a spiritually dry and barren land. Why? Because *YAHveh's* building plan has been set aside for man's inferior and faulty programs!

The Great Shaking

YAHveh is stirring up a remnant; His desire for them is a spirit of holiness and zeal for building a temple for His presence, glory, and name.

> *"'I am with you,' declares YAHVEH." So YAHveh STIRRED UP the spirit of Zerubbabel ... and the spirit of ALL THE REMNANT of the people; AND THEY CAME AND WORKED ON THE HOUSE OF YAHVEH OF HOSTS, THEIR GOD ...* (Hag 1:13-14)

> *"For thus says YAHveh of hosts, 'Once more in a little while, I am going to shake the heavens and the earth, ... AND I WILL FILL THIS HOUSE WITH GLORY,' says YAHveh of hosts. ... 'The latter glory of this house will be greater than the former,' says YAHveh of hosts, 'and in this place I shall give peace,' declares YAHveh of hosts."* (Hag 2:6-9)

YAHveh is also speaking clearly to this generation that will see the establishment of His eternal house described by Haggai as *"this latter house."* He is calling to a remnant of Jews and Gentiles who will be as pure gold refined in His holy fire, individuals who will rejoice to see Zerubbabel's plumb line of truth.

The Holy One of Israel has put a plumb line of immutable truth into the hand of Zerubbabel, the symbolic builder of *YAHveh's* latter day temple. The Great Architect is measuring the hearts of men and women, as well as every religious agenda, according to His eternal standard. He WILL have a holy remnant and a holy temple that are in plumb with His full counsel of truth.

This great shaking has already begun. It will ultimately

remove everything unholy, impure, hypocritical, carnal, and built by man's devices. All that is not rooted in Him is destined to fall as rubble; then a pure, humble, and obedient generation will be formed as *"living stones"* (1Pe 2:5) into God's holy house. *YAHveh* will fill this house with such glory that indeed, *"The latter glory of this house will be greater than the former ..."* (Hag 2:9).

Whitewashed, Bulging Walls Will Fall

The righteous remnant will wholeheartedly rejoice to see the errors and crooked places revealed and rectified. This holy remnant shares the Almighty's desire to have a temple comprised of redeemed *"living stones"* (1Pe 2:5)—Jews and Gentiles—built together on His *correct foundation* with straight walls. It will be a holy and sound spiritual structure that will endure the coming storms.

At the close of the age, it is now time for *YAHveh* to inspect thoroughly all that has been built in the name of religion. With His plumb line extending down from heaven's "architectural suite," He is detecting crooked, bulging walls that are not in line with His standards expressed in Scripture. *YAHveh's* full counsel of truth, His plumb line, is conveyed in both the Old and New Testaments; one without the other is only a partial portrait of the Almighty, His plan of salvation, and His eternal building program.

The Holy One is against all "vain imaginations" (see Ro 1:21) that cause His people to justify the erroneous building programs and traditions. Ezekiel shows us what the Master Builder thinks of spiritual buildings that have been built on faulty foundations—spiritual houses with crooked beams and flimsy walls sloppily covered with man's whitewash.

> *Thus says the Lord YAHVEH, "Woe to the foolish prophets who are following their own spirit and have seen nothing.... . YOU HAVE NOT GONE UP INTO THE BREACHES, NOR DID YOU BUILD THE WALL ... to stand in the battle on the day of YAHVEH." (Eze 13:3-5)*

> *It is definitely because they have misled My people by saying, "Peace!" when there is no peace. AND WHEN ANYONE BUILDS A WALL, BEHOLD, THEY PLASTER IT OVER WITH WHITEWASH; SO TELL THOSE WHO PLASTER IT OVER WITH WHITEWASH, THAT IT WILL FALL. ... Behold, when the wall has fallen, will you not*

be asked, "Where is the plaster with which you plastered it?" (Eze 13:10-12)

SO I SHALL TEAR DOWN THE WALL WHICH YOU PLASTERED OVER WITH WHITEWASH AND BRING IT DOWN TO THE GROUND, SO THAT ITS FOUNDATION IS LAID BARE; *and when it falls, you will be consumed in its midst.* AND YOU WILL KNOW THAT I AM YAHVEH. *Thus I shall spend My wrath on the wall and on those who have plastered it over with whitewash; and I shall say to you,* "THE WALL IS GONE AND ITS PLASTERERS ARE GONE ..." (Eze 13:14-15)

Those who desire truth at any price will forfeit the familiar comfort zone of a man-tainted religious system that has compromised God's standards. Such systems are like whitewashed, bulging walls in the sight of the Great Architect. The holy remnant must seek the ancient foundation of our faith— our holy, Hebrew roots as revealed in the full counsel of Scripture.

Woe to those who continue to exchange His plumb line of truth and righteousness for the crooked standard of man's doctrines and traditions. Woe to those who build their own empires and not His! The whitewashed, bulging walls are doomed to collapse like rubble and fall on all who remain within them in smug complacency.

This is precisely what *YAHveh* showed Zechariah concerning the unsealing of the scroll that would bring His righteous decrees. As the scroll is magnified, a curse of destruction will come upon every unholy house and man-made empire it enters.

"This is the curse that is going forth over the face of the whole land; ... I will make it [the scroll] *go forth," declares YAHveh of hosts, "and it will enter the house of the thief and the house of the one who swears falsely by My name; and it will spend the night within that house and consume it with its timber and stones." (Zec 5:3-4)*

Timber!

Repent! Repent! *"Come forth from her midst, My people, And each of you save yourselves From the fierce anger of YAHveh"* (Jer 51:45). As the wind of His breath blasts upon the earth, the whitewashed, bulging walls of man's vain efforts will collapse. At the same time, the breath of *YAHveh's* Spirit will fill His pure remnant afresh; they will arise by His Spirit into a mighty army.

WE ARE that latter day people to whom the prophet referred. Which foundation do you want to be built on—*the traditions of man* OR *YAHveh's immutable truth*? Which house do you want to live in—*the house built by men* OR *the eternal house built by YAHSHUA, the Master Carpenter?*

Chapter 5

Zipporah's Flint Knife

A *holy temple* built on a *holy foundation* can only be inhabited by a *holy priesthood*. As we have seen in the previous chapter, *YAHveh's* righteous remnant will rejoice when it sees the plumb line of truth in Zerubbabel's hand. This same remnant will also rejoice to see the flint knife that will circumcise their hearts in purity of worship and obedience to the God of Abraham, Isaac, and Jacob.

The concept of circumcision needs to be understood from a biblical perspective, since the word has various uses in Scripture. Its origin in the Old Testament represented *YAHveh's* seal of His covenant with Abraham.[1] But as we will see, *YAHveh* extended this covenant sign to have broader significance and ultimately to be applied, in spirit and in truth, to the Gentile remnant as well.

Circumcision was the outward sign that the individual's identity had a distinguishing mark which separated him from the world and consecrated him in total submission to the service of the Almighty.

Originally this sign of circumcision was for the physical foreskin, then later and more importantly it became an issue of one's heart. The unseen circumcised heart would be outwardly marked by holy behavior and attitudes. The circumcised heart would live distinctly differently and separately from the pagans who did not truly know, love, and worship *YAHveh.*

Whether *YAHveh's* truth comes to us in the form of a plumb line or as a flint knife, it sets His holy remnant free. *YAHshua* longs to circumcise a people to Himself. This circumcision of the heart is designed to separate us spiritually from the defilement of the world and its tainted religious systems

---

[1] "Circumcision was God's appointed 'sign of the covenant,' which signified Abraham's covenanted commitment to the Lord—that the Lord alone would be his God, whom he would trust and serve... . 'If I am not loyal in faith and obedience to the Lord, may the sword of the Lord cut off me and my offspring as I have cut off my foreskin.' Thus Abraham was to place himself under the rule of the Lord as his King, consecrating himself, his offspring and all he possessed to the service of the Lord." Footnote to Genesis 17:10, *The NIV Study Bible* (Grand Rapids: The Zondervan Corporation, 1985).

and traditions. A remnant, circumcised in heart and purified from defiling influences, will move from the outer court of religion into the Holy of Holies—the inner sanctum of YAHveh's glorious presence.

As we have seen, in the days of the Old Testament, circumcision of the flesh was given as a symbolic *foreshadowing of a more vital circumcision: circumcision of the heart.* YAHveh requires circumcision of the heart for Jews and Gentiles—male and female, young and old—in order that we may live in His holy presence now and eternally.

"Moreover YAHveh your God will CIRCUMCISE YOUR HEART *and the heart of your descendants,* TO LOVE YAHVEH YOUR GOD WITH ALL YOUR HEART AND WITH ALL YOUR SOUL, IN ORDER THAT YOU MAY LIVE *[ultimately in the eternal Holy of Holies]."* (Dt 30:6)

Circumcision of Heart Required

This may well be the last generation to be given opportunity and the privilege to enter the eternal Promised Land. We are much like the Israelites, who had wandered for forty years following the Exodus from Egypt and were required to be circumcised again before they could receive their promised blessings.

After the Israelites miraculously crossed the Jordan, the Almighty said to Joshua, *"'Make for yourself flint knives and* CIRCUMCISE *again the sons of Israel the second time.' So Joshua made himself flint knives and circumcised the sons of Israel at Gibeath-haaraloth* [the hill of foreskins]" (Jos 5:2-3). Those who rebelled against YAHveh died in the desert. Through forty years of wandering in the wilderness, YAHveh had purified and prepared a remnant who would heed His voice. This generation had to be circumcised to the Holy One of Israel before they could partake of His memorial Passover Feast and enter and possess the Promised Land.

And their children whom He raised up in their place, Joshua circumcised; ... Then YAHveh said to Joshua, "Today I have rolled away the reproach of Egypt from you." ... (Jos 5:7-9)

The Almighty looks at our hearts. He is calling to men, women, and children who are willing to accept the flint knife of circumcision. Circumcision of the heart will cut away our fleshly and worldly lusts, as well as deceptive doctrines and traditions. It will make us one with Him through the Spirit of Truth. This spirit is called the *Ruach HaKodesh*, which means "the spirit that separates." The *Ruach HaKodesh* (the Holy Spirit) separates the redeemed from all that is false and devised by men, and consecrates them into His priestly service.

Circumcision was and is a scriptural prerequisite for the people of *YAHveh*; Moses was no exception. *YAHveh* anointed him as the deliverer of His chosen people and sent him to Pharaoh on behalf of the enslaved Hebrew nation. At this dramatic juncture in biblical history, something unexpected happened:

Now it came about at the lodging place on the way that YAHveh met him and sought to put him to death. Then ZIPPORAH TOOK A FLINT [knife] and cut off her son's foreskin and threw it at Moses' feet ... (Ex 4:24-25)

Although Moses was called and anointed as the long-awaited deliverer of Israel, his great commission had come to a screeching halt. The voice of the Mighty One said, in essence, "Stop everything! First things first! You forgot something!" *Moses had neglected to circumcise his son to YAHveh, the God of Israel.* The child had to be circumcised or there would be no deliverance and Passover for Israel. The cutting away of foreskin was vital; it had to be accomplished before *YAHveh's* sovereign plan could be fulfilled for His Jewish people.

Zipporah, Moses' Gentile wife, came to his rescue. She took the flint knife and circumcised the boy. It was an unpleasant and painful task but it had to be done! Moses was spared judgment, and Israel was delivered from bondage.

WANTED: Zipporahs who are obedient to *YAHveh* and willing to use the flint knife of circumcision.

Today many congregations are filled with spiritual offspring who sit under leaders who have neglected to circumcise the hearts of the people. Many religious leaders have been preoccupied with fulfilling their divine call. They have been like Moses who neglected to circumcise and consecrate his offspring to the Holy One of Israel. They have not uncompromisingly brought the full counsel of the Word of God.

Multitudes do not know Him as they should or worship Him in spirit and in truth. The Holy One says, *"THIS PEOPLE HONORS ME WITH THEIR LIPS, BUT THEIR HEART IS FAR AWAY FROM ME. BUT IN VAIN DO THEY WORSHIP ME ..."* (Mt 15:8-9) and *"their reverence for Me CONSISTS OF TRADITION ...* [They] *turn things around* [upside down]!"

(Isa 29:13, 16).

It is the Almighty's mercy to send a substitute, like Zipporah, to fulfill His requirements for spiritual circumcision. In this way, He will deter His hand of judgment against the leaders who have neglected the vital biblical mandate of spiritual circumcision. *YAHveh's* commandment still stands: *"Circumcise then your heart, and stiffen your neck no more. "For YAHveh your God is the God of gods and the Lord of lords ..."* (Dt 10:16-17).

The apostle Paul reminded both Jews and Gentiles of the basic issue—circumcision of the heart (Ro 2:29). In Colossians he wrote: *"In whom also ye are circumcised with the circumcision made without hands, in putting off the body of the sins of the flesh* [separated from all unrighteousness unto *YAHveh's* holy standards] ..."* (Col 2:11 KJV — emphasis added).

The Mighty One spoke in anger through the prophet Jeremiah: *"Behold, the days are coming," declares YAHVEH, "that I will punish all who are circumcised* [only in the flesh] *and yet uncircumcised* [in heart] *... for all the nations are uncircumcised, and all the house of Israel are uncircumcised of heart"* (Jer 9:25-26).

How far modern Judaism and organizational Christianity have strayed from *YAHveh's* original intentions. So few are truly circumcised in heart! Churches, synagogues, and other meeting places are filled and pews are warmed by untold numbers of lukewarm, professing believers who love their lives, this world, and their traditions far more than they know and love God. A dedicated remnant, circumcised in heart and consecrated to His service, will joyfully renounce fleshly desires and flee this corrupt world system, including divisive, erroneous doctrines and unholy traditions.

Stephen, a disciple of *YAHshua,* was stoned to death by those he rightly called *"stiff-necked and uncircumcised in heart and ears"* (Ac 7:51). The Scriptures indicate that no Jew or Gentile, uncircumcised in heart, shall enter God's eternal, holy sanctuary or partake of His eternal Passover (see Eze 44:9 and Ex 12:48). Isaiah prophesied of a day when the holy city Jerusalem (*YAHrushalayim*)[2] would no longer be profaned by the uncircumcised in heart:

---

[2] The modern derivative "Jerusalem" means "the peaceful city (or habitation) of *YAHveh.*" It *may* have been derived as follows: Jerusalem< YERushalayim< YAHrushalayim ("*YAHveh SHALOM*"). In Dt 12:5, *YAHveh* designates a place for the worship of His name. Other sources indicate the Hebrew "*YAHveh Shammah*" meaning "*YAHveh* is there" could be a word play from which *Jerusalem* originates.

*Awake, awake, Clothe yourself in your strength, O Zion;
Clothe yourself in your beautiful garments, O Jerusalem,
the holy city. FOR THE UNCIRCUMCISED AND THE UNCLEAN WILL
NO MORE COME INTO YOU.* (Isa 52:1)

YAHveh's cry in the book of Jeremiah emphasizes this point: *"Break up your fallow ground, And do not sow among thorns. CIRCUMCISE YOURSELVES TO YAHVEH AND REMOVE THE FORESKINS OF YOUR HEART ... Lest My wrath go forth like fire And burn with none to quench it, Because of the evil of your deeds"* (Jer 4:3-4).

Some might ask, "But what evil have I done? I go to my congregation, read the Bible, pray, tithe, and help the needy. I'm a good person! I'm saved, and that's enough for me." But is it enough for the One who paid the unfathomable price of His own blood to redeem a holy people for His praise, honor, and glory? In the sobering words of Messiah:

"STRIVE TO ENTER BY THE NARROW DOOR [where only the circumcised in heart may go]; *for many, I tell you, will seek to enter and will not be able. Once the head of the house gets up and shuts the door, and you begin to stand outside and knock on the door, saying, 'Lord* [Master], *open up to us!' then He will answer and say to you, 'I DO NOT KNOW WHERE YOU ARE FROM.' Then you will begin to say, 'We ate and drank in Your presence, and You taught in our streets'* [we went to our congregations and carried out our religious rituals and traditions, doing many good works]; *and He will say, 'I tell you, I do not know where you are from; DEPART FROM ME, ALL YOU EVILDOERS'* [the uncircumcised of heart who do not do the will of the Father]." (Lk 13:24-27)

YAHshua will enter into eternal fellowship only with those who are consecrated by His blood, circumcised in heart, and who do the will of His Father. Only these will stand in His presence as a royal priesthood with *Holy to YAHveh* inscribed on their foreheads.

Abraham, his family, friends, and servants were quick to submit to the flint knife. They wanted to be circumcised and consecrated to Abraham's God. *Do you?*

No one who has a foreskin of flesh over his or her heart can move from the outer court of religion (the court of the uncircumcised) into His sanctuary and Holy of Holies. The flint knife is in Zipporah's hand. The Mighty One of Israel is calling for Jews and Gentiles to be circumcised in heart so that they may stand in His eternal presence.

According to Messiah's word, it is vital for each of us to do the will of His Father, YAHveh, *"Not everyone who says to Me, 'Lord, Lord,' will enter the kingdom of heaven; BUT HE WHO DOES THE WILL OF MY FATHER who is in heaven"* (Mt 7:21). In order to be *doers* of His will, we must be *hearers* of His full counsel, stripped of all traditions, taints, and biases. Messiah was and continues to be repulsed by the hypocritical, self-righteous ways of so many who profess faith in Him.

Joshua was a foreshadowing of YAHshua. Just as the people of Joshua's day were preparing to enter the Promised Land, this end-time remnant is being prepared to enter the heavenly Promised Land. Once more, YAHveh is saying through the Spirit of YAHshua, *"Make for yourself flint knives and CIRCUMCISE AGAIN ..."* (Jos 5:2).

The Mighty One of Israel is looking at our hearts. YAHveh wants to cut away like a foreskin the reproach, defilement, and compromise of the world, including its fabricated religious systems and traditions. He desires to see a "hill of foreskins" from a remnant who are willing to undergo the pain of circumcision of the heart in order to forsake everything for Him and Him alone!

Chapter 6
"Remember"

The plumb line of Zerubbabel and the flint knife of Zipporah are divine symbols; they illustrate the means by which YAHveh intends to bring forth a holy temple and a holy priesthood. The Master Architect drew the blueprints for His temple before the earth was made. His instructions have not changed. When they are followed carefully, these instructions ensure an eternally sound foundation. This sure foundation will give rise to straight beams, pillars, and walls, which will form a dwelling place befitting His name, presence, and glory.

We will study His blueprint carefully with the light of His Word shining on our hearts, eclipsing the dim light of men's doctrines and religious traditions with the light of His full counsel. May He grant you eyes to see, ears to hear, and a tender heart on which to write these vital truths. They are fundamental for a holy temple and priesthood.

Heirs Together with Israel

First century Jewish believers were confronted with a perplexing issue concerning the Gentiles—"was salvation solely for the Jews or was it to include the alien Gentiles?" The apostle Paul was the divinely appointed ambassador to the Gentiles. His mission was to bring them the awesome salvation of YAHshua, the Hebrew Messiah and to instruct them further regarding vital issues pertaining specifically to them as Gentiles within the messianic body.

Ephesians 2 and 3 are foundational support beams for God's holy temple. Paul's powerful words, written almost two thousand years ago, apply to all Gentiles who throughout the centuries have embraced the Messiah of Israel.

Therefore REMEMBER,[1] that formerly you, the Gentiles in the flesh, who are called "Uncircumcision" by the so-called

---

[1] *Remembrance* is an important concept to the Mighty One of Abraham, Isaac and Jacob. YAHveh continually exhorted His people to remember, lest they sin against Him.

"Circumcision," ... REMEMBER *that you were at that time* SEPARATE *from Messiah,* EXCLUDED *from the commonwealth of Israel, and* STRANGERS *to the covenants of promise,* HAVING NO HOPE *and* WITHOUT YAHVEH *in the world. But now in Messiah YAHSHUA YOU WHO FORMERLY WERE FAR OFF HAVE BEEN BROUGHT NEAR BY THE BLOOD OF MESSIAH.* (Eph 2:11-13)

For He Himself is our peace, who MADE BOTH GROUPS INTO ONE, *and* BROKE DOWN THE BARRIER *of the dividing wall* [of hostility] ... *that in Himself* [by dying on the stake] *He might make the two into* ONE NEW MAN, *thus establishing peace, and might* RECONCILE THEM BOTH IN ONE BODY *to YAHVEH through the cross by it having put to death the enmity.* AND HE CAME AND PREACHED PEACE TO YOU [Gentiles] WHO WERE FAR AWAY, AND PEACE TO THOSE [Israelites] WHO WERE NEAR ... (Eph 2:14-17)

So then you are no longer strangers and aliens, but you are FELLOW CITIZENS *with the* [Jewish] *saints, and are of YAHVEH's household* [Israel], *having been built upon the foundation of the* [Jewish] *apostles and prophets, Messiah YAHSHUA Himself being the corner stone, in whom the whole building, being* FITTED TOGETHER *is growing into a* HOLY TEMPLE *in YAHVEH; in whom you also* [Jews and Gentiles] *are being* BUILT TOGETHER *into a* DWELLING OF YAHVEH *in the Spirit.* (Eph 2:19-22)

The highest and purest praise should continually resound from the lips of all humble and grateful redeemed Gentiles as they *remember their origins.* Once they were hopeless aliens, having no place with the God of Israel, His people, and His promises. Paul was aware of human nature, which can cause us to forget, as pride and self-righteousness grow back as a foreskin over the heart. With this concern for Gentile believers, Paul continues his admonition by sharing with them the mystery of Messiah:

"which in other generations was not made known to the sons of men ... to be specific, that the Gentiles are FELLOW HEIRS [together with Israel] *and* FELLOW MEMBERS *of the body, and* FELLOW PARTAKERS [with Israel] *of the promise in Messiah YAHSHUA through the gospel ..."* (Eph 3:5-6)

That Gentiles would turn to the God of Israel and be saved was prophesied in the Old Testament; that they also would become equal with believing Jews, united together as *one new* man, was unexpected. It is important to note that although this "mystery" was not totally revealed to the Hebrew prophets, it was prophesied that Gentiles would be mercifully blessed to worship the God of Israel.

Paul continues: *"To me ... this grace was given, to preach to the Gentiles the unfathomable riches of Messiah, and TO BRING TO LIGHT WHAT IS THE ADMINISTRATION OF THE MYSTERY which for ages has been hidden in YAHVEH, who created all things ..."* (Eph 3:8-9).

This great apostle to the Gentiles was a Jewish Pharisee. He was intimately familiar with the Old Testament Scriptures. No doubt he reflected on the words of Isaiah, Jeremiah, and Zechariah, who spoke of a day when the Gentiles would be granted an eternal place *together* with the children of Israel.

> *Let not the foreigner* [Gentile] *who has joined himself to YAHVEH say, "YAHVEH will surely separate me from His people." ... For thus says YAHVEH ... "foreigners who join themselves to YAHVEH, To minister to Him, and to LOVE THE NAME OF YAHVEH, To BE HIS SERVANTS, every one who KEEPS FROM PROFANING THE SABBATH, And HOLDS FAST My covenant; EVEN THOSE I WILL BRING TO MY HOLY MOUNTAIN, AND MAKE THEM JOYFUL IN MY HOUSE OF PRAYER. ..." The Lord YAHVEH, who gathers the dispersed of Israel, declares, "Yet others* [Gentiles] *I will gather to them, to those* already *gathered."* (Isa 56:3-8)

> *"Then it will come about that if they* [the Gentiles] *will really learn the ways of My people, to swear by MY NAME, 'As YAHveh lives,' even as they taught My people to swear by Baal, then they will be built up in the midst of My people* [Israel]*."* (Jer 12:16)

> *And now says YAHVEH, who formed Me from the womb to be His Servant* [the Messiah], *TO BRING JACOB BACK TO HIM, IN ORDER THAT ISRAEL MIGHT BE GATHERED TO HIM ... He says, "It is too small a thing that You should be My Servant To raise up the tribes of Jacob, and to restore the preserved ones of Israel; I WILL ALSO MAKE YOU A LIGHT OF THE NATIONS* [Gentiles] *So that My salvation may reach to the end of the earth."* (Isa 49:5-6)

> *"Sing for joy and be glad, O daughter of Zion; for behold I am coming and I will dwell in your midst,"* declares

YAHveh. *"And many nations [Gentiles] will join themselves to YAHveh in that day and will become My people."* (Zec 2:10-11)

Glory! Glory! Glory! *YAHshua,* who is the *"glory of Thy people Israel,"* is also a *"light of revelation to the Gentiles"* (Lk 2:32). Through His sacrificial blood, all mankind—including *both* Jews and Gentiles—may be saved and united as *one new man,* to His praise, honor, and glory.

Remember His Mercy

Many of the first Gentile believers remembered their isolation in the outer court of the uncircumcised as they worshiped the Holy One from a distance. They longed to know and embrace the God of Israel. Yet in spite of their heart's desire, the fact remained that there was a spiritual dividing wall separating the Gentiles from God's holy temple.

In the Court of the Gentiles, pious non-Jews could come and worship the God of Israel. That was as close as they could get, though, to the holy portions of the temple, for stern signs were posted upon every gate forbidding Gentiles to pass beyond their court under penalty of death.[2]

Through Messiah's blood, the separating wall was destroyed, and the redeemed Gentiles, circumcised in heart, became one with Israel and her God. All barriers were destroyed. Joy unspeakable, accompanied by humility and gratitude, was to be the perpetual safeguard over Gentile hearts. They were to remember His mercy and praise the Holy One of Israel for making them partakers *together with Israel* in the promised eternal blessings.

This is why Paul wrote:

---

[2] Mitch and Zhava Glaser, *The Fall Feasts of Israel* (Chicago: Moody Press, 1987), p. 93. — "... there was a 'Court of the Gentiles,' with marble screen beautifully ornamented, bearing tablets which, in Latin and Greek, warned Gentiles not to proceed further ..." Alfred Edersheim, *The Life and Times of Jesus the Messiah* (Grand Rapids: Wm. B. Eerdmans Publishing Co., 1971), p. 74.

For I say that Messiah
has become a servant to the circumcision [the Jews]
on behalf of the truth of God
to confirm the promises given to the fathers,
and for the Gentiles to glorify YAHVEH for His mercy;
as it is written,
"THEREFORE I WILL GIVE PRAISE TO THEE AMONG THE GENTILES,
AND I WILL SING TO THY NAME."
And again he says,
"REJOICE, O GENTILES, WITH HIS PEOPLE [Israel]."
And again,
"PRAISE YAHVEH ALL YOU GENTILES,
AND LET ALL THE PEOPLES PRAISE HIM."

(Ro 15:8-11)

Chapter 7
"Life from the Dead"

As the plumb line of the Almighty's truth reveals the crooked foundations and bulging walls of man's doctrines, we begin to see a disparity between man's religious agendas and *YAHveh's* building program for a temple composed of Jewish and Gentile *"living stones"* (1Pe 2:5). Through a study of Romans 11, the flint knife of circumcision will continue to cut away the foreskin of man's doctrines, which has covered our hearts and dulled our understanding of God's sovereign will for a holy remnant.

The apostle Paul, a Jew of Jews, was sent to the Gentiles to bring them the Messiah of Israel and all of His promised blessings. Paul knew well that ignorance, pride, and jealousy of the Jews were common attitudes among the Gentile people. He perceived the potential for age-old anti-Jewish attitudes to grow back like an unholy foreskin over the newly circumcised hearts of these first Gentile converts.

Paul's powerful admonitions to the Gentiles in Ephesians 2-3 and Romans 9-11 were written to destroy latent anti-Jewish attitudes. Unfortunately, these are the very Scriptures the Adversary has attempted to eradicate from Christian theology. *The church's ignorance of these scriptural safeguards has allowed the perpetuation of many distorted doctrines and unbiblical attitudes toward Israel.*

YAHveh has always used *remembrance* as a divine method of ensuring His people's obedience. In Ephesians 2-3 and Romans 11, He reminds the messianic Gentiles of their humble origins as aliens from His eternal promises. These fundamental truths were intended to provide a *safeguard* against Gentile hostility, arrogance, and indifference toward the Jews. Unfortunately, lack of understanding of these truths became the downfall of many professing believers throughout the Gentile Christian era.

Paul prefaces this vital message to the Gentiles by baring his heart regarding His Jewish brethren. He tells the Romans:

I am telling the truth in Messiah ... my conscience bearing me witness in the Holy Spirit, that I have great sorrow and unceasing grief in my heart. For I could wish that I myself were accursed, separated from Messiah for the sake of my brethren, my kinsmen according to the flesh, who are

Israelites, to whom belongs the adoption as sons and the glory and the covenants and the giving of the Law and the temple service and the promises ... (Ro 9:1-4)

Paul continues, *"Brethren, my heart's desire and my prayer to YAHVEH for them* [the Israelites] *is for their salvation"* (Ro 10:1). Paul wanted the Gentiles to share with him the deep love of Messiah; he was emphasizing that through the Jews all the nations of the earth have been mightily blessed. Love and appreciation for the Jewish people were pulsing through his heart, a love so deep that if it were possible, he would have forfeited his own salvation in order to save some of his Israelite brethren.

Following this passionate expression of his feelings for Israel, Paul addresses a question that had arisen in the minds of the new Gentile believers. Was the Almighty finished with the people of Israel because they rejected their Messiah? *"I say then, YAHVEH has not rejected His people, has He? May it never be!* [*YAHveh* forbid!] *For I too am an Israelite ... YAHVEH HAS NOT REJECTED HIS PEOPLE ..."* (Ro 11:1-2).

As a Hebrew scholar, Paul was familiar with the words of the ancient prophets, who continually emphasized the Almighty's unchangeable love and eternal plan for His firstborn people. Jeremiah had written concerning *YAHveh's* love for Israel: *"Thus says YAHveh, 'If the heavens above can be measured, And the foundations of the earth searched out below, Then I will also cast off all the offspring of Israel For all that they have done,' declares YAHVEH"* (Jer 31:37).

Paul also knew that in the book of Isaiah, *YAHveh* asks: *"Can a woman forget her nursing child, And have no compassion on the son of her womb? Even these may forget, but I WILL NOT FORGET YOU* [Israel]. *Behold, I have inscribed you on the palms of My hands; Your walls are continually before Me"* (Isa 49:15-16).

As the light of the prophets' words pierces the darkness of man's traditions, let us continue in Romans: *"I say then, they did not stumble so as to fall, did they? May it never be! BUT BY THEIR TRANSGRESSION SALVATION HAS COME TO THE GENTILES, TO MAKE THEM* [Israel] *JEALOUS"* (Ro 11:11).

It is interesting to note that this Scripture, if taught at all, is usually conveyed *only in part.* Satan's strategies have succeeded in obscuring the most vital phrase of this sentence. Perhaps this phrase sounds familiar to you: *"Rather, [because] of their transgression salvation has come to the Gentiles."* This *portion of Scripture,* taken out of context, leads to a deceptive theology that fosters *ignorance and pride* toward the Jewish people.

The truth is this: corporate Israel was blinded and rejected their Messiah in order that the Gentiles would have the opportunity to receive salvation. Why? So that the Gentiles could replace Israel in *YAHveh's* heart and eternal plan? No! *YAHveh* forbid! Rather, the redeemed Gentiles received *with* their salvation *a divine mandate* to be the vehicle by which the Jews would be lovingly and mercifully drawn to their Messiah, *YAHshua.*

Now if their transgression [in rejecting Messiah] *be riches for the world and their failure be riches for the Gentiles,* HOW MUCH MORE WILL THEIR FULFILLMENT BE! BUT I AM SPEAKING TO YOU WHO ARE GENTILES. *Inasmuch then as I am an apostle of Gentiles, I* MAGNIFY MY MINISTRY, IF SOMEHOW I MIGHT MOVE TO JEALOUSY MY FELLOW COUNTRYMEN AND SAVE SOME OF THEM. FOR IF THEIR REJECTION BE THE RECONCILIATION OF THE WORLD, WHAT WILL THEIR ACCEPTANCE BE BUT LIFE FROM THE DEAD? (Ro 11:12-15)

As much as the great apostle loved all people, his primary hope in ministering to the Gentiles was that the Gospel would flow through their humble hearts as a river of life, drawing the Israelites to their Messiah. He understood the mystery and master plan of *YAHveh's* infinite mercy. This master plan *in no way implies* that the salvation of the Gentiles is any less important to YAHveh than the redemption of His firstborn Jewish people.

The Jews' rejection of *YAHshua* was the catalyst for the prophesied "spring rains," the outpouring of the *Ruach HaKodesh,* the Spirit of Truth, which brought the great harvest of Gentiles into His kingdom. Greater yet, the Jews' acceptance of Messiah will be as the outpouring of the "latter rains" (autumn rains)— (see Dt 11:14; Jer 5:24; Joel 2:23)—which will be such a powerful release of His blessings and salvation that Paul called it *"life from the dead"* (Ro 11:15) ... REVIVAL!

Chapter 8
Holy Root, Holy Fruit

As Paul's mandate to the Gentiles continues, he refers to Israel as a *"thriving olive tree"* (see Ro 11 and Jer 11:16). This tree is of a holy Hebrew root, having originated with Abraham, Isaac, and Jacob. Paul writes:

> *"... if the root be holy, the branches are too. But if some of the branches were broken off, and you* [the Gentiles], *being a wild olive, were* GRAFTED IN *among them* [the Jews] AND BECAME PARTAKER WITH THEM OF THE RICH ROOT OF THE OLIVE TREE [the nourishing sap], DO NOT BE ARROGANT *toward the branches; but if you are arrogant,* REMEMBER *that* IT IS NOT YOU WHO SUPPORTS THE ROOT, BUT THE [Hebrew] ROOT SUPPORTS YOU [the engrafted Gentile branches]." *You will say then,* "Branches were broken off so that I might be grafted in." *Quite right, they were broken off for their unbelief, but you stand by your faith.* DO NOT BE CONCEITED, BUT FEAR; FOR IF YAHVEH DID NOT SPARE THE NATURAL BRANCHES, NEITHER WILL HE SPARE YOU. (Ro 11:16-21)

These scriptural mandates to Gentile believers are foundational and *not optional* for all who truly seek to be *Holy to YAHveh.* The apostle's warning to Gentiles against self-righteousness and conceit is not to be taken lightly. Many Christians throughout the centuries have not known these fundamental truths concerning the Hebrew root. The Mighty One of Israel warns, *"My people are destroyed for lack of knowledge"* (Hos 4:6).

As a result of this ignorance and apathy, many of the "engrafted branches" have become detached from the holy Hebrew root. They have not received the spiritual vitality of its original nourishing sap; and consequently have dried, withered, and produced shriveled fruit that has detracted from the glory of the holy olive tree. Unfortunately, this is the over-all condition of much of Christianity at the close of the Gentile age.

The Spirit of Truth is calling all branches. He is beckoning the "natural" and "wild" olive branches to attach themselves to the holy root. Any branch not directly attached to the holy root will not receive the fullness of its nourishing sap and will inevitably dry and wither. Such a branch will never bear

65

sumptuous spiritual fruit that glorifies the Creator and attracts perishing souls.

At the close of the Gentile age, many engrafted wild olive branches are in jeopardy of being cut off. Paul warned that *arrogance* would be the fatal blow to these engrafted Gentiles, who haughtily believe that they have replaced the natural Jewish branches.

Syntho-Sap

As we study church history as it relates to the Jews, it will become obvious that Satan has succeeded in blighting God's holy olive tree. The Father of Lies has influenced many leaders and laymen to ignore, negate, or despise the Hebrew root and its nourishing sap. Many have replaced it with a counterfeit, man-made, religious syntho-sap. Syntho-sap does not contain *YAHveh's* genuine life-changing spirit.

This false sap will not bring the fullness of *YAHveh's* life to the branches, nor will it bring glory to Him as the Creator. Syntho-sap has been a highly popular product on the religious market for hundreds of years. It comes in a wide variety of flavors and consistencies; it appeals to an assortment of spiritual appetites, lifestyles and needs.

To the basic consumer, this pseudo commodity may look and feel like the real thing; only the discerning, who hunger for righteousness, will notice that it differs from the original holy and nourishing sap. Syntho-sap is widely sold and distributed within many of the various denominations that fill the outer court of religion.

> **WARNING:** *Syntho-sap may have eternally dangerous side-effects!* It should not be used by those who earnestly desire to produce fruit that will remain and pass the heavenly Creator's inspection.

The coming King of Kings strongly advises His people to avoid syntho-sap at any cost. The nourishing original sap, although very rare and spiritually expensive, is still available from the original holy root. The trumpet is sounding from the throne room of the eternal King. He is beseeching a remnant to prepare for the establishment of His righteous kingdom. In His mercy, YAHveh will give to a remnant the *wisdom to discern between the religious and the righteous.*

YAHveh will enlighten this remnant with great spiritual truth. By His Spirit, the *Ruach HaKodesh*, He will separate a people from all that is synthetic; by His might, He will reattach many branches to the holy Hebrew root, then the original nourishing sap will cause them to bear glorious fruit due His holy *memorial-name*.

Many are now being called to choose between "syntho-sap" and the "original sap." May He bless you with discernment to choose wisely.

Chapter 9

"Contrary to Nature"

The great Hebrew apostle continues his admonitions to Gentile believers with a double warning against pride.

> Behold then the KINDNESS and SEVERITY of YAHVEH; to those who fell, severity, but to you [Gentiles], YAHVEH's kindness, IF YOU CONTINUE IN HIS KINDNESS; OTHERWISE YOU ALSO WILL BE CUT OFF. ... For if you [Gentiles] were cut off from what is by nature a WILD OLIVE TREE, and were grafted CONTRARY TO NATURE into a CULTIVATED OLIVE TREE, how much more shall these [the Jews] who are the natural branches be grafted into their own olive tree? (Ro 11:22-24)

Working in an olive grove, the practice is to graft *cultivated* olive branches into a *wild* olive tree in order to improve the fruit of the *wild* olive. If the wild olive is grafted into the cultivated olive tree, the effect is *reverse*; the cultivated olive will run to wildness. Paul was well-aware of the risk of grafting the Gentiles into the holy olive tree because it was "contrary to nature."

Paul warned that the engrafted branches that do not take their nourishing sap from the holy root will eventually become withered; they will be fruitless branches, destined to be cut off as the natural branches (the Jews) are grafted back into their holy olive tree.

To the church at Galatia Paul wrote: *"There is neither Jew nor Greek [Gentile], there is neither slave nor free man, there is neither male nor female, FOR YOU ARE ALL ONE IN MESSIAH YAHSHUA"* (Gal 3:28).

This passage does not negate the fact that Paul wrote of specific roles for males, females, Jews, and Gentiles within the body of Messiah. The Gentiles have been given a specific biblical mandate that is a safeguard against anti-Jewish attitudes, as well as a debt of obedience owed to their Savior.

The Gentile "engrafted branches" are to *remember* their hopeless condition as aliens apart from the God of Israel and His promises. They are to co-labor humbly with *YAHshua*, the Great Shepherd, who is gathering His lost sheep of the house of Israel back to their God. The engrafted branches are to provoke the Jews to envy as they wholeheartedly embrace the holy Hebrew root, receive its nourishing sap, and worship the God of Israel in the reverence and holiness due His name.

The redeemed "wild olive branches" are to reflect *YAHveh's* great mercy—the mercy He showed the Gentiles as He risked polluting the purity and strength of His holy olive tree when He grafted them in. This same mercy is to run as a river of life through the Gentiles as they co-labor with *YAHshua* in sharing His love and salvation with His brethren the Jews.

To this point in Christian history, many Gentile believers have neglected or ignored this vital mandate. It is time for a redeemed, humble remnant to tap into the holy Hebrew root in order to become spiritually healthy olive branches. Let all humble engrafted branches remember to *guard their hearts against arrogance and conceit* as they *remember* the apostle's words to the Gentiles: *"do not be arrogant ... IT IS NOT YOU WHO SUPPORTS THE ROOT, but the* [HEBREW] *root supports you"* (Ro 11:18).

> *For I do not want you, brethren, to be* UNINFORMED OF THIS MYSTERY, *lest you* BE WISE IN YOUR OWN ESTIMATION [conceited] *that a partial hardening has happened to Israel* UNTIL THE FULNESS OF THE GENTILES HAS COME IN; *and thus all Israel* [the surviving Jewish remnant in the last days] *will be saved ... From the standpoint of the gospel they* [the Jews] *are* ENEMIES FOR YOUR SAKE, BUT FROM THE STANDPOINT OF *YAHVEH'S* CHOICE THEY ARE BELOVED FOR THE SAKE OF THE FATHERS [Abraham, Isaac, and Jacob]; *for the gifts and the calling of YAHveh are* IRREVOCABLE. *For just as you once were disobedient to YAHveh, but now have been* SHOWN MERCY *because of their* [the Jews'] *disobedience, so these also now have been disobedient, in order that* BECAUSE OF THE MERCY SHOWN TO YOU THEY ALSO MAY NOW BE SHOWN MERCY [through the redeemed Gentiles]. *For YAHveh has shut up all in disobedience that He might show* MERCY *to all."* (Ro 11:25-32)

May those who have ears to hear heed this warning: *"Do not be conceited, but fear; for if YAHveh did not spare the natural branches, neither will He spare you"* (Ro 11:20-21).

"Sing Aloud with Gladness for Jacob"

YAHshua continues to weep over the *"lost sheep of the house of ISRAEL"* (Mt 10:6). He, along with heaven's host, is longing to hear them say, *"BLESSED IS HE [YAHshua] WHO COMES IN THE*

NAME OF YAHVEH!" (Mt 23:39). Now is the time to favor Zion; those who bring the mercy, love, and Jewish essence of Messiah to His Jewish people are hastening the day of His return.

Let the righteous remnant rejoice with *YAHveh* our Father over his son, Israel, who is like the prodigal son who *"was dead, and has come to life again ... was lost, and has been found"* (Lk 15:24).

Like the prodigal son, a remnant of Israel will return to the Father. In gleaning understanding from this biblical illustration, there is a special warning that can be equally applicable to the Gentile brethren: Do not be like the jealous brother of the parable. Although this brother had been serving his father with sincerity, resentment for his sibling caused such rivalry that he refused to go in to the banquet. Your Father asks you, "Does not all that I have belong to you?" (see Lk 15:31).

Let us obey His commission and rejoice with him. *"For thus says YAHveh, 'Sing aloud with gladness for Jacob, And shout among the chiefs of the nations; Proclaim, give praise, and say, "O YAHveh, save Thy people, The remnant of Israel"'"* (Jer 31:7).

A great spiritual banquet will be given as the remnant of Israel recognizes and embraces her Messiah. As in the parable of the prodigal son, many Jews will return to reverently embrace their heavenly Father. There will be the slaying of the fatted calf, which will bring bountiful blessings *to the whole family of YAHveh.* The main course of this joyful banquet will be a deeper revelation of *YAHveh,* the Father, and *YAHshua,* the Son. Those who come to the banquet will feast on many hidden scriptural treasures, which will be unsealed and presented to the righteous remnant that shares the Father's joy.

We need to heed the words of Isaiah:
For Zion's sake I will not keep silent,
And for Jerusalem's [YAHrushalayim's] sake I will not keep quiet,
Until her righteousness goes forth like brightness,
And her salvation like a torch that is burning. ...
On your walls, O Jerusalem, I have appointed watchmen;
All day and all night they will never keep silent.
You who remind YAHveh, take no rest for yourselves;
And give Him no rest until He establishes
And makes Jerusalem [YAHrushalayim] a praise in the earth.
(Isa 62:1, 6-7)

PART THREE

Dedicated to the Tribes of Dan and Naphtali

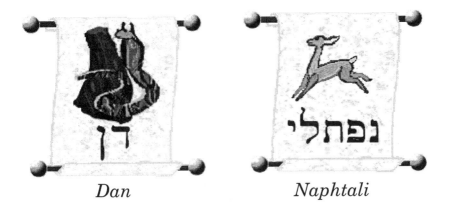

Dan   Naphtali

And you shall say to them, "Thus says YAHVEH," ...
'Why then has this people ... Turned away in continual apostasy?
THEY HOLD FAST TO DECEIT, They refuse to return.
I have listened and heard, THEY HAVE SPOKEN WHAT IS NOT RIGHT
NO MAN REPENTED OF HIS WICKEDNESS, SAYING, "WHAT HAVE I DONE?" ...'
BUT MY PEOPLE DO NOT KNOW THE ORDINANCE [requirements] OF YAHVEH.
'How can you say, "We are wise, And the law of YAHVEH is with us"?'
BUT BEHOLD, THE LYING PEN OF THE SCRIBES HAS MADE IT INTO A LIE. ...
Behold, they have rejected the word of YAHveh,
And what kind of wisdom do they have? ...

BECAUSE FROM THE LEAST EVEN TO THE GREATEST EVERYONE IS GREEDY FOR
GAIN; FROM THE PROPHET EVEN TO THE PRIEST EVERYONE PRACTICES DECEIT.
'And they heal the brokenness of the daughter of My people
[Israel] superficially, Saying, "Peace, peace" … 'WERE THEY
ASHAMED BECAUSE OF THE ABOMINATION THEY HAD DONE?' … "
(Jer 8:4-12)

Who is the wise man that may understand this? And who is he to
whom the mouth of YAHVEH has spoken, that he may declare it?
… THEY HAVE FORSAKEN MY LAW [the full counsel of Scripture,
including the divine mandate to bless the Jews] which I set
before them, and have not obeyed My voice nor walked according
to it, but have walked after the stubbornness of their heart …
(Jer 9:12-14)

"See, I will send venomous snakes among you, vipers that cannot
be charmed, and they will bite you."
(Jer 8:17 NIV)

Chapter 10
Prologue to the Ancient Serpent's Trail

Paul was well aware of intrinsic *pride* and *jealousy* against the Jewish people. He also perceived the looming potential for ancient anti-Jewish attitudes to grow back as a foreskin over the hearts of the newly spiritually-circumcised Gentiles.

In Ephesians 2-3 and Romans 9-11, Paul delivers a powerful admonition to these early messianic Gentiles, warning them against the resurgence of an anti-Semitic mind set. Unfortunately, as previously mentioned, these are the very Scriptures that the Enemy has strategically obscured or obliterated from the mentality of corporate Christianity.

Today in Jerusalem, as plans for the reconstruction of the Almighty's earthly temple are underway, so too is *YAHshua* working to build His spiritual temple for His near return and the establishment of His eternal kingdom. Time is of the essence; the Master Architect is going to remove all hindrances and stumbling blocks from among His people. He is going to build His holy house, His spiritual temple, according to His sovereign blueprints.

Those who call Him "Savior" must know and do His perfect will. *YAHveh's* holy decrees and His plumb line of truth often differ from man's doctrines and religious traditions. We will either yield as *living stones* in the hands of the Master Builder, or we will become *stumbling blocks* to His divine and sovereign purposes. The Almighty says, *"Build up, build up, prepare the way, REMOVE EVERY OBSTACLE out of the way of My people"* (Isa 57:14).

Bearing in mind the mandates and warnings written to Gentile believers and using these Scriptures as our plumb line of truth, let's take a look at how crooked the walls of Christianity have become. May *YAHshua's* Spirit grant us humility and a willingness to see how far man's doctrines and "building agendas" have veered from *YAHveh's* original blueprints. May He impart to us an understanding of His purposes as clearly expressed through the full counsel of both the Old and New Testament Scriptures.

Before we begin this overview, we should be mindful of two important facts. First, *YAHveh* clearly states, *"For My thoughts are not your thoughts, Neither are your ways My ways"* (Isa 55:8).

73

Second, *"our struggle is not against flesh and blood"* (Eph 6:12). The battle is spiritual. It is *"against the powers, against the world forces of this darkness, against the spiritual forces of wickedness in the heavenly places"* (Eph 6:12).

Throughout history, Satan, the ancient Serpent (Rev 12:9 NIV), has strategized relentlessly to thwart the Almighty's glorious eternal plan. The apostle Paul reminds us that we must not be *"ignorant of his schemes"* (2Co 2:11).

Chapter 11
The Serpent's Trail Begins

Anti-Semitism is an ancient hostility toward the Jewish people and their God, *YAHveh*. In order to understand the essence of the hatred of and persistent warfare against Israel, a brief history of anti-Semitism is needed. The battle between God's people and Satan has raged since the Garden of Eden; it has left a bloody trail throughout biblical and world history. The Serpent will continue to spew his anti-Semitic venom until the Messiah crushes him and all of Israel's enemies under His holy, vengeful feet.

The ancient Serpent made his initial appearance in the Garden of Eden. There he injected his lethal venom of deception into the bloodstream of mankind. However, by the Creator's holy vengeance, Satan's ultimate doom was sealed. *YAHveh* declared to His Adversary, *"And I will put enmity Between you and the woman, And between your seed and her seed; He* [Messiah] SHALL BRUISE YOU ON THE HEAD, AND YOU SHALL BRUISE HIM ON THE HEEL" (Ge 3:15).

The Almighty's pronouncement of Satan's future destruction caused the Adversary's hatred to rise to immeasurable proportions. In fury, the Serpent went on a raging quest to destroy the promised "seed," through whom his ultimate defeat would come.

The battle lines were drawn. Satan knew he must kill or be killed. Like all crafty serpents, he hid himself in the dust of the earth. Man, who was created from the dust of the earth, became the vehicle through which he would war against the promised seed of woman. Poised, ready to attack, he waited for the appearance of his prey.

What was the lineage of people through whom the man-child Redeemer would come? The Jewish race—through *Abraham*, his son *Isaac*, Isaac's son *Jacob*, and Jacob's twelve sons—was chosen by *YAHveh* as the lineage through which the Redeemer of mankind and the destroyer of Satan would come.

Don't Thwart *YAHveh's* Blessings

YAHveh made an everlasting promise to Abraham, Isaac, Jacob, and their offspring from the twelve tribes of Israel[1]—the Jewish people. God declared to Abraham:

> *"And I will make you a great nation, And I will bless you, And make your name great; And so you shall be a blessing; AND I WILL BLESS THOSE WHO BLESS YOU, And THE ONE WHO CURSES YOU I WILL CURSE. And in you all the families of the earth SHALL BE BLESSED."* (Ge 12:2-3)

In addition to these promises, *YAHveh* granted Abraham and his descendants (the Jewish people) an area of land from the river of Egypt to the great river Euphrates. The boundaries of this land include all of modern-day Israel, the disputed territories, and much more.

YAHveh gave the Holy Land to His chosen people through an everlasting covenant. Even today, any person or nation that embraces a political or religious doctrine opposed to this biblical fact will inevitably find itself fighting against the Mighty One of Israel. The Bible tells us that this heated controversy over the land of Israel, which has raged since ancient times, will one day climax in the war of all wars, called *Armageddon* (see Rev. 16:16).

Due to the focus of this book, the issue of God's everlasting gift of the land of Israel to the Jewish people will not be addressed. Suffice it to say, however, that those who know the God of Israel and the Messiah will readily accept and affirm this biblical truth.

Ancient Agents of Anti-Semitism

The Almighty, well aware of Satan's vendetta against Israel, took divine precaution and built a wall of protection around His chosen nation. *YAHveh's* declaration to bless all who would bless Abraham's descendants and to curse any person or nation who dared to curse them was and is a safeguard for His people. His warning to the Gentiles is still in effect: *Do not curse those whom*

---

[1] Jacob's name was changed to Israel after he wrestled with *YAHveh* (who came as a messenger in the form of an angel, Ge 32:24-25, 28). His twelve sons are the heads of the twelve tribes of Israel (note the seals of the twelve tribes at the beginning of each "Part" of this book). The Jewish Messiah was born from the tribe of Judah.

YAHveh has commanded you to bless, or you will be under His curse! (see Ge 12:3; Nu 23:19- 20; 24:9).

The Abrahamic covenant is a plumb line of truth by which the Holy One judges individuals and nations, and by which they will ultimately be built up or torn down. Biblical and world history testify to this.

With Abraham's seed targeted for attack, the ancient Serpent formulated his hideous scheme to destroy this chosen nation before the Messiah could be born. His strategy was to inject his venom into the heart and mind of Ishmael, Isaac's brother, and later into Esau, Jacob's brother.

This poison of sibling rivalry—jealousy, hostility, and revenge—has powerfully permeated millions of Ishmael's and Esau's descendants to this day. This venom bred a consuming, obsessive hatred of Israel. Throughout history, as these nations have yielded to anti-Semitism, they have become Satan's primary earthly agents for the destruction of the Jews.

The Bible and many history books are filled with accounts of the Adversary's vicious attacks against the Jews. The consequences of these attacks affirm the sovereignty of *YAHveh's* curses on any agent of Satan who perpetuates this deadly venom of Jew-hatred.

The Edomites and the Amalekites were two biblical nations that descended from Esau, Jacob's jealous and angry brother. The Old Testament is full of prophetic judgments against these enemies of Israel. For example, because the Amalekites continually warred against Israel, *YAHveh* declared in anger, *"Write this in a book as a memorial ... that I will* UTTERLY BLOT OUT THE MEMORY OF AMALEK *from under heaven"* (Ex 17:14).

YAHveh's memory is not a short list of vengeances; it is an eternal scroll of remembrance. In His sovereignty, the Mighty One will completely destroy all of Israel's enemies, sparing only those who bless Israel. Only these will warrant *YAHveh's* promised blessings.

Throughout Scripture, the Edomites[2] (Esau's descendants) are symbolic of any person or nation that harbors Satan's hatred

---

[2] *The NIV Study Bible* (Grand Rapids: The Zondervan Corporation, 1985), p. 1064 (footnote on Isaiah 34:5, regarding Edom: *"Edom.* Symbolic of all the enemies of God and his people, ...") — (footnote on 34:8: "The *Edomites* opposed Israel at every opportunity... But Edom's day would come ...") — (footnote on 34:9: "Edom's destruction is compared with the overthrow of Sodom and Gomorrah.")

for the Jews and continually opposes Israel. *YAHveh's* judgment against Edom for anti-Semitism is clearly stated:[3]

"O how Esau will be ransacked, And his hidden treasures searched out! ... "Will I not on that day," declares YAHveh, "Destroy wise men from Edom? ... "Because of violence TO YOUR BROTHER JACOB, You will be covered with shame, And you will be cut off forever. ... DO NOT GLOAT OVER YOUR BROTHER'S [Israel's] DAY, The day of his misfortune." (Ob vv. 6-12)

Moab was another agent of the Serpent's anti-Semitic venom. Jeremiah prophesied concerning *YAHveh's* judgments on Israel's enemy:

"Moab will wallow in his vomit, and he also will become a laughingstock. Now was not ISRAEL A LAUGHINGSTOCK TO YOU? Or was he CAUGHT AMONG THIEVES [nations, individuals, religions, and doctrines that steal from Israel what is rightfully her inheritance]? *..."* (Jer 48:26-27)

The redeemed remnant must beware of "replacement theology" which Satan has insidiously injected into the bloodstream of Christianity over many centuries. This doctrine resembles the spirit and pride of Edom and Moab. Ishmael, Esau, and their descendants claimed Israel's promises to be their own. In a similar manner, those who embrace replacement theology suppose that Israel's promises now belong to the *Christian church*, which they believe has replaced Israel in God's heart and plan.

Doctrines that have arisen against the knowledge of *YAHveh's* eternal purpose for Israel are destined to be destroyed like the pride of Moab:

"We have heard of the pride of Moab ... Of his haughtiness, his pride, his arrogance and his self-exaltation. ... And Moab will be DESTROYED ... Because he

---

[3] Ibid., p. 1360 (Intro. to Obadiah), "Since the Edomites are related to the Israelites, their hostility is all the more reprehensible. Edom is fully responsible for her failure to assist Israel...") — p. 1361, ("... The day of Edom's destruction; ... Since in O.T. prophecy Edom was often emblematic of all the world powers hostile to God and his kingdom, her judgment anticipates God's complete removal of all such opposition in that day ...") — Obadiah v. 11, "He did not act like a brother but was like one of the strangers." — p. 1362, Ob v. 15, "... *The day of the Lord brings judgment for the nations* [including, but not limited to Edom] *and salvation for the House of Jacob...*"

has become arrogant toward YAHveh" (Jer 48:29, 42).
[Remember Paul's warning regarding Gentile arrogance against the Jews (Ro 11:20-21).]

As we follow the slippery path of the ancient Serpent, we find that his next great strategy was fulfilled by Pharaoh of Egypt. This satanic agent was fearful because of the increasing number of Israelites and their potential power in the land. He plotted the mass murder of all Jewish male infants. Through Pharaoh's paranoia, Satan attempted to terminate the Hebrew race before the Redeemer could be born. Again, *YAHveh* foiled the plans of the Adversary. The Hebrew race was perpetuated, yet the Serpent continued to plot against Israel.

During the 400s B.C.E.[4] Haman, a descendent of King Agag, embraced the ancient anti- Semitism of his Amalekite forefathers. As a high-ranking Medo-Persian official, he became Satan's agent for perpetuating hatred against the Jews. His diabolical plan was to have every Israelite killed in one day. Queen *Hadassah* (Esther) was used by *YAHveh* to intervene, and the Jews were divinely spared.

Before every major move of the Almighty on behalf of Israel, the Enemy attempted to wipe out the Jewish race. At the time of the Redeemer's prophesied birth, Satan launched another massive attack. This time, King Herod was the embodiment of the Serpent's poisonous paranoia. Dread of the coming infant "King of the Jews" provoked Herod to issue a murderous edict. All Hebrew boys under age two were destined for slaughter. *YAHshua*, the man-child Messiah, escaped Satan's vengeful strategies just as His forefather Moses had centuries before.

Although the Serpent's appetite for Jewish blood was temporarily satisfied, his main purpose was foiled again. The Mighty One of Israel is always the victor over His Adversary's schemes! In spite of this hideous plot, the Jewish Messiah, Satan's dreaded conqueror, was born.

The Enemy's blood boiled in his evil veins the day the infant *YAHshua* was circumcised unto the God of Israel. There in the temple, the infant Messiah was heralded by the prophet Simeon and prophetess Anna. He was honored and praised as *"the consolation of Israel"* (Lk 2:25), the *"light of revelation to the Gentiles"* (Lk 2:32), and *"the glory of Thy people Israel"* (Lk 2:32).

---

[4] B.C.E., meaning "before the common era," is used in place of B.C. throughout this book; C.E., meaning "of the common era," is used in place of A.D.

Murderous hatred flared in Satan's nostrils. Enraged and panic-stricken, he again surmised that he must kill or be killed. It was then the Serpent cunningly infused deception into the hearts of the power-hungry, the self-righteous, and the traditionally religious. He stirred up a mob of Jews, Gentiles, religious leaders, and Roman rulers to nail the "King of the Jews" to a tree at Calvary.

As the blood of *YAHshua* spilled out upon the earth, the crafty Serpent must have let out a shout of victory that echoed throughout hell's domain. Little did he realize that this victory shout would soon become a gasp of defeat. The ancient Serpent was ensnared by his own devious devices. Messiah's spilled blood would now redeem and empower an army of Jews and Gentiles, and unite them into *one new man* (Eph 2:15). Satan's ultimate defeat was now *written and sealed in the very blood of the One* he so furiously plotted to destroy.

Chapter 12
"Hisssss" Says the Serpent

NOTE TO THE READER — This next section of the ancient Serpent is written as a childlike satire. Due to the intense nature of this highly sensitive subject, this capricious style will help the reader to understand this issue as spiritual and not a battle between flesh and blood.

Thus we continue to see the unfolding saga of the successive slithery steps of Satan, the slimy Serpent, Hissssss..... The loathsome creature was truly in a revolting development. In his beady-eyed, near-sighted vision, he had not foreseen that the spilled blood of Messiah would bring eternal salvation to Jews and Gentiles. He, like all mankind, had no clue of the "great mystery," that through Messiah's death, the ancient wall of hostility between Israel and the Gentiles would be destroyed (Eph 2:14). The *Gentiles* would be *joined with Jews* to form *one new man* (Eph 2:15) a mighty army under whose feet the Devil's ultimate defeat is sealed.

Oh how the ancient Serpent had cherished that dividing wall separating Jew from Gentile! Although it had been constructed by *YAHveh* to protect His chosen people from Gentile influences, the old Devil found it to be a real asset in his warfare against the Jews. How often Satan and his legions had fortified that dividing wall with their venomous lies.

How diligently the Adversary had worked to keep that wall erect. What was he to do now that the dividing wall was destroyed? Surely there would be a mass exodus of his earthly allied forces over to the ranks of his arch enemy, *YAHshua*. What a major defeat for Satan to see the Gentiles marching as *one new man—together with the Jews*—in bonds of peace, love, and obedience to their Commander in Chief.

YAHveh had outwitted him again! There was big trouble with a capital "T" for the Serpent General and his legions. Satan raged as he remembered how that wall had served his evil purposes for so many centuries. Now in one day, on a tree at Calvary, he outsmarted himself and grossly miscalculated the consequences of his evil plot. The wall was destroyed right in front of his beady eyes. It disintegrated into nothing *under the blood* of the Redeemer of mankind.

But all was not lost for the Adversary. Out of his defeat emerged another diabolical plan. He remembered well from slithering about and spying on his enemy that *YAHshua* had said, *"If a house is divided against itself, that house will not be able to stand"* (Mk 3:25).

With that point in view, Satan devised a new strategy. He must erect another dividing wall to separate the *one new man* back into two opposing peoples. This scheme would ultimately cause the precious spilled blood of *YAHshua* to *appear* ineffective and become a mockery to the world.

This called for a red hot celebration to be given by the crafty Devil and all his demonic cohorts. The Serpent General, puffed with pride over his brilliant brain storm, began chanting one of his old proven satanic slogans. "Divide and Conquer" became the motivating motto and anthem for this new strategy.

All of hell's legions were once again marching to its destructive beat.

In Sheol's conference room, the Prince of Darkness called a meeting of his best diabolical minds. The topic for discussion was how to separate what Messiah had joined together. A devious plan was implemented; they would construct *another dividing wall*.

As this satanic meeting was in session, the Spirit of Truth was working mightily to add Jews and Gentiles to *YAHshua's* army. This army, known as the *one new man*, was inseparably linked together with bonds of peace, love, and unity.

Around the holy camp was a high, thick wall of protection to *safeguard the costly unity and purity of Jew and Gentile which Messiah died to purchase*. The Almighty built this wall with pure truth and reinforced it with the mortar of Paul's warning to the Gentiles in Ephesians 2 and 3, and Romans 11.

Paul, an Israelite and brave spiritual soldier, had once been Satan's puppet. Now, he was *YAHveh's* high ranking ally within Messiah's army. Keenly aware of the Devil's strategies, this spiritual warrior was going to be much trouble to the Serpent General. The protecting wall was partially Paul's handiwork. It served to protect the holiness of the redeemed remnant. More specifically, it guarded the hearts and minds of believing Gentiles from the Serpent's ancient pride and hostility towards the Jews.

Satan knew that once the Jewish apostles died, it was only a matter of time before their teachings and safeguards would be diluted. Then the engrafted Gentiles (Ro 11:17) would become vulnerable to these insidious anti-Semitic attitudes once again.

That day came. The great apostles died; their words were soon misunderstood and distorted through Gentile men. It was prime time for the Serpent General and his troops to advance. He scouted the unguarded area, slithered up and scaled the wall. The coast was clear for him to infiltrate the ranks of *YAHshua's* unsuspecting soldiers.

His evil eyes peered hatefully over the protective wall. His venom boiled when he saw many Gentiles whom he had bound from birth. Once, they had been his agents of anti-Semitism on earth. Now, through the blood of *YAHshua*, they were allied with the Jews.

To his disgust, the Serpent saw Jews and Gentiles marching in harmony as a holy army. Oh, how he hated that unifying love! These redeemed soldiers marched in synchrony, following their Commander in Chief and praising *YAHveh*. This *one new man* battalion was being divinely prepared and empowered to bombard the gates of hell as they went forth in His name.

The Serpent General was enraged as he saw more and more prison doors flying open, and his captives being freed to follow *YAHshua* Messiah. That did it! He was not going to take this lying down. He was no weak little garden snake. He was the ancient Serpent and this was no time to slither back!

He called an emergency meeting and said:

Devious Demons and Crafty Cohorts:

Our name is at stake. Everything we've killed for, all the souls we've captured, and all the venom our fangs have injected into humanity could be lost. Sharpen your fangs. Increase your production of the ancient venom. Be ready to attack!

Then the Serpent continued:

Here's the plan—HISSssssss. Work only in the dark. While some of the soldiers are sleeping, wait for the watchmen to grow weary and look for breaks in the walls. Slither down quickly into their camp and hide in the dust. During the day, look for those who have broken rank—those who are not busy with the Commander's business. These are the ones who usually neglect to put on their full armor; they make perfect targets. Lunge for the heel and inject the FORGETFUL ONES with the ancient venom of hostility, pride and jealousy towards the Jewish people.

The Serpent General and his crafty troops slithered over the wall and through the developing cracks directly into the ranks of the unsuspecting soldiers. The initial attack was subtle. There were only a few who could be caught off guard. The words of the apostle Paul were still sealed in their memories and protected their hearts. The Devil knew he had to be sneaky. The form of venom and its symptoms must not be too obvious or his plot would be in vain.

Lethal Injection

From the second century on, Satan's attacks increased in number. By the fourth century, he had successfully injected his anti-Jewish poison into several key Christian leaders. Consequently, many had become spiritually sick and delirious from his lethal bite.

Before long, these victims began to react in ways that were contrary to the heart and purpose of their Commander in Chief. Indeed, the Serpent had succeeded! By infiltrating *YAHshua's* ranks, he had deceived many Gentile believers and enlisted them to promulgate his anti-Semitic doctrines and traditions.

The wall of division between the Jews and Gentiles was resurrected. This was a time of darkness and gloom in world history. The bright light of *YAHshua's* love and the full counsel of *YAHveh's* Word became obscured behind the doctrines and traditions of Gentile men.

Viper Eggs—The Big Lie

The Serpent General's infiltration of *YAHshua's* ranks was meeting with success. Undetected, he slithered around the camp looking for hearts in which to deposit his viper eggs. As the full counsel of *YAHveh's* Word became increasingly diluted and distorted, many unsuspecting victims became hatcheries for Satan's venomous offspring.

Ignorance of Scripture and of *YAHveh's* heart and plan for Israel became the perfect environment for these "viper eggs" to thrive. There they incubated, later hatched, and then matured as anti-Semitic religious and political doctrines. These doctrines would mobilize many Christians in a diabolical onslaught against Messiah's beloved brethren.

One of the biggest, most destructive lies that the Serpent hatched as a viper egg among Christians was that *Jews are Christ-killers*; so it came to be believed that *Jews are eternally rejected by God.* Based on totally unscriptural foundations, many Christians now began to believe that *the church has **replaced** Israel.*

These venomous lies led to the continued distortion of the Word of YAHveh over the centuries. But Messiah said, *"You shall know the truth, and the truth shall make you free"* (Jn 8:32). Regarding who killed the Savior, Scripture is clear. *YAHshua* predicted to His disciples before His death:

"Behold, we are going up to Jerusalem; and the Son of Man will be delivered up to the CHIEF PRIESTS and SCRIBES [representing only a small fraction of Israel], and they will condemn Him to death, and will deliver Him to the GENTILES to mock and scourge and crucify Him, and on the third day He will be raised up." (Mt 20:18-19)

The Bible tells us: *"For truly in this city there were gathered together against Thy holy servant YAHshua, ... both Herod and Pontius Pilate, along with the Gentiles and the peoples of Israel ..."* (Ac 4:27). Jews, Gentiles, Pilate, Herod, and the Roman government were all partially responsible for Messiah's death. In truth, however, *YAHshua* made it clear that these men had no power to kill Him apart from His Father's perfect will. Indeed, it was *YAHveh's* perfect will that the Son willingly gave His life as the sacrificial Passover Lamb. In this single, glorious act, *YAHshua* redeemed His Jewish brethren and made a way for Gentile aliens to be joined with Israel to partake of Messiah's salvation.

Chapter 13

Do You Know What Hurts Me?

The purpose of the next three chapters is to expose Satan's strategies and lies, many of which have become imbedded in the doctrines and traditions of corporate Christianity. *It is important to note that these chapters are not intended as an indictment against any individual, race, or religious group.*

Throughout the centuries, there has always been a righteous remnant of God's people. These believers have prayed for Israel and blessed the Jewish people with the love of their Messiah. Through their loving obedience, many lost sheep of the house of Israel have been drawn into the kingdom of their long-awaited Messiah. *YAHveh* will certainly be faithful to this remnant and will bestow on them His blessings as promised in Genesis 12:3.

To truly love *YAHveh*, we must be willing to open our hearts to know what hurts Him. There is a story of a Hasidic rabbi whose student comes to him saying, "Master, I love you."

"Do you know what hurts me?" the rabbi asks tenderly.

The student is taken aback. "What do you mean, do I know what hurts you?"

"Unless you know what hurts and grieves me," responds the rabbi, *"you can't possibly love me."*

For almost two thousand years, Messiah's blood has been trampled as His brethren, the Jews, have been persecuted, tortured, driven out of countries, and killed in the name of Jesus Christ. Many Christians have believed the lie that the Jews were "Christ-killers." Consequently, much of Israel's history has been written in the blood of *YAHshua's* slaughtered brethren.

With *YAHveh's* truth as our plumb line, let's examine the foundation and walls of the religious system men have built throughout Christian history. We begin with a brief overview of several famous church fathers—men who are respected as some of the great pillars of the church. It is a grievous paradox that *these same men are infamous to the Jewish people.*

Keeping in mind that *YAHshua* died to make Jewish and Gentile believers into *one new man,* how is it possible that the same "church fathers" are famous and beloved to Christians, yet dreaded and infamous to Jews? *Remember that while Messiah died to tear down the dividing wall between Jew and Gentile, Satan lives to resurrect it.*

May the following accounts serve as the flint knife of circumcision to cut away any ignorance, pride, hostility, and indifference you may have toward the Jews. And may the pain of circumcision sensitize your heart to our heavenly Father's deep sorrow over the tragic treatment of His chosen people throughout church history. Then when you say that you love Him and He asks, "Do you know what hurts Me?" *you will truly know.*

The Darkness of Men's Doctrines

Beginning with Origen (185-254 C.E.), an erroneous foundation of biblical interpretation was laid through an allegorical view of Old Testament prophecy.[1] According to Origen's interpretation, Israel was rejected by God and His covenant with them nullified because of their rejection of Messiah. This venomous lie bred another lie that is still advanced today—the church is now "true Israel" and has replaced the Jewish nation in God's sight. According to this deceptive theology, all of Israel's promises, prophetic blessings, and covenants now belong solely to the church.

> The consequences of this doctrine were subtle at first. The most serious consequence was that the protections provided by the clear Scriptural warnings of God against those who would harm His covenant people were snatched away. A feeling of contempt naturally followed, since, in the eyes of those who held this view, the Jews were clinging to a hope that now belonged only to the Church... . The Church leaders saw no justification for the Jews to remain a distinct people, since in their view, their hopes belonged exclusively to the church forever.
>
> ... when the church began to see itself as God's true Israel, the inheritor of the covenant promises made to Israel, then in the eyes of the Church, the Israelites ceased to have any legitimate purpose or right to exist as a people.[2]

Mr. Lindsey continues:

---

[1] For an in-depth and sobering study, see Dr. Michael Brown's book, *Our Hands Are Stained With Blood*; and Hal Lindsey's book, *Road to Holocaust.*

[2] Hal Lindsey, *The Road to Holocaust* (New York: Bantam Books, 1989), pp. 8-9.

These prophetic views were a complete departure from the original teachings of the Apostolic Fathers of the Church, whose period extended from 33 C.E. to shortly after 100 C.E.... .

... the early Christians ... recognize the Jews as a chosen people with whom God will yet fulfill His promises.

These views also promoted a compassion for the Jews because the Christians saw them as a demonstration of God's faithfulness to His Word. And most important, the early believers held that God would judge anyone who unjustly harmed a Jew in accordance with His promise of protection to him in the Abrahamic covenant. **"I will bless those who bless you, and the one who curses you I will curse."** (Genesis 12:3 — emphasis in source)[3]

Infamous Words of the Famous Fathers

The apostle Paul's warnings to the Gentiles were disregarded by those who promoted these new, anti-Israel interpretations of Scripture. The Serpent's egg had indeed hatched into a new breed of so-called doctrine.

Chrysostom was praised as one of the most dynamic preachers of truth and divine love; even his name means "golden-mouthed." Because of his eloquent preaching, he was revered as one of the notable church fathers. Unfortunately and paradoxically, his exemplary compassion and sensitivity were not demonstrated in his attitudes towards the Jews. Chrysostom wrote:

The synagogue is worse than a brothel ... it is the den of scoundrels and the repair of wild beasts ... the temple of demons devoted to idolatrous cults ... the refuge of brigands and debauches, and the cavern of devils. [It is] a criminal assembly of Jews ... a place of meeting for the assassins of Christ ... a house worse than a drinking shop ... a den of thieves; a house of ill fame, a dwelling of iniquity, the refuge of devils, gulf and abyss of perdition.

As for the Jewish people themselves Chrysostom

---

[3] Ibid., pp. 10-11.

commented, "I would say the same things about their souls." And so, "As for me, I hate the synagogue ... I hate the Jews for the same reason."[4]

Thus billows the voice of a respected church father and pillar of historical Christianity who preached, "It is incumbent on all Christians to hate the Jews."[5] Dr. Michael L. Brown comments:

What happened to Christian love? Paul had wished that he could be cursed in place of his Jewish people. Chrysostom instead cursed them! How much destruction was subsequently ignited by these tragic sermons of malice? The Catholic historian Malcolm Hay is surely right when he says, "For many centuries the Jews listened to the echo of those three words of St. John Chrysostom, the Golden-Mouthed: 'God hates you.'" And thus, "the popular Christian doctrine has always been that anyone, whether pagan or Christian, who has at any time persecuted, tortured or massacred Jews has acted as an instrument of Divine wrath."[6]

St. Jerome attempted to *prove* that the Jews are incapable of understanding the Scriptures and that they should be assigned a place with the base and illiterate. It is nonsensical that the very ones through whom the Scriptures were written should be considered incapable of comprehending them. St. Jerome's teachings were aimed at the severe persecution of the Jews, forcing them to confess the faith of Christianity.

St. Augustine (354-425 c.e.) built on Origen's allegorical method of interpretation. Through Augustine's teaching came a strong theology that would become part of the man-made structure of organized Christianity over the next thousand years. This teaching strengthened the erroneous doctrine that the Christian church was now the inheritor of Israel's promises. Augustine accused the Jew of being the image of Judas Iscariot, who was forever guilty and spiritually ignorant.

These distorted views of Scripture were completely opposed

---

[4] Michael L. Brown, *Our Hands are Stained with Blood* (Shippensburg, PA: Destiny Image Publishers, 1992), pp. 10- 11. Dr. Brown, in his work cited here, is quoting from the following: Raul Hillberg, *The Destruction of the European Jews*—one volume edition (New York: Holmes & Meier, 1985), pp. 7ff. and 27-28.

[5] Erwin W. Lutzer, *Hitler's Cross* (Chicago: Moody Press, 1995), p. 87.

[6] Ibid., p.11.

to the original teachings of the Hebrew fathers of the faith (see Eph 2-3 and Ro 9-11). The ancient Serpent's strategy had succeeded in breeding doctrinal misinterpretations that would perpetuate his venomous lies in the centuries to come.

Raul Hillberg, a noted scholar of the Holocaust, summarizes the essence of Satan's diabolical strategy to infect the church with anti-Semitism as follows:

> Since the fourth century after Christ there have been three anti-Jewish policies: (forced) conversion, expulsion, annihilation. The second appeared as an alternative to the first, and the third emerged as an alternative to the second. ... The missionaries of Christianity had said in effect: You have no right to live among us. The Nazis at last decreed: You have no right to live.
>
> The process began with the attempt to drive the Jews into Christianity. The development was continued in order to force the victims into exile. It was finished when the Jews were driven to their deaths. The German Nazis, then, did not discard the past; they built upon it. They did not begin a development; they completed it.[7]

David cried out in his psalm:

Do you rulers indeed speak justly? Do you judge uprightly among men? No, in your heart you devise injustice, and your hands mete out violence on the earth. Even from birth the wicked go astray ... they are wayward and speak lies. THEIR VENOM IS LIKE THE VENOM OF A SNAKE ... (Ps 58:1-4 NIV — emphasis added)

Anti-Jewish Atrocities

In 313 C.E. the emperor Constantine converted to Christianity and made the Christian faith the official religion of the Roman Empire. Constantine's conversion was a glorious turning point for the persecuted Christians. However, his policies proved destructive to the Jewish people and to the Hebrew foundations of the Christian faith.

Constantine harbored Satan's ancient hostility toward

---

[7] Raul Hillberg, op. cit., p. 7ff.

Israel and labeled the Jews a wicked, villainous, and perverse sect.

> ... by the early fifth century, the Church believed that it was the sole possessor of Israel's covenant promises, including the ownership of the promised land. Acting from this false premise, the Church began to use its new political power to create and enforce anti-Jewish legislation—a practice that became usual in the Middle Ages. In many cases throughout the Middle Ages, the institutional Church either forced Jews to convert by political oppression and terror, or put them to the sword.
>
> Once again, it was the false prophetic premises of the Church that were the basis of the Church's anti-Jewish attitudes and actions. The Church began to act in a way that was in diametric contradiction to the teachings of the Lord Jesus Christ.
>
> ... Persecution followed the Jews wherever they went in the centuries that followed Emperor Constantine.... . Only two years after Constantine made Christianity the official religion of the empire, he initiated a series of repressive edicts, ... Prejudice against the Jews was guaranteed.[8]

The Serpent had succeeded in injecting his ancient venom into the bloodstream of Christianity. In the delirium caused by the cunning Serpent's bite, men laid faulty foundations and gave rise to a form of religion contrary to YAHveh's original building program. As new Christian doctrines and attitudes emerged, these undermined YAHshua's command for Gentile believers to love and bless His Jewish brethren.

> Historian Ausubel reports another important milestone along the infamous road of anti-Semitism: "Two centuries later [i.e., after Constantine's reign], the Emperor Justinian (527-565 c.e.) issued his celebrated code which laid the legal groundwork for anti-Semitism as a PERMANENT CHRISTIAN STATE POLICY. One clause provided: "They (the Jews) shall enjoy no honors. Their statues shall reflect the baseness which in their souls they have elected and desired" (emphases in source).[9]

At times, the Jews were defamed and forced to wear special clothing that depicted humiliation. In the centuries following

---

[8] Hal Lindsey, op. cit., pp. 12-13.
[9] Ibid., pp. 13-14.

Constantine and Augustine, they were alienated from society, forced to live in ghettos, and massacred in diverse places.

Anti-Jewish atrocities reached a pinnacle with the Crusades of 1096 C.E. During the eleventh through the thirteenth centuries, European Christians sent military expeditions to the land of Israel. Determined to retrieve the Holy Land from its Jewish and Muslim inhabitants, these deceived Crusaders targeted the Jews and Muslims as the "enemies of Christianity."

According to the historical account of Solomon bar Samson regarding the Crusades, he states: *"All the Gentiles were gathered together against the Jews in the courtyard to blot out their name, and the strength of our people weakened when they saw the wicked Edomites overpowering them* [the Edomites were the traditional foes of the Jews; here, Christians are meant]*"* (emphasis in source).[10]

> The centuries of misguided sermons about the whole Jewish race being exclusively guilty of the crucifixion of the Lord Jesus, the long history of an official church policy of humiliating and persecuting them, and the clergy-cultivated image of the Jews as being obstinate impostors with no future as a people in God's plan, all began to bear their murderous fruit among the lower class of the Crusaders.
>
> Soon there were cries for the blood of the "Christ-killer" before going to Palestine to deal with the Muslims. There is nothing more dangerous or uncontrollable than a mob which has been deluded into thinking it is doing a religious deed by eliminating an enemy of God.... .
>
> When the Crusaders, led by Godfrey, captured Jerusalem on July 15, 1099, they first entered the city through the Jewish quarter. A terrible slaughter took place. The surviving Jews were sold as slaves. The Jewish community of Jerusalem was obliterated. In all, tens of thousands of Jews were massacred in the name of Christianity as a consequence of the first Crusade.[11]

With banners flying in the name of Jesus Christ and giant crucifixes held high, the Serpent's envoys paraded as Christians to accomplish Satan's diabolical schemes. The Crusaders

---

[10] Jacob R. Marcus, *The Jew in Medieval World* (New York: Atheneum, 1969), p. 116.

[11] Hal Lindsey, op. cit., pp. 14-15.

stormed Jerusalem, rounded up the Jews in their great synagogue, locked the doors, and set it ablaze. As the screams of Messiah's brethren pierced *YAHveh's* heart, the deceived army marched proudly and mercilessly around this Jewish bonfire,[12] waving their Christian banners and singing "Christ We Adore Thee."

The passionate mission of the Crusaders had been ignited through the erroneous doctrine of replacement theology. These Christians believed that Jerusalem no longer belonged to the Jews. The church had replaced Israel, and Jerusalem was to become a Christian city. A leader of the Crusade, Raymond Aguilers, led the army over a carpet of mutilated bodies in the height of satanic victory. As they marched, they sang Psalm 118:24: *"This is the day which the LORD has made; Let us rejoice and be glad in it."*

Indeed the ancient Serpent had won himself quite a victory! The dividing wall of hostility between Jew and Gentile, which had been destroyed through the blood of the Messiah, was now resurrected and stained with the blood of His brethren, the Jews.

The Dark Ages

YAHshua, the glory of Israel, was to be the *"light of revelation to the Gentiles"* (Lk 2:32). Illumined by this light, the Gentiles now would have eyes to see, ears to hear, and a spirit to know, understand, and worship the God and Messiah of Israel. The Gentiles were redeemed and commissioned to labor with *YAHshua* in His harvest field, to go in His divine order and bring the Gospel to the Jews first (Ro 1:16).

But now the bright light of Messiah was overshadowed by Satan's darkness. *YAHshua's* love and truth were overpowered by the Enemy's hatred and lies. The anti-Semitic Crusades ushered in a period of history called *the Dark Ages.* Simply stated, *the degree to which the Church has walked in the light and love of YAHshua toward the Jews is the same degree to which it has had the true light of revelation shining in and through it.*

During the Dark Ages, a common Christian slogan caught on among the people like a catchy tune: "Kill a Jew and save your soul." To the ancient Serpent, this morbid melody echoed like a

---

[12] *Webster's New World Dictionary of the American Language,* s.v. "bonfire" — "[... lit., bone fire, fire for burning corpses] ..."

victory cry from the mouths of thousands of misguided Christians.

If only the light of revelation had not been overshadowed by the darkness of men's doctrines. Many of these unsuspecting Christians would never have become the agents of anti-Semitism. YAHveh's heart cries out, *"My people are destroyed for lack of knowledge"* (Hos 4:6).

Hear the words of Isaiah: *"To the law and to the testimony!* [including the biblical mandate to bless the Jews] *If they do not speak according to this word* [YAHveh's full counsel], *... THEY HAVE NO LIGHT OF DAWN"* (Isa 8:20 NIV).

The *"bright morning star"* (Rev 22:16) has been eclipsed by trumped up doctrines, becoming as dim moonlight. Many Christians have worked diligently in the harvest field as if working by the light of the moon. Because of the darkness, many good crops were inadvertently trampled and never harvested. Many seeds were not planted correctly, nor was the soil prepared properly simply because there was no bright light of truth by which to work. Many seedlings died before maturity because the Son's (sun's) full counsel and radiance was not there to feed them with the proper nutrients. *What a blighted harvest field with so much dry, shriveled fruit!* What a grief to the Creator and a repulsion to the multitudes who see it.

The Iniquitous Inquisitions

The infamous Inquisitions followed the cruel Crusades. Deep darkness was upon the church and the world. Most vestiges of love and mercy toward Messiah's brethren had been buried with the thousands of Jews who were murdered as "Christ-killers."

The Inquisitions lasted several hundred years and helped perpetuate Satan's strategy against the Jews. From the reign of Constantine to the Middle Ages, every religious tradition that did not line up with the teachings of "the Church" was considered heresy. The Jewish people, in their tenacity to maintain their biblical Hebrew roots, were considered a threat to this tainted form of Christianity.

The European Inquisitions were aimed in part at the eradication of all that was Jewish and considered heresy. During these dark years, many Jews were threatened and massacred. If YAHshua, the Jew of all Jews, had lived during that time, the church leaders would have considered His uncompromised Hebraic nature a threat to their form of Christianity.

During the long dark years of the Middle Ages, Jews were frequently given the option of baptism or expulsion, baptism or torture, baptism or death. Every type of degrading law was passed against them: They were forbidden to work good jobs; after all, they were an accursed people, assassins of Christ, so how could they be allowed to prosper? They were forced to listen to humiliating public sermons aimed at their conversion— wasn't this the holy obligation of the Church? Their children were kidnapped and baptized as "Christians," thus saving them from the fires of hell. They were rounded up and beaten as a highlight of Easter celebrations, since they deserved it as murderers of the Lord.[13]

The following is an excerpt from a typical profession of faith that a Jewish baptismal candidate was forced to confess:

I do here and now renounce every rite and observance of the Jewish religion, detesting all its most solemn ceremonies ... In the future I will practice no rite or celebration connected with it, ... promising neither to seek it out or perform it. ... I promise that I will never return to the vomit of Jewish superstition. Never again will I fulfill any of the offices of Jewish ceremonies to which I was addicted, nor ever more hold them dear. [I will] shun all intercourse with other Jews and have the circle of my friends only among other Christians.

[We will not] associate with the accursed Jews who remain unbaptized. ... We will not practice carnal circumcision, or celebrate the Passover, the Sabbath or the other feast days connected with the Jewish religion. ...

I renounce the whole worship of the Hebrews, ... And I absolutely renounce every custom and institution of the Jewish laws ... in one word, I renounce absolutely everything Jewish. ...

If I wander from the straight path in any way and defile the holy Faith, and try to observe any rites of the Jewish sect, or if I shall delude you in any way in the swearing

---

[13] Michael L. Brown, op. cit., p 11.

of this oath ... then may all the curses of the law fall upon me. ... May there fall upon me and upon my house and all my children all the plagues which smote Egypt, and to the horror of others may I suffer in addition the fate of Dathan and Abiram, so that the earth shall swallow me alive, and after I am deprived of this life I shall be handed over to the eternal fire, in the company of the Devil and his Angels, sharing with the dwellers in Sodom and with Judas the punishment of burning; and when I arrive before the tribunal of the fearful and glorious Judge, our Lord Jesus Christ, may I be numbered in that company to whom the glorious and terrible Judge with threatening mien will say, "Depart from Me, evil-doers, into the eternal fire that is prepared for the Devil and his Angels."[14]

In the words of Dr. Brown, "Let us hang our heads in shame. The 'Church' has blood on her hands."[15]

In Spain during the fourteenth century, Jews were forced to convert to Christianity or be massacred and have their bodies dismembered. Seventy communities were destroyed. In Vienna during the fifteenth century, the possessions of Jews were confiscated and their children forcibly converted. Several hundred were burned at the stake.

During the Middle Ages, the Jewish people were forced to wear distinctive clothing to mark them as separate and repulsive to the Gentile communities.

Early in the 16th Century, whole cities of Jews were segregated from the general population into what were called *ghettos*. ... The worst part of the city was sectioned off, and a high wall was built around it. ... They were guarded by Christians whose salaries the Jews were compelled to pay. Ghettos were closed during all Christian festivals such as Easter and Christmas. Those living in the area were required to listen to long sermons aimed at their conversion.[16]

---

[14] Ibid., pp. 95-96.

[15] Ibid., p. 97.

[16] David Levy, "Anti-Semitism in the Middle Ages," *Israel My Glory* Vol. 51, No. 2 (April/May, 1993), p. 21.

Poison in a Pillar

Martin Luther is considered the great pillar of Protestantism—a man whom many in Christendom respect. What did Martin Luther have to say about the Jews? Early in his life, he rallied to their cause. In 1523 he wrote a pamphlet entitled "Jesus Christ Was Born a Jew" in hopes of winning the Jews to Christianity. But toward the end of his life, Luther became frustrated with the Jews because they did not respond to his presentation of the Gospel.

Martin Luther, even with his prominent faith and noteworthy zeal, did not understand the Jews, nor did he understand *YAHveh's* heart and purpose for His chosen people. He did not fully comprehend the sovereignty of the Abrahamic covenant (Ge 12:3) or the mandate for Gentiles to extend love and mercy to the Jews (Ro 11). Moreover, he presented a Savior stripped of His Jewish identity and distorted by Gentile characteristics. *A Gentile portrayal of their long-awaited Messiah never did and never will appeal to the masses of Jews. The Jews await a Jewish Messiah.*

Like many others, Martin Luther was simply a by-product of a religious system that had been permeated by the Serpent's venom. This poison was circulated in his spiritual veins until it flared as a raging infection toward the end of his life.

Jacob R. Marcus, a notable Jewish historian expounds on Luther. "His growing bitterness and sense of disillusionment finally vented itself in 1543 in a series of German anti-Jewish writings of which *Concerning the Jews and Their Lies* is a notorious example. There are no more bitterly anti-Jewish statements in all Christian literature than those who may be found in these writings of the disappointed rebel."[17]

Martin Luther's words have often been used as proof to the Jews that the beloved Savior of the Gentiles could not possibly be their friend, much less their long-awaited Messiah.

What then shall we Christians do with this damned, rejected race of Jews? Since they live among us and we know about their lying and blasphemy and cursing, we cannot tolerate them if we do not wish to share in their

---

[17] Jacob R. Marcus, op. cit., p. 165.

lies, curses, and blasphemy. ... We must prayerfully and reverentially practice a merciful severity. ... Let me give you my honest advice:

First, to set fire to their synagogues or schools and to bury and cover with dirt whatever will not burn, so that no man will ever again see a stone or cinder of them. This is to be done in honor of our LORD and of Christendom. ...

Second, I advise that their houses also be razed and destroyed ...

Third, I advise that all their prayer books and Talmudic writings, in which such idolatry, lies, cursing, and blasphemy are taught, be taken from them.

Fourth, I advise that their rabbis be forbidden to teach henceforth on pain of loss of life and limb ...

Fifth, I advise that safe-conduct on the highways be abolished completely for the Jews. ... Let them stay at home ...

Sixth, I advise that usury be prohibited to them, and that all cash and treasure of silver and gold be taken from them, and put aside for safe keeping ...

Seventh, I recommend putting a flail, an ax, a hoe, a spade, a distaff, or a spindle into the hand of young, strong Jews and Jewesses and letting them earn their bread in the sweat of their brow.[18]

Noted author Erwin Lutzer gives this personal account of leading a tour group in Wittenberg:

When we walk across the Town Square, we come to the Town Church where Luther preached the gospel to the common people of Wittenberg. But if you walk around to the back of the church and look up at the point where the roof and wall meet, you will see the sandstone relief of a pig, a sculpture perhaps three feet long and eighteen inches high.

This pig, as I learned while leading a tour to the sites of the Reformation, is *Judensau* (a "Jewish sow") erected to spite the Jews and commemorate their expulsion from Wittenberg in 1305. The Hebrew inscription reads,

---

[18] Hal Lindsey, op. cit., pp. 23-24 (Lindsey is quoting from *Concerning the Jews and Their Lies*. Luther's words can be found in other works including Jacob R Marcus, *The Jew in the Medieval World*, p. 167; and Erwin W. Lutzer, *Hitler's Cross*, p. 86.)

"Rabine Schem Ha Mphoras," which means, "Great is the name of the one who is blessed." This phrase was used by the Jews to refer to God since they believed that His name should not even be pronounced. Now these words sarcastically refer to them, contemptuously linking them to a pig, an animal regarded by them as being most unholy!

Our tour group looked up with disgust to think that such a symbol of hatred was placed on a Christian church. Our sadness dissipated slightly when we saw a memorial on the ground dated 1988 that was, in effect, an apology for what had happened so many centuries ago. A cross lies against a black background to commemorate the sad fact that millions of Jews had suffered under the very cross that was to be a symbol of forgiveness and reconciliation. A translation of the inscription reads:

The true name of God
The maligned, *"Schem Ha Mphoras"*
Which the Jews even before the dawn of Christianity
Regard as most inexpressibly holy
This name died within six million Jews
Under the symbol of a cross.[19]

As someone has said, "How odd of God to choose the Jew, but not so odd as those who choose the Jewish God and hate the Jew."

---

[19] Erwin W. Lutzer, op. cit., p. 85.

Chapter 14
Anti-Semitism Fanned into Flames

Adolph Hitler, one of Satan's greatest hit men, was inspired by Martin Luther's anti-Semitic writings.

Germany had a long history of "Christian" anti-Semitism, not only from within the Roman Catholic Church, but even from within the Protestant Church. It was Martin Luther, who in his latter years turned upon the Jews with a religious fury, thus paving the way for Adolph Hitler to consummate the Reformer's great desire for the elimination of the Jewish people. Is it any wonder that Hitler cited Martin Luther in *Mein Kampf* as one of the great heroes of the German people.[1]

Christianity did not create the Holocaust; indeed Nazism was anti-Christian, but it made it possible. Without Christian anti-Semitism, the Holocaust would have been inconceivable.... . Hitler and the Nazis found in medieval Catholic anti-Jewish legislation a model for their own, and they read and reprinted Martin Luther's virulently anti-Semitic writings. It is instructive that the Holocaust was unleashed by the only major country in Europe having approximately equal numbers of Catholics and Protestants. BOTH TRADITIONS WERE SATURATED WITH JEW-HATRED.[2]

At the Nuremberg trials, the infamous Nazi war criminal Julius Streicher quoted Luther's anti-Semitic writings in defending the Nazi atrocities. Indeed, it was Luther's work that had provided Adolf Hitler and Nazi Germany with Christian justification for their murderous "final solution" for the Jews. Hitler wrote, "Hence today I believe that I am acting in accordance with the almighty Creator: **by defending myself against the JEW, I am fighting for the work of the Lord.**"[3] Even today,

---

[1] Hal Lindsey, *The Road to Holocaust* (New York: Bantam Books, 1989), p. 5.

[2] Dennis Prager and Joseph Telushkin, *Why the Jews? The Reason for Anti-Semitism* (New York: Simon and Schuster, 1983), p. 104.

[3] Adolph Hitler (trans. by Ralph Manheim), *Mein Kampf* (Boston: Houghton Mifflin Co., 1971), p. 65.

Martin Luther's anti-Semitic tracts are respected by neo-Nazis.

Most Jewish people have lost one or more relatives to anti-Semitism, which was fanned into flames by the writings of Martin Luther. Engraved on the memory of many holocaust survivors are the words which were written across the archways of certain death camps: "We kill you because you killed Jesus."[4]

Dr. Erwin Lutzer comments, "As Gentiles, we forget that Christ is thought of as an enemy of the Jews. A Jewish women told some of us at a Bible study that when she was searching for God, she feared studying the New Testament in case it turned out to be true. She often prayed, 'O God, turn out to be anybody but Jesus!'"[5]

Harbored Hostility

The Nazis were entertained by the suffering and torment of their Jewish victims. Holocaust historian Elie Wiesel is quoted by Michael Brown:

"Imagine: the chief rabbi of the town forced by German officers to clean the pavement, to sweep it with his beard. And all around, proud soldiers, warriors puffed up with their victories, slapped their thighs in merriment. Imagine: a distinguished officer, a man of good family, orders Jewish children to run, like rabbits, and then he takes out his revolver and begins shooting at the terrified living targets, scattering them, mowing them down. Imagine: no, let us not imagine anymore. In those days, the executioners had more imagination than their victims."

Dr. Brown continues:
These were all driven, all impelled, all given over to the humiliation, degradation and extermination of the Jews. Only yesterday they were neighbors and friends!

When the Nazis murdered all the patients of the Lodz ghetto hospitals they threw *newborn babies* out of the upper story hospital windows. Precious Jewish infants

---

[4] Sid Roth, *Time is Running Short* (Shippensburg, PA: Destiny Image Publishers, 1990), p. 31.

[5] Erwin W. Lutzer, *Hitler's Cross* (Chicago: Moody Press, 1996), p. 84.

were splattered on the pavement! But for one teenaged SS soldier this was not enough. He asked permission— and was granted permission—to catch the falling babes on his *bayonet*. Is there no limit to hell's depravity?[6]

Many of these Nazis were considered good family men; many of them were supposed to be God-fearing Catholics and Protestants. With one hand they would clothe, feed, and nurture their families. With the other, they would viciously strip, starve, torture, and kill Jewish families.

These Nazi "shepherds" would herd the Jews into gas chambers. In cold blood, they would hear the tormented screams of Messiah's dying brethren. Many would change their blood-stained clothes to flock "as wolves in sheep's clothing" into their churches. Safe within their Christian cathedrals, they would piously sing choruses such as "Silent Night, Holy Night" and "Christ We Adore Thee."

Dr. Lutzer relates a chilling account of his personal observation in a former German army war ministry building, where "… the pictures that caught my attention were those of Protestant pastors and Catholic priests giving the Nazi salute. I was even more surprised at the pictures of swastika banners that adorned the Christian churches—*swastika banners with the cross of Christ in the center!*"[7]

Lutzer continues with another alarming story about a German man who had lived in Nazi Germany during the Nazi Holocaust:

> I considered myself a Christian. We heard stories of what was happening to the Jews, but we tried to distance ourselves from it, because, what could anyone do to stop it?
>
> A railroad track ran behind our small church and each Sunday morning we could hear the whistle in the distance and then the wheels coming over the tracks. We became disturbed when we heard the cries coming from the train as it passed by. We realized that it was carrying Jews like cattle in the cars!
>
> Week after week the whistle would blow. We dreaded to hear the sound of those wheels because we knew that we

---

[6] Michael L. Brown, *Our Hands are Stained with Blood* (Shippensburg, PA: Destiny Image Publishers, 1992), p. 160.

[7] Erwin W. Lutzer, op. cit., p. 12.

would hear the cries of the Jews en route to a death camp. Their screams tormented us.

We knew the time the train was coming and when we heard the whistle blow we began singing hymns. By the time the train came past our church we were singing at the top of our voices. If we heard the screams, we sang more loudly and soon we heard them no more.

Years have passed and no one talks about it anymore. But I still hear that train whistle in my sleep. God forgive me, forgive all of us who call ourselves Christians yet did nothing to intervene.[8]

The ancient Serpent, in all his diabolical cunning, had succeeded in turning Christianity upside down. He had divided the *one new man* and cursed both the Jews and the Gentiles whom Messiah had died to bless. Today is it any wonder that the majority of Jews in the world respond in horror and dread to the name Jesus Christ? The name that is above all names to Christians has become a curse word to them, reeking with the stench of torment and death, and never to be spoken in Jewish homes. Dr. Brown again:

Let me translate for you the words of an Israeli writer who expresses the heart of many of his people:

"Instead of bringing redemption to the Jews, the false Christian messiah has brought down on us base libels and expulsions, oppressive restrictions and burning of [our] holy books, devastations and destructions. Christianity, which professes to infuse the sick world with love and compassion, has fixed a course directly opposed to this lofty rhetoric. The voice of the blood of millions of our brothers cries out to us from the ground: 'No! Christianity is not a religion of love but a religion of unfathomable hate! All history, from ancient times to our own day, is one continuous proof of the total bankruptcy of this religion in all its segments.'"[9]

Dr. Brown continues, quoting Professor Eugene Bares: "We might be more inclined to give Christian claims some credence had we seen Christians through the ages behave as models of a redeemed humanity. Looking

---

[8] Erwin W. Lutzer, op. cit., pp. 99-100.
[9] Ibid., pp. 89-90.

through the window of history we have found them in as much need of saving as the rest of humankind. If anything, their social failings are especially discrediting of their doctrine for they claim to be uniquely free of human sinfulness and freshly inspired by their faith to bring the world to a realm of love and peace. ... Until sinfulness ceases and well-being prevails, Jews know the Messiah has not come."

"The fact that a leading Jewish thinker like Elixir Berkovits could speak of 'the moral bankruptcy of Christian civilization and the spiritual bankruptcy of Christian religion' should cut us to the heart."[10]

"After nineteen centuries of Christianity, the extermination of six million Jews, among them one-and-a-half million children, carried out in cold blood in the very heart of Christian Europe, encouraged by the criminal silence of virtually all Christendom including that of an infallible Holy Father in Rome, was the natural culmination of this bankruptcy. A straight line leads from the first act of oppression against the Jews and Judaism in the fourth century to the holocaust in the twentieth."[11]

The Holy One of Israel has not changed. The eternal words He spoke against the enemies of Israel are as appropriate today as they were in the days of Edom. In Scripture, Edom is symbolic of any individual or nation that harbors Satan's enmity toward God's chosen people. *YAHveh* prophesied against Edom and all of Israel's enemies.

"Because you have had EVERLASTING ENMITY *[an ancient hostility] and have delivered the sons of Israel to the power of the sword* AT THE TIME OF THEIR CALAMITY, *at the time of the punishment of the end, therefore, as I live," declares the Lord YAHveh, "I will give you over to bloodshed, and bloodshed will pursue you; ..."* (Eze 35:5-6)

*Thus says the Lord YAHveh concerning Edom ... "*THE ARROGANCE OF YOUR HEART *[toward the Jewish people]* HAS DECEIVED YOU ... *"Though you build high like the eagle ... I will bring you down ..."* (Ob vv. 1-4)

---

[10] Ibid., p. 90.
[11] Ibid.. p. 91.

"Will I not on that day," declares YAHveh, "Destroy wise men from Edom ... "Because of violence TO YOUR BROTHER JACOB, You will be covered with shame, And you will be cut off forever. "On the day that YOU STOOD ALOOF ... "DO NOT GLOAT OVER YOUR BROTHER'S DAY, THE DAY OF HIS MISFORTUNE." (Ob vv. 8-12)

Because the Serpent's eggs hatched within Christian theology, the church became an enemy of Israel, causing the brethren of YAHshua to be driven far from the truth and love of their Messiah. *The fullness of the Savior's glorious presence and His promised blessings have been blocked by Christianity's sins of omission and commission with regard to the Jews.* The hands of corporate Christendom are stained with blood. The prophet Isaiah cries out:

"YOUR INIQUITIES HAVE SEPARATED YOU FROM YOUR GOD; YOUR SINS HAVE HIDDEN HIS FACE FROM YOU, so that he will not hear. For YOUR HANDS ARE STAINED WITH BLOOD, your fingers with guilt. YOUR LIPS HAVE SPOKEN LIES ... No one calls for justice ... THEY HATCH THE EGGS OF VIPERS ... WHOEVER EATS THEIR EGGS WILL DIE ..." (Isa 59:2-5 NIV — emphasis added)

Alas, sinful nation, People weighed down with iniquity, Offspring of evildoers, Sons who act corruptly! THEY HAVE ABANDONED YAHVEH, THEY HAVE DESPISED THE HOLY ONE OF ISRAEL, THEY HAVE TURNED AWAY FROM HIM [and His mandate to bless the Jews]. *Where will you be stricken again, As you continue in your rebellion? The whole head is sick, And the whole heart is faint. FROM THE SOLE OF THE FOOT EVEN TO THE HEAD THERE IS NOTHING SOUND IN IT ... "I WILL HIDE MY EYES FROM YOU, YES, EVEN THOUGH YOU MULTIPLY PRAYERS, I WILL NOT LISTEN. YOUR HANDS ARE COVERED WITH BLOOD. "WASH YOURSELVES, MAKE YOURSELVES CLEAN ... CEASE TO DO EVIL, LEARN TO DO GOOD ..."* (Isa 1:4-6, 15-17)

Those who call themselves children of God must stand in the gap and repent for the multitudes of Jews killed in the name of Jesus Christ and Christianity. Messiah's words to the self-righteous religious leaders of His day are applicable to us upon whom the end of the age has come. YAHshua said, *"This generation will be held responsible for the blood ... Yes, I tell you, this generation will be held responsible for it all"* (Lk 11:50-51 NIV).

You and I did not sing Satan's tune, "Kill a Jew and save your soul." We did not march around flaming synagogues singing

"Christ We Adore Thee" as the screams of the Jewish people pierced heaven's gates and *YAHveh's* heart. There were many, however, who *stood aloof in shameful silence* as the Jews were mercilessly slaughtered by the Nazis.

The Spirit of Truth asks us to examine our hearts. The humble will willingly acknowledge to one degree or another that they have fallen prey to ignorance, indifference, spiritual pride, hostility, and even the rejection of Messiah's brethren. *The venom of anti-Semitism must be thoroughly purged from individual hearts in order that we might be Holy to YAHveh.*

King David was required to make restitution for the Gibeonite blood that King Saul had shed. David was not guilty, nor was he responsible for Saul's sin. However, the nation of Israel suffered a great famine *"on account of Saul and his BLOOD-STAINED HOUSE"* (2Sa 21:1 NIV — emphasis added). In the purity of his heart, David understood that *the stain of blood had to be repented for* in order for the curse of famine to be reversed (see 2Sa 21:14).

Today *YAHveh* is raising up a "David generation" that will repent for the blood-stained house of Christendom. These stains were brought about by a "Saul generation" who did not rightly discern *YAHveh's* will and love for Israel. Instead of drawing Messiah's brethren in with cords of lovingkindness, some throughout Christian history have driven them away with whips of hate and violence.

Through prayer and repentance, the "David generation" will help reverse the biblical curse incurred by a form of religion that has not blessed Abraham's descendants. The *spiritual famine* will end, and a banqueting table will be set for those who *weep over the slain of Jacob* (see Jer 9:1) and repent for the blood-stained house of historical Christianity.

Do Not Stick Your Finger in His Eye

The prophet Zechariah proclaimed: *"for he who touches you [Israel], touches the apple [pupil] of His eye. For behold, I will wave My hand over them, so that they will be plunder ..."* (Zec 2:8-9).

Serpents don't have fingers, but men do. *YAHveh* is posting His warning: *Do not stick your finger in My eye!* YAHveh is so identified with His people Israel that their pain is His pain. According to Isaiah, *"In all their affliction He was afflicted"* (Isa

106

63:9). If we say that we love Him, we too will grieve with Him in all His pain.

Concerning His Jewish brethren, Messiah emphatically said, *"Whatever you did for one of the least of these brothers of mine, you did for me"* (Mt 25:40 NIV). He explained that nations and peoples will one day be judged—separated as sheep from goats to receive eternal blessings or curses. Their fate will ultimately be determined by their obedience to the Abrahamic covenant as recorded in Genesis 12:3.

Scripture reminds us that *"YAHveh is not a man, that He should lie, Nor a son of man, that He should repent; Has He said, and will He not do it? Or has He spoken, and will He not make it good?"* (Nu 23:19).

A Slippery, Dark Path

The Abrahamic covenant and the issue of the Jews will soon become a threshing instrument in God's hands. *YAHveh* will use these to separate the humble, redeemed "wheat" from the arrogant, deceived "tares" (see Isa 41:15-16 and Mic 4:13). Those who are ambassadors of the Father of Truth will be as the wheat. Those who are agents of the Father of Lies will be the tares. Satan has succeeded in leading the whole world astray through deception (see Rev 12:9), but more shockingly, he has deceived many professing Christians by leading them down a slippery, dark path.

"FOR BOTH PROPHET AND PRIEST ARE POLLUTED; Even in My house [including the church] *I have found their wickedness," declares YAHveh. "Therefore their way will be like SLIPPERY PATHS to them, They will be driven away into the GLOOM and fall down in it; For I shall bring calamity upon them, The year of their punishment," declares YAHveh.* (Jer 23:11-12)

Jews and Christians continue to sit in darkness, apart from the full truth, light, and love of Messiah. By and large, the church has not reflected the bright light of the Son, *YAHshua*, but rather the dimness of man's doctrines and traditions. Multitudes languish in sin and wither in bondage. They are waiting for the truth to set them free. Messiah's purpose will soon be completed. The true redeemed body for which He died, including both Jews and Gentiles, must be reconciled into *one new man*. It is time for

Jews and Gentiles to unite against our common enemy, to form a mighty army under whose feet Satan and all of his anti-Semitic venom will be crushed.

We Must Not Keep Silent

Today throughout the world, we see the ancient Serpent rearing his ugly head and spewing out his anti-Semitism because he knows that his time is short. We must take heed and learn a lesson from historic Christianity's attitude toward the Jews. If many devout pillars of the faith fell prey to Satan's ancient venom, how much more could we?

A time is coming soon that is called *"Jacob's trouble"* (Jer 30:7 NIV). Daniel prophesied that it will be *"a time of distress such as never occurred since there was a nation until that time"* (Da 12:1).

During this time of great tribulation, the Serpent's obsessive hatred for Israel will reach its culmination. At this ominous juncture in history, all of the world's nations will unite together in the common bond of Jew-hatred. According to Scripture, two-thirds of the Jewish people are slated for destruction, and only a remnant will repent and *"call on the name of YAHveh"* and be *"delivered"* (Joel 2:32).

"And it will come about in all the land," Declares YAHveh, "That two parts [of the Israelites] in it will be cut off and perish; But the third will be left in it. ... THEY WILL CALL ON MY NAME, And I will answer them; I will say, 'They are My people,' And they will say, 'YAHveh is my God.'" (Zec 13:8-9)

"Now it will come about in that day THE REMNANT OF ISRAEL, ... will truly rely on YAHveh, the Holy One of Israel. A REMNANT WILL RETURN, the remnant of Jacob, to the mighty God. For though your people, O Israel, may be like the sand of the sea, ONLY A REMNANT WITHIN THEM WILL RETURN; A destruction is determined, overflowing with righteousness." (Isa 10:20-22)

With this in mind and in view of the resurgence of anti-Semitism throughout the world, *YAHveh's* righteous remnant must obey His expressed will. We must bring salvation in His biblical order: *"to the Jews first"* (Ro 1:16).

The Devil is planning his final attack on Messiah's Jewish brethren. The Holy One of Israel commands us not to keep silent in regard to His chosen people and nation. He will sovereignly judge all who *stand aloof* and do not listen to His heart as expressed through His prophets. We are to *give Him no rest* as we cry out from merciful hearts, *"'O YAHveh, SAVE THY PEOPLE, THE REMNANT OF ISRAEL'"* (Jer 31:7).

Scripture teaches that when we know the right thing to do and don't do it, it is sin. Messiah said to His disciples, *"My mother and My brothers are these who hear the word of YAHveh and do it"* (Lk 8:21).

Queen *Hadassah* (Esther) was divinely used to thwart the Serpent's plot to destroy the Jews. The true body of Messiah, the holy remnant, should be as Queen *Hadassah*. If we *"remain silent at this time, relief and deliverance for the Jews will arise from another place, ..."* (Est 4:14 NIV) *"For such a time as this ..."* (Est 4:14), the obedient remnant, like Esther, must go in humility before her king on Israel's behalf. Because of her irresistible beauty, which will radiate from a heart filled with love for her Jewish brethren, the eternal King will extend his *"golden scepter"* (Est 5:2) and welcome her into His glorious presence.

The apostle Paul admonished Gentiles to follow his example of love for his Jewish people:

"Brethren, my heart's desire
and my prayer to YAHveh for them [the Israelites]
is for their salvation."
(Ro 10:1)

"How then shall they call upon Him in whom they have not believed?
AND HOW SHALL THEY BELIEVE IN HIM
WHOM THEY HAVE NOT HEARD [a Hebrew Messiah
with a Hebrew name]?
And how shall they hear without a preacher?
And how shall they preach unless they are sent?"
(Ro 10:14-15)

How lovely ...
Are the feet of him who brings good news ...
Who announces salvation [YAHshua],
And says to Zion, "Your God reigns!"
(Isa 52:7)

Chapter 15
The Divine Remedy

The prophet Jeremiah understood *YAHveh's* grief and cried out, *"Oh, that my head were waters, And my eyes a fountain of tears, THAT I MIGHT WEEP DAY AND NIGHT FOR THE SLAIN ... OF MY PEOPLE!"* (Jer 9:1). This is the heart of *YAHveh* and the heart of *YAHshua*; this is the heart of His prophets, His apostles, and of a holy remnant.

This also is the heart of Basilea Schlink, a German nun who cries out for more people to shed tears of repentance for what has been done to the beloved brethren of the Savior. Her profoundly contrite heartbeat speaks to humble persons of all faiths. She says, "Whoever wants to know the heart of God will do so by acquainting himself with His people Israel."[1]

... Do not our consciences smite us after we have learnt of the Jews' suffering, brought on by our silence, ... ? ...

Yet at Christian conferences and elsewhere how seldom grief is voiced, ... Where are the troubled consciences? Where are the large repentance gatherings? Where is the church that regularly holds prayers of repentance for our crime against Israel? We pray for revivals, but they fail to come. A curse lies upon the Christian community, a curse of unrepented guilt towards Israel.

What has been done to atone for our guilt? Where are those who submit to God's verdict, not because they are forced to but of their own free will, and who on account of this guilt have served His people gladly and with sacrificial love?[2]

This dear godly saint goes on to say:

... But one thing we do know is that the number of those who are currently living in such a state of repentance, atoning for their sin, and showing love to Israel wherever they can is infinitesimal and scarcely deserve mention. Yet the Lord is waiting for the

---

[1] Basilea Schlink, *Israel, My Chosen People* (Old Tappan, NJ: Fleming H. Revell Company, 1987), p. 96.
[2] Ibid., p. 53.

completion of a certain number who are willing to be convicted and to atone for the sin-stained past.

Yes, God is waiting. He is waiting with infinite patience. For so many years now He has waited for our repentance. Should we not do all we can now to rejoice the Father's heart with our repentance? If there is joy in heaven with Him who is heaven's Lord and with His angels when a soul repents, how much more so when we Christians at last come to repentance for what we have done to His people![3]

It is through humble, repentant people like Basilea that Messiah will pour out His tears, bathing Israel in a healing balm of compassion and love. These tears will be His remedy to cure the unfathomable wound in Jewish hearts—a wound that was inflicted by corporate Christianity, which harbored the Serpent's anti-Semitic venom and *"stood aloof"* (Ob v. 11) at the time of her calamity.

*"COMFORT, O COMFORT MY PEOPLE," SAYS YOUR GOD. "SPEAK
KINDLY to Jerusalem* [and to individual Jews]; *And CALL OUT
TO HER, that her warfare has ended, That her iniquity has
been removed* [by YAHshua her Messiah], ..." (Isa 40:1-2)

This divinely prescribed remedy of prayers mixed with tears of repentance will prepare Jewish hearts to behold and receive their Messiah through obedient *"ambassadors of reconciliation"* (see 2Co 5:18-20).

The uncultivated, thorny ground of Christianity will not become a fertile harvest field until a humble and repentant remnant begins to weep over the Jewish people. These tears will fall as spring rain from heaven; they will break up the desert-like ground. The tears of a "David generation" will be as rains that end the spiritual drought and famine and help wash away the stain of blood.

As the holy remnant beseeches the master of the harvest to open a flood of repentance through their hearts, they will begin to weep for the slain of Israel. Their tears will act as a spiritual catalyst causing grief and repentance to pour out from many Jewish hearts because of Israel's continual rejection of Messiah. Zechariah prophesied of Israel's sorrow saying:

*"they will look on Me whom they have pierced; and they
will mourn for Him, as one mourns for an only son, and*

---

[3] Ibid., p. 57.

they will weep bitterly over Him, like the bitter weeping over a first-born." (Zec 12:10)

Godly sorrow and true repentance from the hearts of the righteous remnant over Christian anti-Semitism, combined with Israel's bitter grief and repentance over the rejection of their Messiah, will bring about the prophesied "latter day rain" (Joel 2:23-26) upon the harvest field of this earth. As *one new man*, we should *"Ask rain from YAHVEH at the time of the spring rain— YAHVEH who makes the storm clouds; And He will give them showers of rain, ..."* (Zec 10:1).

As Gentiles and Jews are circumcised in heart and reconciled to *YAHveh* and to one another, the harvest field of the earth will become as a desert in bloom. Isaiah prophesied of this glorious event saying, *"In the days to come Jacob will take root, Israel will blossom and sprout; And they will fill the whole world with fruit"* (Isa 27:6). One of the greatest fruits of the salvation of Israel will be the increased knowledge of *YAHveh* that will fill the earth with His glory.

Regarding the salvation of the Jews, Paul wrote, *"Now if their transgression be riches for the world and their failure be riches for the Gentiles, HOW MUCH MORE WILL THEIR FULFILLMENT BE!"* (Ro 11:12).

> Death to life ...
> Fallow ground to fertile fields ...
> Drought to latter day rains ...
> Withered branches to vibrant vines ...
> Blighted harvest to bountiful fruit ...
> Famine to feast.

Indeed, our famine will turn to feasting at the Father's banquet table, which will be set for all brethren who share His joy over Israel, His returning prodigal nation.

> *"So rejoice, O sons of Zion, And be glad in YAHveh your God; For He has given you the early rain for your vindication. AND HE HAS POURED DOWN FOR YOU THE RAIN, THE EARLY AND LATTER RAIN as before. ... You shall have plenty to eat and be satisfied And PRAISE THE NAME OF YAHVEH YOUR GOD, ..."* (Joel 2:23, 26)

Epilogue to the Trail of the Serpent

Many in the body of Messiah have labored in vain as they've built on a faulty foundation, which has given rise to cracked, irregular, and bulging walls. They would not heed the Holy One of Israel and His precepts. Many have preferred man's ways over *YAHveh's* commands. Scripture tells us, *"There is a way which seems right to a man, But its end is the way of death"* (Pr 14:12).

YAHveh declares through Isaiah:

> *Now go,* WRITE IT *on a tablet before them And* INSCRIBE IT *on a scroll, That it may serve* IN THE TIME TO COME *As a witness forever. For this is a rebellious people, false sons,* SONS WHO REFUSE TO LISTEN *To* THE INSTRUCTION OF YAHVEH; *Who say ... to the prophets, "You must not prophesy to us what is right, Speak to us pleasant words ...* GET OUT OF THE WAY, TURN ASIDE FROM THE PATH, LET US HEAR NO MORE ABOUT THE HOLY ONE OF ISRAEL." *Therefore thus says the Holy One of Israel, "Since you have* REJECTED THIS WORD, *And have put your trust in oppression and guile, and have relied on them,* THEREFORE THIS INIQUITY WILL BE TO YOU LIKE A BREACH ABOUT TO FALL, A BULGE IN A HIGH WALL, WHOSE COLLAPSE COMES SUDDENLY *in an instant."* (Isa 30:8-13)

> In Ezekiel it is written:
> *"... '*LISTEN TO THE WORD OF YAHVEH!' *... "Woe to the foolish prophets* [religious leaders and teachers] *who are following their own spirit and have seen nothing. ... "*YOU HAVE NOT GONE UP INTO THE BREACHES, NOR DID YOU BUILD THE WALL AROUND THE HOUSE OF ISRAEL TO STAND IN THE BATTLE ON THE DAY OF YAHVEH. *... "It is definitely because they have misled My people ... when anyone builds a* [flimsy] *wall* [by men's doctrines], BEHOLD, THEY PLASTER IT OVER WITH WHITEWASH [men's religious traditions]; SO TELL THOSE WHO PLASTER IT OVER WITH WHITEWASH, THAT IT WILL FALL. *... I* SHALL TEAR DOWN *the wall which you plastered over with whitewash and bring it down to the ground, so that its* FOUNDATION [anti-Semitic doctrines and traditions of men] IS LAID BARE [exposed] *... I shall say to you, 'The wall is gone and its plasterers are gone ...'"* (Eze 13:2-5, 10-11, 14-15)

From Constantine to Martin Luther to replacement theology in the church, many of God's people have embraced a form of religion and its traditions. We have exchanged His plumb line of truth for the crooked foundation of fabricated doctrines and spurious traditions.

"*An appalling and horrible thing Has happened in the land: The prophets* PROPHESY FALSELY, *And the priests* [preachers and teachers] RULE ON THEIR OWN AUTHORITY [not by *YAHveh's* truth]; AND MY PEOPLE LOVE IT SO! BUT WHAT WILL YOU DO AT THE END OF IT?" (Jer 5:30-31)

With broken and contrite hearts, the remnant will weep with *YAHshua* over His brethren, the Jews. They will stand in the gap and repent for a church system that has neglected His mandates to love and comfort God's chosen people. The curses of anti-Semitism will be broken as this remnant fully realizes how far the church has strayed from *YAHveh's* plumb line of truth.

Dear Heavenly Father—*God of Abraham, Isaac, and Jacob—You're the sovereign judge over all people. You show no favoritism to Jew or Gentile. You reward those who obey Your commands and You judge those who rebel against Your righteous decrees. Father, I ask Your forgiveness for my sins and the sins of the church system in their historic neglect, hostility, and shameful violence against Your firstborn people, Israel. I recognize that the Jews are my brethren. I pray that in Your mercy You'll cleanse me and a remnant of Your people of all anti-Semitic venom, and of any way in which it has poisoned the spiritual bloodstream of Your redeemed body. With grief and lament, I ask You to break all curses that have been incurred through my ancestors and the church fathers who've been "Satan's" ambassadors against the Jewish people. I pray that the curse of the Abrahamic covenant will be reversed to the blessings of the Abrahamic covenant as the David generation begins to cry out on behalf of Your people. Forgive me for arrogance against the original branches of Your olive tree, Israel.*

Thank You for the blood of the Lamb that cleanses me and the repentant remnant of all sins and transgressions. Thank You for the blood that destroyed the dividing wall that separated the Gentiles from Your promises to Israel. Thank You for not leaving me a Gentile outcast, far away from Your eternal promises. Thank You for the pain of the flint knife, which circumcised my heart that I might know what hurts

You and that I might love and obey You with all my heart.

Having prayed this prayer, you will find comfort in the words of Micah:

WHO IS A GOD LIKE THEE,

WHO PARDONS INIQUITY

AND PASSES OVER

THE REBELLIOUS ACT OF THE REMNANT OF HIS POSSESSION? ...

He will again have compassion on us;

He will tread our iniquities under foot.

Yes, Thou wilt cast all their sins Into the depths of the sea.

THOU WILT GIVE TRUTH TO JACOB [and the holy remnant]

And UNCHANGING LOVE TO ABRAHAM

[and his spiritual offspring, redeemed by Messiah's blood],

WHICH THOU DIDST SWEAR TO OUR FOREFATHERS

FROM THE DAYS OF OLD.

(Mic 7:18-20)

PART FOUR

Dedicated to the Tribes of
Isaachar and Zebulun

Issachar   Zebulun

"... you said to me,

'No, but a king shall reign over us,'

although YAHveh your God was your king. ...

"If you will fear YAHveh and serve Him,

and listen to His voice and not rebel

against the command of YAHveh,

then both you and also the king who reigns over you

will follow YAHveh your God.

"And if you will not listen to the voice of YAHveh,

but rebel against the command of YAHveh,

then the hand of YAHveh will be against you,

as it was against your fathers. ...

"For YAHveh will not abandon His people

on account of His great name,

because YAHveh has been pleased

to make you a people for Himself. ...

"But if you still do wickedly,

both you and your king shall be swept away."

(1Sa 12:12, 14-15, 22, 25)

Chapter 16
The Saul Generation

Throughout the ages, the church has been lacking the full measure of the glory and presence of the Almighty. Christianity is not standing as a bright beacon in this dark and decaying world. In these last days, the church has become quite accomplished at bringing the message of salvation. However, it has not been overwhelmingly successful in bringing the multitudes out of darkness.

As we have seen, the body of Messiah has fallen prey to the doctrines and traditions of men. These have given way to the darkness of apathy, complacency, lukewarmness, and discontent. Empty forms of religion have evolved, becoming increasingly offensive and repulsive, rather than glorious and appealing, to the multitudes.

As the third- and fourth-century church grew unfamiliar with the Old Testament Scriptures and the knowledge of *YAHveh*, the Mighty One of Israel, Christianity became detached from its holy Jewish root. New doctrines and traditions, rather than the presence of the Spirit of Truth, began to dominate the church. Centuries before, Paul had warned:

> For the time will come when they will not endure sound doctrine; but wanting to have their ears tickled, they will accumulate for themselves teachers [forming a man-made religious system] in accordance to their own desires; (2Ti 4:3)

A study of King Saul's reign over Israel reveals lessons that help us understand historic Christianity. During the time of Saul, Israel was fiercely persecuted. The sole authority of *YAHveh* as protector and king over Israel was no longer welcomed. The people cried to God for human leadership, saying, *"we want a king to rule over us"* (1Sa 12:12 NIV). Consequently, Israel received Saul as their leader.

In the days of Israel, a "Saul mentality" gave rise to a compromised "Saul generation." Like the people of Israel prior to Saul's rule, the early believers suffered great persecution before Constantine's reign. History repeated itself; like Israel, the corporate body of believers no longer welcomed the sole authority of *YAHveh* almighty as their leader. They wanted human leadership and man's intervention to protect and lead them—they wanted a king! Christianity now began to embrace an organized religious system and eventually its many diversities and divisions. The result is that another Saul-like generation has arisen within much of historic Christianity.

YAHveh's response to the demands of Israel is the same response He made to Christians under Constantine:

"IF YOU WILL FEAR YAHVEH AND SERVE HIM, AND LISTEN TO HIS VOICE AND NOT REBEL AGAINST THE COMMAND OF YAHVEH, then both you [the church] *and also the king* [Christian leadership] *who reigns over you will follow YAHveh your God* [good!]. *And if you will not listen to the voice of YAHveh, but rebel against the command of YAHveh, then the hand of YAHveh will be against you, as it was against your fathers."* (1Sa 12:14-15)

Saul's greatest rebellion parallels Christianity's greatest error. Saul was commanded to annihilate Israel's ancient enemies, the Amalekites.

"Thus says YAHveh of hosts, 'I will punish Amalek for what he did to Israel, how he set himself against him on the way while he was coming up from Egypt. Now go and strike Amalek and UTTERLY DESTROY ALL THAT HE HAS, and do not spare him; but put to death both man and woman, child and infant, ox and sheep, camel and donkey.'" (1Sa 15:2-3)

It is important to remember that the Almighty keeps records of Israel's enemies; His promise to *"utterly blot out the memory of Amalek from under heaven"* (Ex 17:14) had been sovereignly proclaimed and written by Moses in a scroll of remembrance centuries before. Even that which seemed harmless and good in the enemy camp (which may be paralleled with our world system today) was to be destroyed—never to be brought into the holy camp.

The redeemed remnant is to understand and obey YAHveh's perfect will. We are to separate ourselves completely from the pagan world and rid our lives of all vestiges of carnality, lust, greed, pride, lies, and pagan traditions. Like Saul and his army who were commanded to blot out Amalek, God's present-day army is to actively combat Israel's arch enemy, anti-Semitism. There must be no trace of it within YAHshua's holy camp.

But Saul and the people SPARED Agag and THE BEST of the

sheep, the oxen, the fatlings, the lambs, and all that was good, and WERE NOT WILLING TO DESTROY THEM UTTERLY; *but everything despised and worthless, that they utterly destroyed. Then the word of YAHveh came to Samuel* [who is a type and symbol of the Holy Spirit], *saying, "I* REGRET *that I have made Saul king,* FOR HE HAS TURNED BACK FROM FOLLOWING ME, AND HAS NOT CARRIED OUT MY COMMANDS." ... (1Sa 15:9-11)

Church history bears witness that many church leaders and individuals have been the embodiment of the "Saul mentality." In self-justified disobedience, they have misinterpreted and distorted the Word of *YAHveh*, which resulted in many erroneous religious doctrines and traditions. *YAHveh* had proclaimed this would happen, saying, *"every man's own word will become the oracle, and* YOU HAVE PERVERTED THE WORDS OF THE LIVING GOD, YAHVEH OF HOSTS, OUR GOD" (Jer 23:36).

The Filleting of Messiah

The distortion and manipulation of *YAHveh's* truth into man-made doctrines may also be called *the filleting of Messiah*. Over the centuries, many leaders have *picked and chosen* the preferred aspects of Messiah that would appeal to the religious appetites of the formerly pagan masses. The parts of *YAHshua's* character that convey His Hebrew lineage and Jewish background have been deemed unappealing or discarded as unimportant to corporate Christendom. Notice how they epitomize the "Saul mentality."

Grieved by Saul's behavior, Samuel sought out the rebellious king. He found Saul puffed up with pride, having *"set up a monument in his own honor"* (1Sa 15:12 NIV). Saul, arrogant and self-deceived, justified his disobedience by saying, *"I have carried out the command of YAHveh"* (1Sa 15:13).

This is the tendency of rebellious human nature—to rationalize its disobedience in the face of the truth. There are many religious systems, groups, and individuals who have compromised the perfect will of God. Many are in self-righteous deception as they justify their desires, agendas, and programs they have set up in their own honor.

Samuel's reply to Saul (and the Holy Spirit's reply to all who compromise His Word) was:

"What then is this bleating of the sheep ... and the lowing of the oxen which I hear?" [The hypocritical King Saul answered], *"They [the soldiers] have brought them from the Amalekites, FOR THE PEOPLE SPARED THE BEST of the sheep and oxen, to sacrifice to YAHveh your God; but the rest we have utterly destroyed."* (1Sa 15:14-15)

Samuel continues as if speaking to us today:
"YAHveh sent you on a mission, and said, 'Go and UTTERLY DESTROY the sinners, the Amalekites, and fight against them until they are exterminated.' WHY THEN DID YOU NOT OBEY THE VOICE OF YAHVEH, BUT RUSHED UPON THE SPOIL [pounced on the plunder] *AND DID WHAT WAS EVIL IN THE SIGHT OF YAHVEH?" Then Saul said to Samuel, "I did obey the voice of YAHveh ... But the people took some of the spoil, sheep, and oxen, the choicest of the things devoted to destruction, to sacrifice to YAHveh your God ... "And Samuel said, "Has YAHveh as much delight in burnt offerings and sacrifices As in obeying the voice of YAHveh? BEHOLD, TO OBEY IS BETTER THAN SACRIFICE ... For rebellion is as the sin of divination* [witchcraft], *And insubordination is as iniquity and idolatry. BECAUSE YOU HAVE REJECTED THE WORD OF YAHVEH, HE HAS ALSO REJECTED YOU FROM BEING KING."* (1Sa 15:18-23)

Saul began to squirm in the face of truth. Like many people today, Saul justified his disobedience by shifting the blame, saying, *"I feared the people and listened to their voice"* (1Sa 15:24). Many religious leaders and professing believers speak only what itching ears want to hear. They rationalize their hypocrisy in order to maintain their reputations, programs, congregational numbers, and self-made monuments. Saul's heart was more concerned with his reputation than grieved over his sins. At times we can all shamefully relate to this.

Saul begged Samuel, *"return with me, that I may worship YAHveh"* (1Sa 15:25). The outraged prophet replied, *"I will not return with you; for YOU HAVE REJECTED THE WORD OF YAHVEH, AND YAHVEH HAS REJECTED YOU from being king over Israel"* (1Sa 15:26). We have witnessed the downfall of many Christian denominations, leaders, and individuals. With self-justification, they have set their own agendas and built monuments honoring themselves rather than walking in humble obedience to the Almighty's commands. Their fate is similar to King Saul's; Saul grieved *YAHveh*, causing His Holy Spirit to depart. In panic, Saul grabbed hold of Samuel's robe and it tore.

So Samuel said to him, "YAHVEH HAS TORN THE KINGDOM OF ISRAEL FROM YOU TODAY, AND HAS GIVEN IT TO YOUR NEIGHBOR WHO IS BETTER THAN YOU [the coming David generation]. *AND ALSO THE GLORY OF ISRAEL WILL NOT LIE OR CHANGE HIS MIND; for He is not a man that He should change His mind.*" (1Sa 15:28-29)

Rather than godly sorrow leading to true repentance (see 2Co 7:10), Saul was consumed with his own self-image and interests. He begged Samuel, *"please honor me now before the elders of my people and before Israel, and go back with me ..."* (1Sa 15:30).

And Samuel did not see Saul again until the day of his death; for Samuel grieved over Saul. AND YAHVEH REGRETTED THAT HE HAD MADE SAUL KING OVER ISRAEL. ... NOW THE SPIRIT OF YAHVEH DEPARTED FROM SAUL ... (1Sa 15:35; 16:14)

The Spirit left Saul an empty, tormented, jealous man. He continued to reign by his own fleshly might as his life deteriorated into spiritual and emotional turmoil. Such has been the condition of multitudes throughout the history of the church. Perhaps even you and I have fallen into turmoil at various times because of self-will and compromise. Don't forget that the Word of God reminds Gentile believers to pay close attention to Israel's history.

Now these things happened as EXAMPLES FOR US,
THAT WE SHOULD NOT CRAVE EVIL THINGS, AS THEY ALSO CRAVED.
... and they were WRITTEN FOR OUR INSTRUCTION,
upon whom the ends of the ages have come.
Therefore LET HIM WHO THINKS HE STANDS TAKE HEED
LEST HE FALL.
(1Co 10:6, 11-12)

Chapter 17
Pouncing on the Plunder

The Holy Spirit spoke to King Saul after he had compromised *YAHveh's* instructions, and in a similar manner He is speaking to those with a "Saul mentality" today. *YAHshua's* Spirit desires to reveal the many compromises that a "Saul generation" has brought into Christianity over the centuries. As Samuel asked Saul, *"What then is this bleating of the sheep ... and the lowing of the oxen which I hear?"* (1Sa 15:14), the Spirit asks us, "What have you brought in from the pagan world and mixed with my holy things? Why do you justify your compromise by claiming that you 'spared the best' for Me? Do you not realize that I require *obedience* more than your *sacrifice?"* (see 1Sa 15:22).

    YAHveh has redeemed a remnant of Jews and Gentiles to be a "royal priesthood"—a priesthood that will distinguish between the holy and the profane, the righteous and the unrighteous. He has called this priesthood out of the pagan world system to be separate from all that is impure and grievous in His sight. The Holy One will not tolerate the mixing of the common with the holy.

    True disciples of *YAHshua* must be willing to count the cost to follow Him, forsaking the love and approval of men. True disciples must choose between their familiar and often sentimental traditions and the pure, holy worship of *YAHveh.*

    The Almighty has redeemed His priesthood to be separate from all that is unholy, fleshly, worldly, and pagan-tainted. May He prepare your heart to take an honest look at the compromises of a "Saul mentality," which have brought many impure, pagan elements into His holy camp. The compromises of corporate Christianity have often times caused His Spirit to grieve and even to depart as it did during Saul's reign of compromise.

    Let us take a brief look at some of the plunder that a "Saul generation" has pounced on in the enemy's camp and has brought into the holy camp of the redeemed. Just as Saul spared the fattest sheep and cattle, likewise Constantine and many early church leaders spared the best pagan elements, identified them as "good," and *sacrificed* them to God.

    The popular pagan celebration known as "the birthday of the unconquered sun" (also called "Winter Solstice") was spared.

123

This festival, celebrated annually on December 25, was for the worship of the great "invincible sun God"—"Zeus Soter" or "Zeus the Savior."

Zeus the father of gods and men. Zeus, known as Jupiter, "the light bringer," by the Romans was viewed as a supreme, perhaps pantheistic deity, the beginning and end of all things.[1]

The infamous Antiochus IV (Epiphanes), one of Satan's great ambassadors, was determined to destroy the Jewish religion and the worship of *YAHveh* almighty.

In his [Antiochus'] opinion, the greatest possible unifying force was Grecian thought and the Grecian way of life. It was particularly necessary that all, no matter what their nationalities or beliefs, adopt a common faith... . [He gave] explicit orders to stamp out Judaism and in its place establish the worship of the greatest of the deities of the Greeks, the supreme sovereign of the universe, Olympian Zeus.[2]

Epiphanes instituted strict edicts against honoring the biblical Sabbath (Saturday), the holy feasts, circumcision, and other scripturally sacred Jewish customs. According to Nelson Beecher Keys, "The temple was robbed, and then a statue of Zeus or Jupiter, as he was known to the Romans, was set up in the Holy of Holies. All the sacred books that could be found were burned."[3]

To further desecrate *YAHveh's* temple and to appall the Jews, Epiphanes offered the flesh of a swine upon the altar of Zeus, which had been erected on top of the traditional Jewish altar of burnt offering. According to some historians, Antiochus Epiphanes commanded that the twenty-fifth day of each month be honored as a memorial of this desecration of *YAHveh's* holy temple (see 1Mc 1:59).[4]

Constantine "spared" this beloved pagan day, December 25. He conveniently whitewashed this unholy festival and mixed it with the pure messianic faith. The pagan festival in honor of the sun deity was so popular and sacred to the Gentile masses who

---

[1] *Webster's New Riverside University Dictionary*, 2d ed., s. v. "Zeus."

[2] Nelson Beecher Keyes, *Story of the Bible World* (Pleasantville, NY: The Reader's Digest Association, 1962), p 109.

[3] Ibid., p. 109.

[4] *The New Jerusalem Bible* (New York: Doubleday, 1985), p. 680.

had converted to Christianity, that it was *spared as good* and erroneously identified as the Savior's birth date. In other words, *the unholy festival that had honored the "sun god" was expediently substituted with the honoring of the birth of the "Son of God."*

Pagan celebrations on December 25 had included feasting, dancing, lighting bonfires, decorating homes with greens, and giving gifts. So when this became a Christian festival, the customs continued, but with a Christian meaning imparted to them.[5]

The popular pagan use of Christmas trees is a tradition commonly shared by Christians and non-Christians alike. YAHveh had warned His holy remnant against such customs.

"DO NOT LEARN THE WAYS OF THE NATIONS ... FOR THE CUSTOMS OF THE PEOPLES ARE WORTHLESS; THEY CUT A TREE OUT OF THE FOREST ... THEY ADORN IT WITH SILVER AND GOLD; THEY FASTEN IT WITH HAMMER AND NAILS SO IT WILL NOT TOTTER." (Jer 10:1-4 NIV — emphasis added)

Many Bible scholars interpret these verses to be warning against the folly of making man-made idols. Nevertheless, many do the same thing in principle by *idolizing* the pagan origins of the Christmas tree. Like idolatry, this can lead one down the road to vanity and preoccupation with *worthless* things.

Throughout history there has often been a righteous minority attempting to expose the pagan roots of Christmas in order to purify Christianity.

Throughout the Middle Ages, Christmas was a richly varied religious holiday. However, during the Commonwealth, the English Puritans, repelled by both the pagan practices and the religious ceremonies, forbade any religious or secular celebration of Christmas. The English celebration returned with the restoration of the Stuarts, but Christmas observances were still outlawed in Puritan New England for many years; and not until the 19th century did Christmas become a legal holiday in America.[6]

---

[5] *Encyclopedia International*, s.v. "Christmas."
[6] Ibid.

Messiah Fulfills Holy Hebrew Feasts

In truth, the Messiah's birth, death, and resurrection were the divine fulfillments of the holy feasts of Israel. Most historians and Bible scholars concur that the scriptural details surrounding His birth point to the early fall. *YAHshua's* birth is likely the fulfillment of the fall feast called *Sukkot* (also known as "the Feast of Booths" or "the Feast of Tabernacles"), when *YAHshua* came to "tabernacle" (or dwell) among men.

Sukkot is outlined in Leviticus 23:23-44. The Feast of Booths began on the fifteenth day of the seventh month and lasted seven days. *"These are the appointed times of YAHveh which you shall proclaim as holy convocations, to present offerings by fire to YAHveh ... It shall be a perpetual statute throughout your generations; ..."* (vv. 37,41).

During the Feast of Tabernacles, the Israelites temporarily left the comforts of their well-built homes and dwelt in fragile *sukkahs* (booths), where they were exposed to the elements. So *YAHshua* left heaven to indwell the body that was prepared for Him (see Heb 10:5). He risked exposure to many treacherous elements to do the will of the Father. The Feast of Tabernacles speaks of His incarnation; *"And the Word became flesh, and dwelt among us ..."* (Jn 1:14).

The celebration of *Sukkot* is in remembrance of *YAHveh's* provision of shelter for Israel during her wilderness journeys. This feast will ultimately be fulfilled by *YAHshua*, who will be the shelter for His redeemed throughout His eternal kingdom. From the fulfillment of the Feast of Tabernacles on earth at His birth, to its eternal fulfillment in the Father's kingdom, *YAHshua is the beginning and the end.*

With this in mind, it becomes easier to understand Zechariah's prophecy regarding the millennial period.

"... any who are left of all the nations [Gentiles] that went against Jerusalem will go up from year to year to WORSHIP THE KING, *YAHveh of hosts, and to* CELEBRATE THE FEAST OF BOOTHS *[Tabernacles]. And it will be that whichever of the families of the earth does not go up to Jerusalem* TO WORSHIP THE KING, YAHVEH OF HOSTS, *there will be no rain on them. ... it will be the plague with which YAHveh smites the nations [Gentiles] who do not go up to* CELEBRATE THE FEAST OF BOOTHS *[Sukkot]."* (Zec 14:16-18)

Zechariah foresaw the final, jubilant regathering and

restoration of Israel. He also saw the gathering of Gentile nations to worship *YAHveh* almighty. The Feast of Tabernacles was appropriately fulfilled when *YAHveh* came as *YAHshua* to dwell among men. *YAHveh* also memorialized the *Sukkot* as a future mandatory event to be observed throughout His millennial reign—the messianic kingdom to come.

Messiah is the fulfillment of every "jot and tittle" of all the holy feasts of Israel—even to the exact hour of the exact day. The spring feasts were fulfilled with precision by His death, resurrection, and the outpouring of His Spirit. *YAHshua's* death and resurrection were the fulfillment of the holy Feast of Passover and the Feast of Firstfruits. It had no connection with the worship of the Babylonian fertility goddess Ishtar, from which we've derived the modern celebration and name of Easter.

Early Christians observed Easter on the same day as Passover (14-15 Nisan, a date governed by a lunar calendar). In the 2nd century, the Christian celebration was transferred to the Sunday following the 14-15 Nisan. ... [7]

The Council of Nicaea Changes the Date of Easter, 325 ...
At this meeting [at Nicaea] the question concerning the most holy day of Easter was discussed, and it was resolved by the united judgment ... that this feast ought to be kept by all and in every place on one and the same day [Sunday]. ...

... it appeared an unworthy thing that in the celebration of this most holy feast we should follow the practice of the Jews, who have impiously defiled their hands with enormous sin, and are, therefore, deservedly afflicted with blindness of soul. For we have it in our power, if we abandon their custom, to prolong the due observance of this ordinance to future ages, ... It is far more probable that the early Christians determined their date for the celebration of the resurrection of Jesus by the date of the Jewish Passover.

Let us then have nothing in common with this detestable Jewish crowd; for we have received from our Savior a different way. ...

---

[7] J. Gelb and R. M. Whiting, *Multimedia Encyclopedia*, Ver. 1—a CD-ROM (New York: Grolier Electronic Publishing, 1992), s. v. "Easter."

... it has been determined by the common judgment of all, that the most holy feast of Easter should be kept on one and the same day [Sunday].[8]

Easter, like Christmas, was spared by the "Saul generation" and identified as a worthy sacrifice unto God. This by-product of paganism was incorporated into Christianity, replacing the Hebrew roots of our faith and the full understanding of the Messiah's death and resurrection.

What is commonly known to the Gentiles as the "Last Supper" was a *Passover Seder* (the ceremonial evening meal with which Passover begins). Messiah and His twelve disciples, being devout Jews, partook of this memorial dinner directly before He gave His life as the Lamb of God for the forgiveness of our sins.

According to *YAHveh's* infinite mercy and sovereign plan, *YAHshua* was crucified as the perfect Passover Lamb. In Jerusalem, at the same time that multitudes of Jews were sacrificing their *"spotless male lambs"* (see Ex 12:3-7), *YAHshua* died as our sacrifice. For those who accept Him, His blood covers the door posts of their hearts and protects them from the *angel of* eternal *death* (see Ex 12:12).

Messiah died after only six hours rather than the usual three days on the stake. He had a limited time in which to be *buried*, in order to fulfill the second spring feast, the Feast of Unleavened Bread (see Lev 23:6 and 1Co 5:7-8). *YAHshua* was *resurrected* as the fulfillment of the third spring feast, the Feast of Firstfruits (Lev 23:9-14). *YAHshua* is the *"sheaf of the first fruits of harvest"* (Lev 23:10) presented before *YAHveh*, the Mighty One of the harvest. He is "the firstfruits" of those to rise from the dead (1Co 15:23) promising resurrection and eternal life to the multitudes who are covered in His (the Passover Lamb's) blood. We are deprived of a vital scriptural truth and its richest promise by not using the correct biblical term "firstfruits" and substituting it with the pagan term Easter.

Shavuot (Pentecost), biblically referred to as the Feast of Weeks (Lev 23:15-22), was fulfilled precisely on divine schedule when *YAHshua* poured out His Holy Spirit (*Ruach HaKodesh*) at Jerusalem exactly fifty days after the Feast of Firstfruits (His resurrection). On the Day of Pentecost (Ac 2:1-4), also known as the Feast of Harvest, three thousand Jewish souls were brought

---

[8] Jacob R. Marcus, *The Jew in the Medieval World* (New York: Atheneum, 1969), p. 105.

into the kingdom of *YAHveh* as a *summer harvest*. The fall feasts of Israel will soon be fulfilled by *YAHshua* with the same accuracy as the spring feasts.

Through the centuries, most Jews have continued to reject their Messiah, just as most Gentile believers neglect the holy Hebrew root of their faith and continue to cling to customs and traditions that are rooted in paganism. As the whitewash is removed and the pagan customs of Christianity are rejected, the true image of the Jewish Messiah will be reflected through His redeemed and holy people. Finally, *YAHshua* will be recognized and embraced by a remnant of His brethren, the Jews.

Chapter 18

What Happened to the Sabbath?

For those who seek to obey all of *YAHveh's* righteous decrees, it might well be noted that the fourth commandment, *"Remember the Sabbath day, to keep it holy"* (Ex 20:8), was never meant to be tampered with by man. Many throughout history have tried to abolish the Sabbath, or at best, to superimpose it on another day.

The Jews suffered great judgments from the hand of *YAHveh* for desecrating or neglecting the holy Sabbath. The Old Testament is filled with the accounts of these awesome judgments. *YAHveh* and His Jewish people will never recognize any other Sabbath than the one sovereignly ordained at Mount Sinai.[1]

When Moses received the Law on Mount Sinai, *YAHveh* did not introduce the Sabbath as a new institution, but reminded them of what He had previously ordained at creation (Ge 2:2-3). Like *YAHveh's* holy name, the Sabbath was to be remembered and observed as a memorial of the Creator's work and rest. It is the only day of the week that was given a name—the Sabbath. It is the day by which all other days of the week are measured, as in "one day before the Sabbath" or "three days after the Sabbath." No other day of the week can ever be the Sabbath. It is called in Scripture *"a Sabbath of YAHveh your God"* (Ex 20:10) and not "the Jewish Sabbath," although the Jews have kept it through the ages because it is *Holy to YAHveh.*

According to the Almighty's timepiece, the days of the week begin at sundown and end at sundown the next day (Gen 1:5). Therefore, the biblical Sabbath (the seventh day) begins at sundown on Friday and ends at sundown on Saturday. All seven days of the week should be filled with reverent worship and the praises of His people. This, however, does not nullify *YAHveh's* fourth commandment.

YAHveh was very explicit about the need for wholehearted obedience to His Ten Commandments. He said, "YOU SHALL NOT ADD TO *the word which I am commanding you,* NOR TAKE AWAY *from it, that*

---

[1] Note for Nehemiah 9:14: "*holy Sabbath.* According to the rabbis, 'the Sabbath outweighs all the commandments of the Torah.' See 10:31-33; 13:15-22." *The NIV Study Bible* (Grand Rapids: The Zondervan Corporation, 1985), p. 707.

you may KEEP THE COMMANDMENTS *of YAHveh your God which I command you"* (Dt 4:2).

The Almighty further emphasized the Sabbath commandment by saying to Israel:

"... 'YOU SHALL SURELY OBSERVE MY SABBATHS; FOR THIS IS A SIGN BETWEEN ME AND YOU THROUGHOUT YOUR GENERATIONS, THAT YOU MAY KNOW THAT I AM YAHVEH WHO SANCTIFIES YOU. *Therefore you are to observe the Sabbath, for it is holy to you. ... as a* PERPETUAL COVENANT.'" (Ex 31:13-16)

The early Christians, most of whom were Jews, kept the seventh day as a Sabbath, but since the resurrection of their Lord was the most blessed day in their lives, they began very early also to meet for worship on the first day of the week (Ac 2:1), and designated it as the Lord's day. ... As the split between the Jews and Christians widened, the Christians came gradually to meet for worship only on the Lord's day and gave up the observance of the seventh day.[2]

During Constantine's reign, anti-Judaism began to permeate the church. This caused a growing repugnance to the biblical Sabbath. "The Romans misrepresented the Sabbath and the Sabbath year as caused by laziness."[3]

In 321 Constantine made Sunday a public holiday and put into effect what might be called the world's first "blue laws." The edict proclaimed, "All judges, city people, and craftsmen shall rest on the venerable day of the Sun. Despite the edict, many Christians continued the long-standing practice of observing the Jewish Sabbath (Saturday) as well, until the mid-360's when the church forbade it.[4]

It was not until 789, in the days of Charlemagne, that the Christian Sunday actually took over the characteristics of the Jewish Sabbath completely and became not merely a day of worship but also a day of rest.[5]

---

[2] *Zondervan Pictorial Bible Dictionary*, s. v. "Sabbath."

[3] Footnote for Ne 10:31. *The NIV Study Bible*, op. cit., p 710.

[4] Gayla Visalli, ed., *After Jesus—The Triumph of Christianity* (Pleasantville, NY: The Reader's Digest Association, Inc., 1992), p. 239.

[5] Jacob R. Marcus, *The Jew in Medieval World* (New York: Atheneum, 1969), p. 104.

The emperor Constantine had been an avid sun-worshiper before he made Christianity the state religion of the Roman Empire. With a half-hearted attitude toward the holy Scriptures, he fused parts of true messianic worship with parts of popular pagan worship. Many Christian doctrines evolved from this unholy fusion.

The official transition from observance of the Sabbath to Sunday as the day of rest occurred at the Council of Laodicea. The edicts from this council forbade Christians to observe the biblical Sabbath. This practice was identified as "Judaizing" and was deemed totally unacceptable to the Christian religion. Christians were required to work on that day in order to prove their irreverence toward *YAHveh's* ordained Sabbath.

Following the Council of Laodicea, the *seventh* day of the week—the true Sabbath—lost its biblical name. This holy day was now being called by its *pagan name*, "SATUR-day." The state religion of Rome transferred the biblical day of rest from the seventh day (the Sabbath) to "SUN-day." Instead of the seventh day being dedicated to *YAHveh*, its name was replaced with "SATUR-day," honoring the pagan deity, Saturn. Thus *YAHveh's* Sabbath was nullified and perverted through a worship system rooted in paganism.

The ancient Serpent had once again *cunningly hidden the holy Hebrew root* under that which is rooted in *profane paganism.*

Tradition above Scripture

During the dark centuries of the Middle Ages, ordinary people had no access to the Scriptures. When the Bible became available through the printing press during the Reformation, the infallible authority of the Word was contested by the religious leaders of that day. These leaders blatantly declared that *tradition stood above Scripture* and insisted that *the authority of the church was not bound to the authority of the Scriptures.* Thus the failure to observe *YAHveh's* Sabbath as He had commanded was openly stated to have been *by the church's own authority* and not by the command of Messiah.

YAHveh had warned His people through the prophet Ezekiel:

"*Her priests* [religious leaders] *have done violence to My law and have profaned My holy things;* THEY HAVE MADE NO

DISTINCTION BETWEEN THE HOLY AND THE PROFANE, and they have not taught the difference between the unclean and the clean; and THEY HIDE THEIR EYES FROM MY SABBATHS ..." (Eze 22:26)

For such transgressions of *YAHveh's* commandments, Israel was mightily judged. Nehemiah rebuked God's people with these words:

"What is this evil thing you are doing, BY PROFANING THE SABBATH DAY? Did not your fathers do the same so that our God brought on us, and on this city, all this trouble? Yet you are adding to the wrath on Israel by PROFANING THE SABBATH." (Ne 13:17-18)

YAHshua the Messiah spoke vehemently to the hypocritically religious about their man-made traditions.

"... YOU INVALIDATED THE WORD OF YAHVEH FOR THE SAKE OF YOUR TRADITION. You hypocrites, rightly did Isaiah prophesy of you, saying, 'THIS PEOPLE HONORS ME WITH THEIR LIPS, BUT THEIR HEART IS FAR AWAY FROM ME. 'BUT IN VAIN DO THEY WORSHIP ME, TEACHING AS DOCTRINES THE PRECEPTS OF MEN.'" (Mt 15:6-9)

According to *YAHveh's* fourth commandment, we are to remember the Sabbath day by keeping it holy. The Sabbath is blessed in the Creator's sight and carries a special blessing for all who reverence it as *Holy to YAHveh*. Those who seek more of His glorious presence will truly find Him to be the "*Lord* [Master] *of the Sabbath*" (see Mk 2:27-28).

Concerning His Father's commandments, *YAHshua* said:

"For truly I say to you, until heaven and earth pass away, not the smallest letter or stroke shall pass away from the Law ... WHOEVER THEN ANNULS ONE OF THE LEAST OF THESE COMMANDMENTS, AND SO TEACHES OTHERS, SHALL BE CALLED LEAST IN THE KINGDOM OF HEAVEN; BUT WHOEVER KEEPS AND TEACHES THEM, HE SHALL BE CALLED GREAT IN THE KINGDOM OF HEAVEN." (Mt 5:18-19)

YAHshua said, *"The Sabbath was made for man, and not man for the Sabbath. Consequently, the Son of Man is Lord [Master] even of the Sabbath"* (Mk 2:27-28). Every day should be a day of worship of the Almighty; however the true issue is that the day which *YAHveh* calls "holy" must not be tainted through man's irreverent distortions and misinterpretations.

The Sabbath is the crowning day of the week. It serves as a vivid illustration of the coming messianic kingdom—the hope of the righteous remnant. According to *YAHveh's* time table, *"one day is as a thousand years, and a thousand years is as a day"* (2Pe 3:8) After six thousand years of human history, we are approaching the seventh "day," which will be a thousand-year rest. This culmination of the ages will be the ultimate *Shabbat Shalom*, the long-awaited Sabbath peace of *YAHveh's* messianic kingdom, often referred to as *the Millennium.*

Listen to what *YAHveh* says concerning His eternal Sabbath:

"For just as the new heavens and the new earth Which I make will endure before Me," declares YAHveh, "So your offspring and your name [Israel] will endure. And it shall be from new moon to new moon And from SABBATH TO SABBATH, All mankind will come to bow down before Me," says YAHveh. (Isa 66:22-23)

Long ago the prophet Isaiah recorded *YAHveh's* unchanging words of promise to redeemed Jews and Gentiles who would be joined through the blood of *YAHshua:*

Thus says YAHveh ... "DO RIGHTEOUSNESS, FOR MY SALVATION IS ABOUT TO COME And my righteousness to be revealed. HOW BLESSED IS THE MAN WHO DOES THIS, And the son of man who takes hold of it; WHO KEEPS FROM PROFANING THE SABBATH ... Also the foreigners [Gentiles] who join themselves to YAHveh, To minister to Him, and to LOVE THE NAME OF YAHVEH, To be His servants, EVERY ONE WHO KEEPS FROM PROFANING THE SABBATH, AND HOLDS FAST MY COVENANT; Even those I will bring to My holy mountain, And make them joyful in My house of prayer. ..." (Isa 56:1-2, 6-7)

"If because of the Sabbath, you turn your foot From doing your own pleasure on My holy day, AND CALL THE SABBATH A DELIGHT, THE HOLY DAY OF YAHVEH HONORABLE ... I will make you ride on the heights of the earth; And I will feed you with the heritage of Jacob your father, For the mouth of YAHveh has spoken." (Isa 58:13-14)

The observance of the Sabbath is the one commandment of God that gives an outward sign that we, as children of the Mighty One, have become separate from the world system. It is a visible indication that we have chosen to obey *YAHveh* rather than man. If we are to be priests who have no inheritance in the land (the world), then *YAHveh* alone is to be our exceedingly great reward.

Let those who wholeheartedly desire to understand and

obey *YAHveh's* commandments seek Him with all their heart, soul, and strength while He may be found. Let us pray.

Dear Heavenly Father: *We ask You to lead us on the path of righteousness for Your name's sake. We beseech You to have mercy on us for we have walked in the dim light of the only truth available. Forgive us for our transgressions and teach us to walk in all Your ways. Your Word says, "This is the love of YAHveh, that we keep His commandments; and His commandments are not burdensome" (1Jn 5:3). Please give us wisdom and clarity regarding all that You require in obedience to Your commandments, especially the commandment, "Remember the Sabbath day, to keep it holy" (Ex 20:8).*

Thank You that You are the rewarder of those who diligently seek You. Your perfect will is the desire of our hearts. May we be righteous instruments through which Your will is done on earth as it is in heaven. In the name of YAHveh the Father, YAHshua the Son, and the Spirit of Truth, Amen.

As the apostle Paul wrote:

"Let YAHveh be found true,

though every man be found a liar."

(Ro 3:4)

135

Chapter 19
Touch Not the Plunder under the Ban

The Holy One is sounding a trumpet. His righteous decrees have been emphatically spelled out that a righteous remnant might heed His warnings. The hour is upon us for separating from our lives and practices all that is profane and unholy. In His mercy, His words to Israel of old speak directly to our hearts today. Man's justified mixing of the holy with the common and pagan rooted are nothing less than a grievous abomination in the sight of a holy God and King.

Let us not be deceived and mock YAHveh "*for whatever a man sows, this will he also reap*" (Gal 6:7). Let us not partake of doctrines sown by the flesh and not by His Spirit of Truth and in so doing jeopardize our intimate relationship with a holy God. "*YAHveh is not mocked*" (Gal 6:7).

That which has pagan roots cannot be camouflaged and dressed up to appear righteous. *YAHveh's* penetrating eyes search the hearts of men and the heart of religion and its traditions. He sees the essence of all things. Those pagan roots which were sown like tares into His harvest field will certainly not escape His righteous judgments. These judgments are destined to go forth like a sickle in His mighty hand to separate the wheat (the holy) from the tares (the unholy and profane).

The Almighty adamantly warned His people not to mix the holy with the profane (Lev 10:10) and not to mix the pure worship of *YAHveh* with the unholy, pagan practices of the Gentiles. "*Thus you are to keep My charge, that you* DO NOT PRACTICE ANY OF THE ABOMINABLE CUSTOMS *which have been practiced before you, so as* NOT TO DEFILE YOURSELVES *with them; I am YAHveh your God*'" (Lev 18:30).

"YOU SHALL NOT BEHAVE THUS TOWARD YAHVEH YOUR GOD, *for every abominable act which YAHveh hates they have done for their gods ...* WHATEVER I COMMAND YOU, YOU SHALL BE CAREFUL TO DO; YOU SHALL NOT ADD TO NOR TAKE AWAY FROM IT.*"* (Dt 12:31-32)

YAHveh implored His people to remain at a great distance from the practices of the pagan nations around them. He admonished them to respond to even rumors regarding the unholy practices of the Gentiles entering the holy camp and worship of *YAHveh*. He continues to emphasize that all who seek righteousness *"SHALL INVESTIGATE AND SEARCH OUT AND INQUIRE THOROUGHLY"* (Dt 13:14) regarding any inkling of such forbidden compromises.

He continued by saying, *"If it is true and the matter established that this abomination has been done among you* [the mixing of pagan practices with *YAHveh's* holy requirements]*"* (Dt 13:14), then all that was impure was to be *"utterly destroyed"* (Dt 13:15) and given up as a sacrificial offering to *YAHveh* who had placed these things under His sovereign ban, never to be touched again. He further emphasized, *"Nothing from that which is put UNDER THE BAN shall cling to your hand, in order that YAHveh may turn from His burning anger and show mercy to you, and have compassion on you and make you increase, ..."* (Dt 13:17).

> *"I will not be with you anymore unless you DESTROY THE THINGS UNDER THE BAN FROM YOUR MIDST* [the plunder which was devoted to destruction]. *... You cannot stand before your enemies until you have removed the things under the ban from your midst."* (Jos 7:12-13)

There is a chronic malaise and despondency in many members of the religious system; many who truly believe in the Living God and His Messiah are discouraged, spiritually empty, and confused. Could it be that *YAHveh's* presence has long departed because these traditions, like "pounced on plunder," have not been destroyed from their midst?

> *Yet YAHveh warned ... "TURN FROM YOUR EVIL WAYS AND KEEP My COMMANDMENTS, My STATUTES ..." However, they did not listen, but stiffened their neck like their fathers, who did not believe in YAHveh their God. And they rejected ... His warnings with which He warned them* [let us learn from their mistakes] *...* (2Ki 17:13-15)

Sadly, this is the condition of the religious multitudes who love this world and follow the compromised traditions of men. Through Jeremiah, *YAHveh* expressed His displeasure in tainted forms of religion.

> *"... 'Obey My voice, and I will be your God, and you will be My people; and you will walk in all the way which I command you, that it may be well with you.' Yet THEY DID NOT OBEY OR INCLINE THEIR EAR, but walked in their own counsels and in the STUBBORNNESS of their evil heart, and WENT BACKWARD AND NOT FORWARD."* (Jer 7:23-24)

HOWEVER, THEY DID NOT LISTEN, BUT THEY DID ACCORDING TO THEIR EARLIER CUSTOM. So while these nations feared YAHveh, THEY ALSO SERVED THEIR IDOLS [any person, thing, attitude, even religious tradition that is treasured above YAHveh and His commandments]; *their children likewise and their grandchildren, as their fathers did, so they do to this day.* (2Ki 17:40-41)

YAHveh spoke strong words through His prophet Isaiah: *"You have made your bed on a high and lofty hill* [your man-made traditions]; *there you went up to offer your sacrifices. BEHIND YOUR DOORS AND YOUR DOORPOSTS YOU HAVE PUT YOUR PAGAN SYMBOLS* [pagan-rooted practices]. ... *Whom have you so dreaded and feared THAT YOU HAVE BEEN FALSE TO ME, and have neither remembered me nor pondered this in your hearts? Is it not because I have long been silent that you do not fear me? I WILL EXPOSE YOUR RIGHTEOUSNESS AND YOUR WORKS, AND THEY WILL NOT BENEFIT YOU."* (Isa 57:7-8, 11-12 NIV — emphasis added)

Such is the condition of Christianity and its members who have unknowingly perpetuated the traditions of their forefathers and a religious system tainted with the profane and unholy. Israel had mixed the pure worship of *YAHveh* with the unholy, pagan practices of the surrounding peoples. The prophet Elijah was sent to apostate Israel to turn them back to the pure worship of *YAHveh.*

Both the prophet Malachi and *YAHshua* the Messiah prophesied that at the close of the age, the spirit of Elijah would be sent forth to a compromised and apostate religious generation. The spirit of Elijah is crying out, "Forsake all that is compromised, man-made and pagan tainted. *Turn back to the pure, wholehearted obedience and worship of YAHveh the Almighty!"*

PART FIVE

Dedicated to the Tribe of Levi

Levi

"... I will raise up for Myself

a faithful priest who will do according

to what is in My heart and in My soul;

and I will build him an enduring house

and he will walk before My anointed always."

(1Sa 2:35)

Chapter 20
Prelude to the David Generation

"the Glory of Israel will not lie or change His mind" (1Sa 15:29)

YAHveh sovereignly instituted His holy feasts and days as a preview of the promised Redeemer. By fulfilling these feasts, *YAHshua* gave further evidence to His people that He indeed was their long-awaited Messiah.[1]

The ancient Serpent, however, has used many strategies to keep Israel from recognizing her Savior. The Enemy countered *YAHveh's* plan of using the feasts to point to *YAHshua* by superimposing pagan festivals over the holy feast days. Through this anti-Semitic plot, Satan succeeded in stripping the Messiah of His Hebrew identity and presented Him in pagan, Gentile trappings, which *YAHveh* had warned His people *never to touch*.

The "Saul generation," like Israel's first king, has not heeded *YAHveh's* commands or followed His instructions; yet His Word to us has not changed. His requirements are the same, but we have compromised His Word and justified our rebellion. Much of organizational Christianity has *"spared as good"* (1Sa 15:9) that which has been designated by *YAHveh* for destruction. In the truest sense, the holy has been mixed with the profane. The Almighty's words echo to this compromising generation: *"Why then did you not obey the voice of YAHveh, but rushed upon the spoil and did what was evil in the sight of YAHveh?"* (1Sa 15:19).

The David Generation

And Samuel did not see Saul again until the day of his death; for Samuel grieved over Saul. And YAHveh regretted that He had made Saul king over Israel. (1Sa 15:35)

The Holy Spirit grieves over the "Saul generation" of today's apostate religious systems. Many denominations, churches,

---

[1] There are many books available on the holy feasts of Israel. This literature will certainly enhance one's knowledge and understanding of the Hebraic roots of the Savior and the holy roots of our faith.

synagogues, leaders, and individuals are steeped in traditions but devoid of the glorious presence of the Almighty. *YAHveh* is not interested in the pomp and grandeur of human programs and religious empires. Just as King Saul continued to reign for a period of time, these compromised religious systems will continue for a season—not by His Spirit, but by the might and power of men.

The Holy Spirit's words are for the "Saul generation" of today: *"YAHveh has torn the kingdom ... from you today, and has given it to your neighbor who is better than you"* (1Sa 15:28).

"But now your kingdom shall not endure. YAHVEH HAS SOUGHT OUT for Himself A MAN AFTER HIS OWN HEART, and YAHveh has appointed him as ruler over His people, because YOU HAVE NOT KEPT WHAT YAHVEH COMMANDED YOU." (1Sa 13:14)

Even now, the Spirit that separates men and women unto *YAHveh* is searching for a "David generation." Like David, they will be men and women *"AFTER MY [YAHveh's] HEART, who will do all My will"* (Ac 13:22).

"Many are called, but few are chosen" (Mt 22:14). So it was when the prophet Samuel called together all of David's brothers to anoint the one who was the chosen "man after *YAHveh's* heart" (see Ac 13:22). Today there are many who, like David, are surrounded by religious brethren who seem more pious and of greater spiritual stature, but whose hearts are not consumed with knowing and doing *YAHveh's* will. Many are called—as were David's seven brothers—yet only a pure remnant is chosen. *YAHveh* is looking at hearts. With wholehearted devotion, the "David generation" will joyfully proclaim:

"... I will bow down toward your holy temple and will PRAISE YOUR NAME ... for you have EXALTED ABOVE ALL THINGS YOUR NAME AND YOUR WORD" (Ps 138:2 NIV — emphasis added). — *"Teach me Thy way, O YAHveh; I will walk in Thy truth; UNITE MY HEART TO FEAR THY NAME. I will give thanks to Thee, ... AND WILL GLORIFY THY NAME FOREVER"* (Ps 86:11-12).

The Holy Spirit has a horn of oil that is now being poured out upon a "David generation," anointing them to go forth in the *name of YAHveh*, the Holy One of Israel. *"Then Samuel took the horn of oil and anointed him in the midst of his brothers; and the Spirit of YAHveh came mightily upon David from that day forward ..."* (1Sa 16:13). These divine words are magnified through the psalmist to their privileged hearts: *"I have found David My servant; With My holy oil I have anointed him, ... My faithfulness and My lovingkindness will be with him, AND IN MY NAME HIS HORN* [strength] *WILL BE EXALTED"* (Ps 89:20, 24).

David's fame as *YAHveh's* servant was quickly established when he confronted and killed the enemy Goliath. The humble "David generation" will join with David in saying to the Adversary, *"I COME TO YOU IN THE NAME OF YAHVEH OF HOSTS [YAHVEH SABAOTH], the God of the armies of Israel, whom you have taunted"* (1Sa 17:45). The "David generation" will desire to live obediently and whole heartedly serve *YAHveh*, and will give Him *the glory due His name.* Many from the varied traditional religious systems will be threatened and even envious of this generation's uncompromised obedience to *YAHveh's* holy standards.

A word of caution to those enlisting in David's ranks: *Beware of Saul's flying spears!* Jealousy causes strange behavior. In Saul's case, jealousy drove him to insanity! Yet David's response to Saul must be the example for *YAHveh's* purified, latter-day remnant.

"... know and perceive that there is no evil or rebellion in my hands, and I have not sinned against you, though you are lying in wait for my life to take it. ... YAHveh therefore be judge and decide between you and me; and may He see and plead my cause [to walk in obedience to His perfect will], *and deliver me from your hand." ... "YAHVEH FORBID THAT I SHOULD STRETCH OUT MY HAND AGAINST YAHVEH'S ANOINTED ..."* (1Sa 24:11-12, 15; 26:11). — *"DAVID GREW STEADILY STRONGER, but the house of Saul grew weaker continually"* (2Sa 3:1).

As the holy anointing oil pours out over this last day "David generation," we will see numbers of people added to David's army. Simultaneously, we will see a weakening of Saul's compromised ranks.

YAHshua is David's eternal heir and the Commander in Chief of *YAHveh's* army. He is summoning a remnant who will count the cost and defect from man-made traditions and worldly preoccupations to join the ranks of David's (*YAHshua's*) holy army.

"... DAY BY DAY MEN CAME TO DAVID TO HELP HIM, UNTIL THERE WAS A GREAT ARMY LIKE THE ARMY OF GOD. ... " (1Ch 12:22, 38). — *"And David became greater and greater, for YAHveh God of hosts was with him"* (2Sa 5:10). — *"And*

David realized that YAHveh had established him as king over Israel, and that He had exalted his kingdom FOR THE SAKE OF HIS PEOPLE ISRAEL" (2Sa 5:12).

Over the centuries, the distorted truths propagated by many in corporate Christianity have led to the persecution of the Jews. This ancient hostility will be replaced with the love, mercy, and salvation of *YAHshua* when a "David generation" remembers it's God-ordained responsibility to bless Israel. *YAHveh* is calling out to the Gentiles of the "David generation":

"Behold, I will LIFT UP MY HAND [beckon] TO THE NATIONS [Gentiles], And set up My standard to the peoples; And THEY WILL BRING YOUR SONS [Israel] in their bosom, And your daughters will be carried on their shoulders [back to YAHveh]. And kings [including the 'David generation'] will be your guardians, And their princesses your nurses. They will bow down to you with their faces to the earth, And lick the dust of your feet; And you [the Jews] will know [from the display of humility and love] THAT I AM YAHVEH; ..." (Isa 49:22-23)

YAHveh will have COMPASSION ON JACOB; once again he will choose Israel and will settle them in their own land. ALIENS [Gentiles] WILL JOIN THEM AND UNITE WITH THE HOUSE OF JACOB. Nations will take them and bring them to their own place. ... (Isa 14:1-2 NIV — emphasis added)

Isaiah prophesies of a remnant of Gentiles who *"'shall bring all [their] brethren [the Jews] from all the nations as a grain offering to YAHveh ... to My holy mountain Jerusalem ... just as the sons of Israel bring their grain offering in a clean vessel to the house of YAHveh'"* (Isa 66:20). "Gentiles will bring back the remnant [of Jews] ... *as an offering* [a tithe to *YAHveh*] ... As the Israelites were to bring their tithes and offerings" (emphases added)[2]

It is very common today for religious leaders to cry out for tithes and offerings to facilitate their building programs, while neglecting to build *YAHveh's* temple of holy "living stones." The typical message on tithing often includes Malachi's words:

"Will a man rob God? Yet you are robbing Me! But you say, 'How have we robbed Thee?' In tithes and offerings. You

---

[2] Note on Isa 66:20. *The NIV Study Bible* (Grand Rapids: The Zondervan Corporation, 1985), p. 1114.

are cursed with a curse, for you are robbing Me, the whole nation of you! Bring the WHOLE *tithe into the storehouse, so that there may be* [spiritual] *food in My house ...*" (Mal 3:8-10)

Those who bring the sons and daughters of Israel to *YAHveh* through the love of *YAHshua* their Messiah are truly *bringing the whole tithe into His storehouse!* Now is the time to favor Zion. Flex those muscles and carry His "treasured possession," the children of Israel, back to the pure worship of *YAHveh* their God through *YAHshua* their Messiah! *"test Me now in this,"* says *YAHveh* of hosts, *"if I will not open for you the windows of heaven, and pour out for you a blessing until it overflows"* (Mal 3:10).

The "David generation" will be a remnant of men and women after *YAHveh's* own heart. They will wholeheartedly obey all of His holy commands, including the mandate to bless the Jewish people by bringing them the love, mercy, and saving truth of *YAHshua.* They will fervently *"pray for the peace of Jerusalem"* (Ps 122:6); they will *"comfort"* His people and *"speak kindly"* to them (Isa 40:1-2). They will carry the lost sheep of the house of Israel back as *"tithes and offerings"* to *YAHveh.* Then, as prophesied, He will throw open heaven's floodgates to pour out the unfathomable blessings promised to the Gentiles in the Abrahamic covenant (Ge 12:3). *"'Test Me now in this,'* says *YAHveh"* (Mal 3:10).

Chapter 21

The Royal Priesthood of the David Generation

Messiah's blood has purchased a holy priesthood from among Jews of every tribe of Israel and Gentiles of every nation. *YAHshua's* blood opened the way for a priesthood to enter the holy sanctuary of God; it tore the veil that had separated the people of *YAHveh* almighty from His divine presence.

The cost was immeasurably high for *YAHveh* to purchase this priesthood for His glory. We must not take lightly such a great sacrifice, nor should we neglect this awesome privilege and responsibility.

His Spirit says to us (as He said to Aaron and his sons, the Levites), *"I am giving you the service of THE PRIESTHOOD AS A GIFT. ... You will have NO INHERITANCE IN THEIR LAND [THE WORLD], nor will you have any share among them; I AM YOUR SHARE AND YOUR INHERITANCE"* (Nu 18:7, 20 NIV — emphasis added). The "Saul generation," which does not wholeheartedly obey the Most High, will not have access to the most holy things of *YAHveh.* Yet the "Saul generation" will continue to exist in the *outer court of religion* causing conflict and confusion in the minds of the brethren because of their false teachings and compromising doctrines.

This *outer court* is the domain of the *uncircumcised in heart.* It is a vast religious system that sits in close proximity to the world—as if a flimsy, man-made wall labeled "religion" is the only thing separating this court from the world. It was therefore inevitable that *the world's influence* would enter in and pollute this outer court with carnality, hypocrisy, rebellion, pagan customs, and sectarian pride, resulting in *lukewarmness.* This double-minded hypocrisy has defamed the holiness and sanctity of the living God.

YAHveh warned against placing man's doctrines, traditions, and empty religious forms next to the threshold of His holy sanctuary. In anger He said:

When they PLACED THEIR THRESHOLD NEXT TO MY THRESHOLD and their doorposts beside my doorposts, WITH ONLY A WALL BETWEEN ME AND THEM, THEY DEFILED MY HOLY NAME BY THEIR DETESTABLE PRACTICES. ... (Eze 43:8 NIV — emphasis added)

YAHveh is a consuming fire! He sits enthroned between the cherubim of the ark of the covenant in the Holy of Holies of His sanctuary. Few Jews or Gentiles who profess to know Him have truly experienced this awesome King of Kings. Donald McCullough summarizes this pitiful and yet prevalent condition:

> The God of the Scriptures is a holy God—wholly other, radically different from anything else in creation, terrifying in greatness, and utterly awesome in love. This is a God who transcends our understanding and is unknowable except by divine revelation—the God described by the author of Hebrews as "a consuming fire."
>
> But the church has reduced this God of glory to more manageable proportions. We have trivialized the God of glory.[1]

The New Testament warns us, "offer to God an acceptable worship with reverence and awe; for indeed our God is a consuming fire" (Hebrews 12:28-29). But reverence and awe have often been replaced by a yawn of familiarity. The consuming fire has been domesticated into a candle flame, adding a bit of religious atmosphere, perhaps, but no heat, no blinding light, no power for purification.[2]

Through the blood, He redeemed a priesthood who would be privileged to leave the outer court of religion and enter the Holy of Holies *to stand in His fiery, life-changing presence.*

In the book of Revelation, John told of a religious system that would lightly esteem this God of glory; they would trivialize the call to be a holy priesthood and the divine blood that purchased it. The members of this Laodicean-type religious system would remain uncircumcised in heart. They would, as it were, be constrained to the outer court filled with tainted religious traditions, money changers, and those who have embraced the lusts of the world. This apostate priesthood would be *so close to the ice-cold dying world* that inevitably, by sheer proximity, it would become *lukewarm* in nature.

---

[1] Donald W. McCullough, *The Trivialization of God* (Colorado Springs: NavPress, 1995), copy inside jacket cover.

[2] Donald W. McCullough, op. cit., p. 13 (footnote).

Messiah said that He would rather a people be either *hot* as they wholeheartedly embrace *YAHveh* and minister as priests in His holy presence, or *cold* as they wholeheartedly embrace the dying world.

"And to the angel of the church in Laodicea write: The Amen, the faithful and true Witness, the Beginning of the creation of YAHveh, says this: 'I know your deeds, that you ARE NEITHER COLD NOR HOT; I would that you were cold or hot. So because you are LUKEWARM, and neither hot nor cold, I WILL SPIT YOU OUT OF MY MOUTH.'" (Rev 3:14-16)

Destruction of the Outer Court

Scripture tells us that when *YAHshua* entered Jerusalem and went to the temple, he *"looked around at everything"* (Mk 11:11 NIV). As the righteous High Priest, He saw His Father's house filled with an abominable mixture of the holy and the profane. With righteous indignation, He turned over the tables of the money changers who filled the outer court and robbed the temple of its sanctity. *"Is it not written, 'MY HOUSE SHALL BE CALLED A HOUSE OF PRAYER FOR ALL THE NATIONS'?"* YAHshua asked. *"But you have made it a ROBBERS' DEN"* (Mk 11:17). This display of holy zeal was a symbolic warning of YAHveh's righteous judgments to come.

Directly before *YAHshua* was slaughtered as the Passover Lamb, He cleansed the "outer court" of the temple of its tangible atrocities. When *YAHshua* comes again it will not be as a meek sacrificial lamb, but as the roaring Lion of the Tribe of Judah. With mighty indignation He will mangle His foe and devour His Father's enemies. He will enter His temple built with the living stones He purchased by His blood. With eyes like a flame of fire (see Rev 1:14; 2:18; 19:12), He will once again look around at everything within the temple.

The Messiah will see far more than human eyes are able to perceive. He will look deep into our hearts, which are to be holy temples for *YAHveh's* glory. The multitudes who confess Him with their lips but whose hearts remain far from His Father's heartbeat will be lukewarm and nauseating to Him.

The Lion of the Tribe of Judah will search both the religious systems and the individual hearts of professing believers. Any unholiness, including pagan influences and abominable mixtures of the holy and the worldly, will be vehemently uprooted; *YAHshua* will not tolerate the desecration of His Father's holy temple.

May His piercing words penetrate our hearts and cleanse our holy temples, just as He cleansed His Father's temple long ago. *"'Get these* [compromises that desecrate] *out of here! How dare you turn My Father's house into a market!' His disciples remembered that it is written: 'Zeal for your house will consume me'"* (Jn 2:16-17 NIV — emphasis added).

The coming purification of *YAHveh's* temple will not be a merely symbolic overturning of the greedy money changers' tables. It will be the total destruction of the entire religious outer court occupied by those who are uncircumcised in heart. *YAHshua* will not allow His Father's house to be a laughingstock. Messiah gave His life to build a *holy house* filled with *holy priests*. It is to be a *temple* built of *living stones*. He will tear down every lifeless stone laid on the foundation of man-made doctrines. Not one stone was left standing when God's earthly temple was destroyed by the Roman army. In a similar manner, the Mighty One will destroy completely any house that has not been built by His Spirit, on His foundation, and according to His plumb line of truth. As John wrote in Revelation:

> *And there was given me a measuring rod like a staff; and someone said, "Rise and measure the temple of YAHveh, and the altar, and those who worship in it. AND LEAVE OUT THE COURT* [of the uncircumsised in heart] *WHICH IS OUTSIDE THE TEMPLE, AND DO NOT MEASURE IT, FOR IT HAS BEEN GIVEN TO THE NATIONS* [Gentiles] *..."* (Rev 11:1-2)

The Spirit was showing John a day when *YAHveh* will cleanse His temple once and for all, purifying it of all desecrating, defiling, and compromising influences.

At *YAHshua's* first cleansing of His Father's house, He drove out *"those who were buying and selling in the temple"* (see Mk 11:15-16). He overturned the tables of the money changers and did not allow anyone to carry goods through the temple. The next cleansing, as envisioned by John, will not be the superficial cleansing of the outer court. It will be the *radical purification of the temple through the elimination of the entire outer court. No longer will there be a merciful provision within YAHveh's temple for the compromised and uncircumcised in heart.* This court, though densely populated with many who have made a profession of faith, is a taint to the holiness of His house and is slated for destruction. The words of Isaiah speak to us today: *"DEPART,*

DEPART [evacuate], GO OUT FROM THERE, Touch nothing unclean; Go out of the midst of her, PURIFY YOURSELVES, You who carry the vessels of YAHveh" (Isa 52:11).

Now is not the time to freeze in your spiritual tracks or to dig your self-righteous heels into the ground. Flee from the destruction to come! Do not remain lukewarm! Leave the doomed outer court and its unholy mixture of worldly and religious affairs! Consecrate yourselves! Be hot! Be holy! For without holiness, no man will stand in His fiery presence.

Only those who are circumcised in heart will be able to enter His temple to worship before His holy altar. These are the "living stones," redeemed by YAHshua and built by His hands as a temple that is Holy to YAHveh. This is the priesthood that will stand eternally in His glorious presence in the New YAHrushalayim. Of this eternal kingdom Isaiah prophesied, "For the uncircumcised and the unclean Will no more come into you" (Isa 52:1).

YAHshua is sounding a trumpet and crying out, "Come out of her, my people, that you may not participate in her sins" (Rev 18:4). Repent and depart from the love of the world, the lusts of the flesh, and from all religious errors that transgress YAHveh's holy commands. The outer court of the lukewarm religious masses, like the golden cup of wrath in His hand, is soon to reach its fill of abominations. It will inevitably overflow its brim. Then the Lamb's mercy and grace will become the Lion's righteous judgments. The Lion of the Tribe of Judah will mangle and destroy everything that profanes and desecrates His Father's eternal, holy temple.

If a trumpet is blown in a city will not the people tremble? ...

Surely YAHveh God does nothing

Unless He reveals His secret counsel

To His servants the prophets.

A LION HAS ROARED! WHO WILL NOT FEAR?

YAHVEH GOD HAS SPOKEN! WHO CAN BUT PROPHESY?

(Am 3:6-8)

Chapter 22
Religious Masses or Righteous Remnant?

In the final book of the Old Testament, the prophet Malachi addressed a religious community whose worship had degenerated into a lifeless perpetuation of empty forms and traditions. The name *Malachi* means "messenger of *YAHveh*," probably derived from "a shortened form of *Mal'ak-ya*"[1] (or Mal'ak-*YAH*). It was through this prophet that *YAHveh* issued a message of rebuke to His faithless priesthood. The prophet exhorted the people to repent and reform their ways in order to regain *YAHveh's* blessings rather than the prophesied judgments to come.

Just as *YAHveh's* heart grieved over Saul's rebellion generations before, so it grieves again over the compromising priesthood of the religious masses today. Listen to the heavenly Father's cry as recorded in the book of Malachi:

> "'A son honors his father, and a servant his master. Then if I am a father, where is My honor? And if I am a master, WHERE IS MY RESPECT?' says YAHveh of hosts to you, O priests who despise MY NAME. ... You are presenting defiled food [hypocritical sacrifices] upon My altar. ... "
> (Mal 1:6-7)

In Malachi's days, priests were to bring *YAHveh* sacrifices that were undefiled and worthy of His holiness. Today God's royal priesthood of believers is to present Him holy sacrifices of their broken and contrite hearts, and the offerings of their dedicated lives placed upon His altar. Instead, many have brought defiled sacrifices of religious services and good works done with self-righteous motives and people-pleasing aspirations.

The Holy One abhors half-hearted, compromised religious sacrifices and says to His priesthood:

> "Oh that there were one among you who would SHUT THE GATES, that you might not USELESSLY KINDLE FIRE [the fiery fervor of religious rituals and traditions] ON MY ALTAR! I am not pleased with you," says YAHveh of hosts, "nor will I accept an offering from you." (Mal 1:10)

---

[1] *The New Open Bible (NASB)*, study edition (Nashville: Thomas Nelson Publishers, 1990), p. 1045.

150

Hands that have touched the unholy, common things of the world and have mixed them with the holy things of YAHveh are offensive and unacceptable in His sight. The worship and sacrifice offered by these defiled hands are merely ineffectual rituals and meaningless forms. The Holy One responds with these words:

"For from the rising of the sun, even to its setting, MY NAME WILL BE GREAT AMONG THE NATIONS, and in every place INCENSE [holy prayer] *is going to be OFFERED TO MY NAME, and a grain offering that is pure; for MY NAME WILL BE GREAT AMONG THE NATIONS* [Gentiles]," *says YAHveh of hosts. "But you are profaning it, in that you say, 'The table of YAHveh is defiled, and as for its fruit, its food is to be despised.' You also say, 'My, how tiresome it is!' And you disdainfully sniff at it,"* *says YAHveh of hosts* [Many will say, "I do not like the flavor of this Hebrew root with its holy requirements" as they sniff at YAHveh's table with haughty disdain.] ... (Mal 1:11-13)

The Almighty's full counsel, including the Old and New Testaments, is also His banquet table. YAHveh desires to take a righteous remnant up the mountain of His glorious presence. There in the midst of His Shekinah glory, He has prepared many delicacies of truth reserved for this last great hour. The redeemed remnant will rejoice as they feast at His table; but the religious masses will turn up their haughty noses as they "sniff" at His feast with contempt.

And YAHveh of hosts will prepare a lavish banquet [great spiritual blessings] *for all peoples on this mountain; A banquet of aged wine* [He has saved the best wine for last], *choice pieces with marrow* [spiritual nourishment], *... And on this mountain He will swallow up the covering* [of deception including religious apostasy] *which is over all peoples, Even the veil which is stretched over all nations. He will swallow up death for all time ...* (Isa 25:6-8)

He is inviting the humble and spiritually hungry to be blessed as they partake of this holy banquet. In Messiah's words: *"Blessed are those who hunger and thirst for righteousness, for they shall be satisfied"* (Mt 5:6).

A Kingdom of Priests

Through the sacrificial blood of the Lamb, men were purchased for *YAHveh* from every tribe of Israel and every Gentile nation. *YAHshua* has *"made them to be A KINGDOM AND PRIESTS to our God"* (Rev 5:10).

The priests of the Old Testament were chosen *"to stand and serve IN THE NAME OF YAHveh forever"* (Dt 18:5). They were commanded to *"SWEAR BY HIS NAME"* (Dt 10:20) and *"to stand before YAHveh to serve Him and to BLESS IN HIS NAME until this day"* (Dt 10:8). It was to be a sacred privilege to bless the people in the name of *YAHveh*.

Then YAHveh spoke to Moses, saying, "Speak to Aaron and to his sons [the priesthood], *saying, 'Thus you shall bless the sons of Israel. You shall say to them: YAHveh bless you, and keep you; YAHveh make His face shine on you, And be gracious to you; YAHveh lift up His countenance on you, And give you peace.' So THEY SHALL INVOKE MY NAME ON THE SONS OF ISRAEL* [and all Gentiles joined with her], *AND I THEN WILL BLESS THEM."* (Nu 6:22-27)

This repetition of *YAHveh's* name three times over the people marked them as His treasured possession and holy nation. The blessing and covering of *YAHveh's* name marked them as chosen people and as heirs to His promised blessings.

A Modern-Day Priesthood

When *YAHveh* called Israel to be His people, they were to be a forerunner and example of His modern-day priesthood, the redeemed as *one new man*. He spoke these words to Israel:

"'Now then, if you will indeed OBEY MY VOICE and keep My covenant, then you shall be My own possession among all the peoples, for all the earth is Mine; and you shall be to Me A KINGDOM OF PRIESTS AND A HOLY NATION.' ..." (Ex 19:5-6)

Through the New Testament, *YAHshua* commissioned the righteous remnant of both Jews and Gentiles to become priests in the service of the Most High.

And coming to Him ... you also ... are being built up as a spiritual house for a holy priesthood, to offer up spiritual sacrifices [of your pure and spotless lives] *acceptable to YAHveh through YAHshua Messiah. ... But you are A*

CHOSEN RACE, A ROYAL PRIESTHOOD, A HOLY NATION ... *that you may proclaim the excellencies of Him who has called you out of darkness into His marvelous light* ... (1Pe 2:4-5, 9)

YAHveh had intended for the entire nation of Israel to be His priests. This priesthood was to be a testimony to the Gentile nations of His glorious presence with His chosen people. Unfortunately, Israel compromised *YAHveh's* righteous decrees, mixed the holy with the profane, and gradually moved farther and farther away from her priestly call.

When *YAHshua* appeared, He found a Jewish religious system that was striving to be a separated people through legalistic regulations. *YAHshua* found the religious masses in Israel steeped in the doctrines and traditions of men. To this tainted system and its many hypocritical leaders He pronounced, *"Therefore I say to you, the kingdom of YAHveh will be taken away from you, and be given to a nation producing the fruit of it"* (Mt 21:43).

Messiah poured out His life blood to purchase a people for His honor and glory. *YAHshua "loves us, and released us from our sins by His blood, and He has made us* to be *a kingdom,* PRIESTS TO HIS GOD AND FATHER;" (Rev 1:5-6). Revelation says this remnant *"will be priests of YAHveh and of Messiah and will reign with Him for a thousand years"* (Rev 20:6).

God's redeemed people must look at Israel's example and learn from her mistakes. *YAHveh* did not tolerate Israel's apostate priesthood; *YAHshua* did not tolerate her man-tainted traditions. Likewise, He will not tolerate our compromised religious traditions and doctrines.

Set Your Heart to Honor My Name

Malachi's admonition to a compromising priesthood is also an admonition to God's redeemed remnant today.

"... I am a great King," says YAHveh of hosts, *"and* MY NAME IS FEARED *among the nations." And now,* THIS COMMANDMENT IS FOR YOU, O PRIESTS. *"If you do not listen, and if you do not* TAKE IT TO HEART TO GIVE HONOR TO MY NAME," *says YAHveh of hosts, "then I will send the curse upon you, and I* WILL CURSE YOUR BLESSINGS; AND INDEED, I HAVE CURSED THEM ALREADY, *because you are not taking* it *to heart."* (Mal 1:14-2:2)

153

It is not difficult to see the consequences of this curse on today's religious systems.

"My covenant with him [the priesthood] *was one of life and peace, and I gave them to him* [through the sacrifice of blood] *as an object of reverence; so he revered Me, and STOOD IN AWE OF MY NAME."* (Mal 2:5)

Distinguish between the Holy and the Common

"True instruction was in his mouth, and unrighteousness [the compromises and doctrines of men] *was not found on his lips; he walked with Me in peace and uprightness, and HE TURNED MANY BACK FROM INIQUITY. For the lips of a priest should preserve knowledge* [the uncompromised full counsel of truth], *and men should seek instruction from his mouth; for he is the messenger of YAHveh of hosts."* (Mal 2:6-7)

"Moreover, they shall teach My people THE DIFFERENCE BETWEEN THE HOLY AND THE PROFANE, and cause them TO DISCERN BETWEEN THE UNCLEAN AND THE CLEAN." (Eze 44:23)

"But as for you, you have turned aside from the way; YOU HAVE CAUSED MANY TO STUMBLE BY THE INSTRUCTION; YOU HAVE CORRUPTED THE COVENANT OF LEVI [the priesthood],*"* says YAHveh of hosts. *"So I also have made you despised and abased before all the people, JUST AS YOU ARE NOT KEEPING MY WAYS, BUT ARE SHOWING PARTIALITY IN THE INSTRUCTION* [picking and choosing, mixing and matching, adding to and deleting from God's instruction according to man's teachings and traditions].*"* (Mal 2:8-9)

Much hypocrisy and unholiness in Christianity and Judaism have caused them to be "despised and abased" by much of the world. For untold numbers, these corporate religious systems have become a mockery and a laughingstock rather than a holy priesthood that is turning many from sin to righteousness.

Ezekiel writes of YAHveh's glory departing from a sanctuary that had become filled with deception and idolatry. YAHveh sent a messenger to *"put a mark on the foreheads of the men who SIGH AND GROAN OVER ALL THE ABOMINATIONS which are being committed in its midst"* (Eze 9:4). This small group of Jews was spared, while the religious masses who walked in apostasy and compromise were mercilessly killed. In fury, *YAHveh* said, *"'Utterly slay old men, young men, maidens, little children, and women, but do not touch any man on whom is the mark; and you shall start from My sanctuary.' So they started with the elders* [leaders] *who were before the temple"* (Eze 9:6).

Peter warned of similar judgments at the close of this age: *"For it is time for judgment to begin with the household of God; and if it begins with us first, what will be the outcome for those who do not obey the gospel of YAHveh?"* (1Pe 4:17).

Today *YAHveh* is making a clear distinction between the wheat and the tares, the holy and the common, the "Saul generation" and the "David generation." He is separating the doctrines and religions of men from his holy, scriptural requirements. He is creating a chasm between the apostate priesthood and His holy priesthood. The righteous Judge will ultimately distinguish between those who are pure, spotless, and blameless, and those who have been defiled by that which is detestable in His sight.

The Mighty One is coming to judge every transgression of His righteous commandments. His holy priesthood will serve Him in purity according to His plumb line of truth.

"Behold, I am going to send My messenger [the spirit of EliYAHu], *and he will clear the way before Me. And the Lord* [Master], *whom you seek, will suddenly come to His temple* [to root out all unholiness, including pagan-tainted traditions]; *... But who can endure the day of His coming? And who can stand when He appears? For He is like a refiner's fire and like fullers' soap. ... and HE WILL PURIFY the sons of Levi* [the priests] *and refine them like gold and silver, SO THAT THEY MAY PRESENT TO YAHVEH OFFERINGS IN RIGHTEOUSNESS. Then the offering ... will be pleasing to YAHveh, as in the days of old and as in former years."* (Mal 3:1-4)

Then those who feared YAHveh spoke to one another, and YAHveh gave attention and heard it, and a book of remembrance was written before Him for those who FEAR YAHVEH and who ESTEEM HIS NAME. "And they will be Mine," says YAHveh of Hosts, "On the day that I prepare My own possession, AND I WILL SPARE THEM as a man spares his own son who serves him." So you will again DISTINGUISH BETWEEN

THE RIGHTEOUS AND THE WICKED, *between one who serves God and one who does not serve Him.*" (Mal 3:16-18)

"*For behold, the day is coming, burning like a furnace; and all the arrogant and every evildoer will be chaff; ...*" "*But for you who* FEAR MY NAME *the sun of righteousness will rise with healing in its wings; and you will go forth and skip about like calves from the stall.*" (Mal 4:1-2)

EliYAHu Will Come

"*Behold, I am going to send you Elijah the prophet before the coming of the great and terrible day of YAHveh.*" (Mal 4:5)

Malachi named Elijah as the forerunner of the "*great and terrible day of the Lord [YAHveh]*" who will "*turn the hearts of fathers to their children and the hearts of children to their fathers*" (Mal. 4:5-6). Jewish writers have often taken up the same theme in their literature: Elijah will "restore the tribes of Jacob" (Ecclus 48:10); ...

Some Bible scholars believe that Elijah will return as one of the two witnesses of the end times (Rev. 11:3-12), in fulfillment of Malachi's prophecy that he is to come before the dreadful judgment day of God. (emphasis added)[2]

The spirit of the Hebrew prophet Elijah is being sent now at the close of this age to prepare a holy people for *YAHshua's* return. The prophet's Hebrew name truly reflects his mission. *EliYAHu* (Elijah) means "my God is *YAHveh*." On Elijah's first mission he was sent to turn apostate Israel away from a pagan-tainted religious system and back to the pure worship of *YAHveh*. *YAHshua* Messiah prophesied that *EliYAHu* would surely come again to restore all things back to the pure worship of *YAHveh* as in days gone by.

How Long Will You Waver?

The spirit of *EliYAHu* was sent again to Israel through John the Baptist (*YAHchanan*[3] *the Immerser*) as a messenger (see Mt 11:10)

---

[2] *Baker Encyclopedia of the Bible, Vol. 1*, s.v. "Elijah."

to clear the way for *YAHshua's* first appearance. As prophesied, the voice of this messenger is now crying out again for the preparation of Messiah's near return. Even through this book, the spirit of *EliYAHu* is beseeching a remnant as He did through John the Baptizer.

"Repent, for the kingdom of heaven is at hand." For this is the one referred to by Isaiah the prophet, saying, *"THE VOICE OF ONE CRYING IN THE WILDERNESS, 'MAKE READY THE WAY OF YAHVEH, MAKE HIS PATHS STRAIGHT!'"* (Mt 3:2-3)

The *EliYAHu* spirit is exhorting a remnant to depart from every compromise of *YAHveh's* commands. Israel had forsaken and forgotten the pure worship of their God and had substituted His most holy name with the name of Baal. As *YAHveh* grieved then, so does He now over religious apostasy and the neglect of His holy name. *EliYAHu* says:

"... you have FORSAKEN THE COMMANDMENTS OF YAHVEH, and you have followed the Baals [by replacing His *memorial- name* with the common title, 'LORD'].*" ... "How long* will *you HESITATE BETWEEN TWO OPINIONS? If YAHveh is God, follow Him; but if Baal, follow him." ...* (1Ki 18:18, 21)

If God's name is *YAHveh*, why not proclaim it? He waits for and is worthy of the glory due His most holy name! *EliYAHu* said, *"Then you call on the name of your god, and I WILL CALL ON THE NAME OF YAHVEH, and the God who ANSWERS BY FIRE, He is God"* (1Ki 18:24). His spirit is urging true and obedient followers to begin calling on the name of *YAHveh* instead of the generic title of "God" or "LORD." As you call on His holy name with a pure and humble heart, He will begin to answer you with the *fire* of His presence, power, and glory—**HalleluYAH!**

The psalmist wrote:

"Like fire that burns the forest, And like a flame that sets the mountains on fire, ... Fill their faces with dishonor, That they may SEEK THY NAME, O YAHVEH. ... That they may know that Thou alone, WHOSE NAME IS YAHVEH, Art the Most High over all the earth." (Ps 83:14, 16, 18)

Then Elijah said to all the people, "Come near to me [leave the ranks of religious compromise and lukewarm complacency].*" ... AND HE REPAIRED THE ALTAR OF YAHVEH WHICH HAD BEEN TORN DOWN. And Elijah took twelve stones*

---

[3] The meaning of the Hebrew name *YAHchanan* is "*YAHveh* is gracious."

*according to the number of the tribes of the sons of Jacob
... with the stones* HE BUILT AN ALTAR IN THE NAME OF *YAHVEH*
... (1Ki 18:30 32)

Truly the altar of *YAHveh's* name lies in ruins. Just as the purified remnant will rejoice to see the plumb line in Zerubbabel's hand, so will it rejoice to see the holy altar rebuilt in *YAHveh's* name.

Against all odds, the sacrifice Elijah made in *YAHveh's* name was miraculously consumed.

Then the fire of YAHveh fell, and consumed the burnt offering and the wood and the stones and the dust, and licked up the water that was in the trench. And when all the people saw it, they fell on their faces; and they said, "YAHVEH, HE IS GOD; YAHVEH, HE IS GOD." (1Ki 18:38-39)

Revival came to people's hearts as they turned back to *YAHveh* and called out His rightful name. The apostate form of worship had been struck a devastating blow; and after the people cried out, *"YAHveh, He is God!"* the curse of their rebellion was broken. The long-awaited rains poured out on the people, bringing the curse of drought and famine (both physical and spiritual) to an end.

Just as the people of Israel needed rain, so we today need the spiritual latter-day rains prophesied in Scripture! We need *YAHveh's* Spirit to pour out and end the curse of spiritual drought and famine! We are living in the final days before the great and dreadful day of the Almighty's wrath (cf. Mal 4:5 and Rev 6:16-17). As *YAHshua* promised, *"Elijah is coming and will restore all things"* (Mt 17:11). Elijah is going forth with divine mercy to turn a righteous remnant back to the pure worship of *YAHveh*, the God of Israel.

Be Holy Because I Am Holy

The Most High has always purposed to have a holy priesthood who could stand in His presence and bring His glory to a lost world. Initially He performed mighty acts of deliverance on behalf of Israel to create a kingdom of priests and a holy nation. Israel fell short by neglecting *YAHveh's* holy requirements. In order to fulfill the desires of His heart, *YAHveh* sent His Son to redeem both Jews and Gentiles to become His eternal holy priesthood.

YAHveh is very specific about the righteous requirements

of this priesthood. He is raising up a remnant, a "Zadok priesthood," that is distinctly unique from the ranks of professing believers. *Zadok* means "righteous."

During David's reign he (Zadok) served jointly as high priest with Abiathar (2Sa 8:17).

Both ... fled from Jerusalem with David when the king's son Absalom attempted to take over the throne. They brought the ARK OF THE COVENANT out with them. ...

When David was dying, another of his sons, Adonijah, tried to take the throne. This time only Zadok remained faithful to the king. When David heard of the plot, he ordered Zadok and the prophet Nathan to anoint Solomon king (1Ki 1:7-8, 32-45).

Consequently, ... Zadok held the high priesthood alone (1Ki 2:26-27). In this way the high priesthood was restored to the line of Eleazar, son of Aaron.[4]

The Zadokites served during David's reign and are symbolic of the holy priesthood that will accompany the "David generation."

As a reward for Zadok's loyalty to Solomon and as punishment for the sins of Eli's sons, Zadok's descendants (the line of Eliezer) replaced the descendants of Ithamar as the leading priests. The developing role of Jerusalem as the exclusive center of Israel's worship furthered the position of the Zadokites.[5]

The Mighty One expresses great disgust toward those who do not follow carefully His instructions. His words to the Levitical priests of old pertain to a latter-day priesthood that has compromised His holy standards.

"'ENOUGH OF ALL YOUR ABOMINATIONS ... *you brought in foreigners, uncircumcised in heart* [carnal, half-hearted believers] ... *to be in My sanctuary to profane it* [and defamed My name and character], ... *And you have not kept charge of My holy things yourselves, but you have set foreigners to keep charge of My sanctuary.*'" (Eze 44:6-8)

The priests were admonished for their negligence and apathy toward *YAHveh's* holy things. The Almighty was grieved that the leaders had not circumcised the hearts of the people

---

[4] *Nelson's New Illustrated Bible Dictionary*, s.v. "Zadok."

[5] *Holman Bible Dictionary*, s.v. "Zadokites."

before bringing them into His midst. He was disgusted over the self-appointed, man-fearing leaders who had no concept of the holy requirements of the God they professed.

Many today who call Him "Lord and Savior" have neglected their priestly responsibilities through either ignorance of His will or indifference to His mandate for holiness. *YAHveh* said to Aaron and all the priests who would follow him:

> "... *it is a* PERPETUAL STATUTE *throughout your generations—* AND SO AS TO MAKE A DISTINCTION BETWEEN THE HOLY AND THE PROFANE [common], *and between the unclean and the clean, and* SO AS TO TEACH ... ALL THE STATUTES *which YAHveh has spoken to them ...*" (Lev 10:9-11)

The holy priesthood must not mix what *YAHveh* has purposely separated. He is a holy God who calls His people to a separated life, free from all mixtures and compromises. The Hebrew word for "holy" is *kadosh,* which means "separate." Messiah reminds His redeemed that He has given "... *THE SERVICE OF THE PRIESTHOOD AS A GIFT.*" (Nu 18:7 NIV author's emphasis) The holy remnant has no inheritance in this world; YAHveh alone is their double portion and exceedingly great reward.

> *"Therefore,* COME OUT FROM THEIR MIDST AND BE SEPARATE," *says YAHveh. "*AND DO NOT TOUCH WHAT IS UNCLEAN; *And I will welcome you. ... And you shall be sons and daughters to Me," Says YAHveh Almighty. Therefore, having these promises, beloved, let us cleanse ourselves from all defilement of flesh and spirit, perfecting holiness in the fear of YAHveh.* (2Co 6:17 - 7:1)

The Almighty addressed a priesthood who *went astray* and *wandered* from Him, going after idols that consisted of worldly lusts and religious rituals:

> *"And they shall not come near to Me to serve as a priest to Me, nor come near to any of My holy things, to the things that are most holy; but they shall bear their shame and their abominations which they have committed. "Yet I will appoint them to keep charge of the house, of all its service, and of all that shall be done in it."* (Eze 44:13-14)

In *YAHveh's* infinite mercy, He has made a provision for the multitudes who are redeemed through the Messiah's blood, yet who have been double-minded and have held unholy standards. Many believers will enter His eternal kingdom *"as* [those] *escaping through the flames"* (1Co 3:15 NIV — emphasis added), losing all of their eternal rewards and saving only their souls. Although they are "saved," they will not touch His most holy things because of their disregard for His holy precepts. *"But the Levitical priests, the sons of Zadok,[6] who KEPT CHARGE of My sanctuary when the sons of Israel* [and Christians] *went astray ... shall come near to Me to minister to Me; and they shall stand before Me ..."* (Eze 44:15)

The Almighty stresses His special provisions and blessings on the faithful priesthood which Zadok symbolizes. In describing the division of the Holy Land in the coming messianic kingdom, Ezekiel wrote of a special portion which is for YAHveh's sanctuary. *"This will be for the consecrated priests, the Zadokites, WHO WERE FAITHFUL IN SERVING ME AND DID NOT GO ASTRAY. ... It will be a special gift to them from the sacred portion of the land, a most holy portion, ..."* (Eze 48:11-12 NIV).

YAHshua concludes the holy Scriptures with these words:

"... let the one who is righteous, still practice righteousness;

and let the one who is holy, still keep himself holy."

"Behold, I am coming quickly, and My reward is with Me,

to render to every man according to what he has done."

(Rev 22:11-12)

---

6 "... the Zadokites received special consideration because of their faithfulness. ... This elevation of the Zadokites and demotion of the Levites were part of the concern for ritual purity, ... Only the fittest were to serve." *The NIV Study Bible* (Grand Rapids: The Zondervan Corporation, 1985), footnote to Eze 44:16-17.

Chapter 23
Standing in the Shekinah

Throughout the scriptures it is clear that only a priesthood properly consecrated and cleansed can enter into *YAHveh's* presence. Although many profess to have faith in Him, *only a remnant will truly function as holy priests.* This priesthood will draw near to *YAHveh* and stand in His presence, enveloped in His Shekinah glory.

Through the progression of this book, the Holy Spirit has been circumcising hearts. Through repentance, He has been bringing a remnant from the outer court of their human religious systems into His holy sanctuary. Ultimately He is preparing a "Zadok priesthood" of men and women who will distinguish between the holy and the profane. These will be eligible, through *YAHshua's* blood, to stand in His presence.

This priesthood will have the very mind of Messiah. *YAHshua's* thoughts will cover their minds as a turban covered the head of every Hebrew priest. They will also wear symbolically a sacred golden diadem over their foreheads, sealing them with the inscription, *Holy to YAHveh.*

And they made the plate of the holy crown [the sacred diadem] *of pure gold, and inscribed it like the engravings of a signet, "Holy to YAHveh." And they fastened a blue cord to it, to fasten it on the turban ...* (Ex 39:30-31)

Consecrate Yourselves

No impure or unconsecrated priest could ever enter His Most Holy Place—the place where His presence dwelled as a "consuming fire." All that is unholy and detestable, anything that transgresses His righteous commands, is sin in the sight of a holy God. *Sin is combustible, and it will burn in YAHveh's fiery presence!* In His great mercy, *YAHveh* warns His people not to approach the fire of His presence with any hint of sin.

Since creation *YAHveh* has longed for a priesthood that would live in His presence and reflect His glory. *However, sin has separated man from a holy God. YAHveh* provided a way to reconcile sinful man to Himself. His divine provision of the blood

162

sacrifice for the redemption and consecration of a holy priesthood is as "a scarlet cord of redemption" inseparably tying the Old and New Testaments together.

YAHveh's plan to have a *"treasured possession"* and a *"kingdom of priests and a holy nation"* (Ex 19:5-6 NIV) was initiated through Israel and is being fulfilled through the redeemed remnant of Jews and Gentiles—the *one new man* (see 1Pe 2:9 and Rev 5:9-10).

YAHveh appeared to the Hebrew nation on top of Mount Sinai. There He descended dramatically as a consuming fire, enveloped in dense clouds and to the sound of loud trumpet blasts. *The Holy One of Israel had come down to tabernacle among men!* Mount Sinai was ablaze with His fiery presence. No man would dare touch even the foot of the mountain lest he die. Boundaries were placed around this holy mountain, the throne of YAHveh's glorious presence (see Ex 19:12). YAHveh gave Moses strict instructions to convey to an awestruck, fearful nation: *"Go to the people and CONSECRATE THEM today and tomorrow, and let them wash their garments; and let them be ready for the third day ..."* (Ex 19:10-11).

YAHveh came down to His holy mountain in the sight of men. His presence required the great preparation of prayer, repentance, and purification on the part of the people. Without such preparation, no person was able to approach His glory and live. This call to be cleansed and ready by the *"third day"* has prophetic significance for us today. Nearly two thousand years have elapsed since YAHshua's first appearance. The apostle Peter wrote, *"But do not let this one fact escape your notice, beloved, that with YAHveh one day is as a thousand years, and a thousand years as one day"* (2Pe 3:8).

We are approaching the third day. *We must be consecrated and ready* for the sounding of the last *shofar* (trumpet). As Moses came down from YAHveh's presence to consecrate Israel and bring the people up the holy mountain, so too is YAHshua Messiah consecrating a remnant that will ascend with Him into His Father's eternal presence.

YAHshua has already fulfilled the first four holy feasts of Israel. Many believe that the next feast, the Feast of Trumpets (*Yom Teruah*), commonly called the Jewish New Year (*Rosh HaShanah*), will be fulfilled at His return. Then will YAHshua call out His elect to ascend to His Father's presence.

"For the Lord [Master] *Himself will descend from heaven*

with a shout, with the voice of the archangel, and with the trumpet of YAHveh; and the dead in Messiah shall rise first. Then we who are alive and remain shall be caught up together with them in the clouds to meet the Lord in the air, and thus we shall always be with the Lord" (1Th 4:16-17). — *"Therefore, beloved, since you look for these things,* BE DILIGENT TO BE FOUND BY HIM IN PEACE, SPOTLESS AND BLAMELESS *..."* (2Pe 3:14). — *"what sort of people ought you to be in holy conduct and godliness, looking for and hastening the coming of the day of YAHveh ..."* (2Pe 3:11-12).

Do Not Force Your Way Through

From the midst of the dense clouds of His glory, *YAHveh* spoke these words for all who are called as a priesthood into His glorious presence:

"... 'Go down, warn the people, lest they break through to YAHveh to gaze, and many of them perish. And also let the priests who come near to YAHveh consecrate themselves, lest YAHveh break out against them'" (Ex 19:21-22). — *"The people cannot come up Mount Sinai, because you yourself warned us, 'Put limits around the mountain and set it apart as holy.'"* (Ex 19:23 NIV).

Mount Sinai is the first symbol in Scripture of the Most Holy Place where *YAHveh's* throne—His presence and glory—dwells. Later a moveable tabernacle would become His throne room, and later still He would inhabit the Holy of Holies of a grand temple. These earthly dwellings for *YAHveh's* presence foreshadowed the temple of human hearts, which when cleansed by *YAHshua's* blood, would become His home. Ultimately, He will tabernacle eternally among His redeemed priesthood in the New Jerusalem (see Rev 21:3).

The Response of the Remnant

The people remained at a distance while Moses approached the thick darkness where *YAHveh* was concealed (see Ex 20:18-21). Moses became the first mediator or high priest who would lead the way for hundreds of high priests (the Levites) to go before

YAHveh on behalf of Israel. *YAHshua* Messiah was the ultimate fulfillment of God's priesthood; He is the eternal High Priest who stands between the remnant of redeemed Jews and Gentiles and *YAHveh* their God.

Moses read the people *YAHveh's* commands and *"all the people answered with one voice, and said, 'ALL THE WORDS WHICH YAHVEH HAS SPOKEN WE WILL DO!'"* (Ex 24:3). Upon agreeing to obey *YAHveh's* commands, the blood covenant was instituted between *YAHveh* and Israel; it was sealed in the sacrificial blood of bulls. The people of Israel had to *count the cost and agree to obey all of YAHveh's holy commands* before they were sealed in the blood covenant.

Like Moses, *YAHshua* Messiah exhorted His followers to *"count the cost"* (Lk 14:28 NKJV) in their agreement to *wholeheartedly do the will of His Father*. Eternal salvation is not cheap. It is not a shallow confession of the lips or a pious adherence to religious doctrines. It is a forsaking of everything in this world, including its tainted forms of religion. *We must not take lightly such a great salvation.*

It Hinges on the Blood

Moses sprinkled the people with the blood of sacrificial bulls to symbolize and affirm the covenant between Israel and *YAHveh.* The new covenant was initiated by *YAHshua* the Lamb, who covers a believing remnant eternally with His precious blood. *Why does so much hinge on the blood?*

Israel had already witnessed the saving power of the blood of a lamb at the first Passover. The lamb's blood was placed over the door posts of Hebrew homes so that the Almighty would "pass over" them and deliver them from the death-plague of Egypt (Ex 12:13). *YAHveh's* institution of a blood sacrifice was His divine provision to bring sinful men into His holy presence.

"'For the life of a creature is in the blood, and I have given it to you to make atonement for yourselves on the altar; IT IS THE BLOOD THAT MAKES ATONEMENT FOR ONE'S LIFE'" (Lev 17:11 NIV — emphasis added). — *"without shedding of blood there is no forgiveness* [of sins]" (Heb 9:22).

Through the system of blood sacrifices He instituted with Israel, the blood of animals became the cleansing agent to prepare a chosen people for *YAHveh's* glory and honor. And through the blood sacrifice, a priesthood was consecrated to stand in purity of body, soul, and spirit before their holy God. *YAHshua* was the ultimate fulfillment of the beautiful Old Testament picture of the shedding of blood as an atonement for sin. As the Passover Lamb, He redeemed with His blood a remnant for eternal salvation. As the ultimate *Yom Kippur* sacrifice, His blood is continually available for the daily purification and consecration of a holy priesthood.

The high calling of a holy priesthood is emphasized throughout the book of Leviticus. *YAHveh's* continual warning to His chosen nation was *"be holy, because I am holy"* (Lev 11:44 NIV). The apostle Paul echoed these words in his warning to the church: *"Pursue peace with all men, AND THE SANCTIFICATION* [holiness] *WITHOUT WHICH NO ONE WILL SEE YAHVEH"* (Heb 12:14).

Aaron's sons, Nadab and Abihu, were ordained priests. They approached *YAHveh* irreverently in an unconsecrated state and *"fire came out from the presence of YAHveh and consumed them, and they died before YAHveh"* (Lev 10:2). In response to the death of two negligent priests and as a warning to all priests who would follow, Moses said to Aaron, *"It is what YAHveh spoke, saying, 'By those who come near Me I will be treated as holy, And before all the people I will be honored'"* (Lev 10:3).

The blood-redeemed priesthood exists for *YAHveh* and not vice versa. *YAHveh* is a jealous God. He will not tolerate any rivals. *He requires total, exclusive allegiance.* YAHshua's blood was sacrificed to purchase a priesthood that would forsake everything to be set apart as *Holy to YAHveh.*

"'They [the priests] *shall therefore keep My charge, so that they may not bear sin because of it, and die thereby because they profane it; I AM YAHVEH WHO SANCTIFIES THEM* [makes them holy].'"* (Lev 22:9)

The Atoning Blood on the Mercy Seat

Israel was continually reminded of her grievous inability to live up to *YAHveh's* standard for holiness. Time and again He drew the attention of His people to their undeniable need of a blood sacrifice to cover their sins. The blood humbled the people of Israel by reminding them that a life must be forfeited to atone for their sinful lives.

In *YAHveh's* tabernacle was the most sacred place called

the *Holy of Holies*. Within this glory-filled chamber, the blood of the sacrificed animal was poured out upon the mercy seat or atonement cover.[1] This golden lid covering the top of the ark of the covenant was *YAHveh's* throne—the place where His divine mercy was granted. The ark of the testimony and His mercy seat, which was covered with blood, were to be the utmost focal points for Israel.

"Make an atonement cover of pure gold— ... And make two cherubim out of hammered gold at the ends of the cover. ... The cherubim are to have their wings spread upward, overshadowing the cover with them. The cherubim are to face each other, looking toward the cover. Place the [atonement] cover [mercy seat] on top of the ark and put in the ark the Testimony [the Ten Commandments], which I will give you. There, above the cover between the two cherubim that are over the ark of the Testimony, I will meet with you and give you all my commands for the Israelites." (Ex 25:17-22 NIV — emphasis added)

The ark contained the tablets of the Ten Commandments. As men and women transgressed any of these holy commandments, they fell short of *YAHveh's* glory and became candidates for His righteous judgment. In His great mercy, the Holy One provided the blood of a spotless sacrifice to cover the sins of His people and to deliver them from judgment. *YAHveh* is a God of both mercy and judgment. In Him, judgment and mercy meet over the ark. There on the mercy seat, the sins of men could be atoned for through the covering of blood.

In reverence and awe, the priests of *YAHveh* were to remain faithful and obedient to His every command as they served Him daily in His tabernacle. They were to go before Him as mediators to ensure Israel's continued sanctification.

The people of Israel were delivered from bondage and sanctified by the blood to fulfill their divine commission as witnesses of *YAHveh's* name and glory to the entire Gentile world (see Isa 43:12). The nation and her priesthood were intricately bound to the blood of sacrificial animals. Likewise we, His royal priesthood, are to be inextricably linked with the blood of our sacrificial Lamb, *YAHshua*. His precious blood is on the mercy

---

[1] The original Hebrew word is *kapporeth*, from the root *kaphar*, meaning "to cover," "to make propitiation," or "to make atonement."

seat for the continual cleansing and consecration of the redeemed remnant. The royal priesthood is commissioned to live holy lives as they witness to the world that *YAHveh* is God and *YAHshua* is Messiah!

Chapter 24

The Divine Approach

YAHveh's awesome appearance on Mount Sinai was followed with the construction of a tabernacle to house His glory as the nation of Israel traveled throughout the wilderness. *YAHveh* gave detailed instructions for the building of this sanctuary, which was *"a copy and shadow of the heavenly things"* (Heb 8:5). He warned Moses: "SEE ... THAT YOU MAKE ALL THINGS ACCORDING TO THE PATTERN WHICH WAS SHOWN YOU ON THE MOUNTAIN" (Heb 8:5).

YAHveh's presence, His Shekinah, dwelt in this transportable tent in the midst of His people during their wilderness journey. Many years later, King Solomon built a magnificent temple in Jerusalem as a dwelling for *YAHveh's* presence and glory. Someday His presence will dwell in a new temple, which was prophesied by Ezekiel and seen by John as recorded in the book of Revelation.[1]

Both Ezekiel and John stressed the mandatory requirement of perfect holiness for all who will enter this temple; it will even have a wall around it *"to separate the holy from the common"* (Eze 42:20 NIV).

"Son of man ... the house of Israel [and all redeemed Gentiles joined with her] *will not again defile My holy name, neither they nor their kings* [including religious leaders], *by their harlotry* [spiritual adultery] *..." ... "Now let them put away their harlotry* [worldly lusts and pagan traditions] *... and I will dwell among them forever.* "As for you, son of man, DESCRIBE THE TEMPLE TO THE HOUSE OF ISRAEL, THAT THEY MAY BE ASHAMED OF THEIR INIQUITIES; AND LET*

---

[1] "Three interrelated ideas dominate. First is the concept of the martyr church, whose faithful members in [*YAHveh's*] temple surmount the spiritual Zion as the material temple did ancient Jerusalem (3:12; 14:1). ... Another aspect is the temple as the place of judgment (11:19; 14:15; 15:5 - 16:1). Finally, any temple in the new age is unnecessary, *'for its temple is ... the Almighty and the Lamb'* (21:22). The ultimate state would be [*YAHveh's*] dwelling with men (21:3). The cube-like proportions of the city may even suggest the immediate presence of [*YAHveh*] in the Holy of Holies (21:16). All lesser types fade away in the glorious reality of [*YAHveh's*] supremacy (1 Cor 15:28) ..." *Baker Encyclopedia of the Bible*, Vol. 2, s.v. "Tabernacle, Temple" (emphases added).

THEM MEASURE THE PLAN ... *write it in their sight, so that they* *may* OBSERVE ITS WHOLE DESIGN *and all its statutes ..."* (Eze 43:7-11)

According to *YAHveh's* sovereign blueprint, His holy temple was designed with areas of *decreasing dimensions,* which allowed only a *decreasing remnant* to approach His Shekinah glory within the Most Holy Place. Both the measuring process and *YAHveh's* pattern for the temple were to serve as expressions of His holiness. The arrangement of the courts and the pattern for measuring were to impress upon the people their need for personal holiness, stimulating their desire for *YAHveh's* presence and His merciful atonement.

In Messiah's day, the *outer court of the Gentiles* surrounded the temple. This was a huge court that served as *YAHveh's* gracious provision for any Gentile who chose to forsake the worship of pagan gods for the worship of Israel's God. Gentiles were free to worship *YAHveh* but were strictly prohibited from going past this "court of the uncircumcised."[2]

As one moved inward from the large outer court, the next court was the *court of Israel.* Although it was smaller, it was large enough for all the attending Jewish men to worship; outside this court was the court of the women where they viewed the service from tall balconies. Just as the Gentiles were constrained to their court, the masses of Jews were constrained to their designated area of worship.

The next area of the temple was called the Holy Place. The Almighty had specified this place as off limits for all Jews except the priests. Only a select and appointed few—consecrated priests adorned in ceremonial clothing—could pass from Israel's outer court into the Holy Place, *YAHveh's* sanctuary. The Holy Place was the arena of sacrifice and service to *YAHveh.*

A thick, heavy veil partitioned the Holy Place from a small, fifteen-foot square area called the Most Holy Place. The Holy of Holies was the dwelling of *YAHveh's* glorious Shekinah presence. It was off limits to all except one man, the high priest. Only he, after a ritual of washing with water and consecration with blood, could go through the veil into the Holy of Holies to stand before

---

[2] Footnote for Ac 21:28. "*brought Greeks into the temple area.* Explicitly forbidden according to inscribed stone markers (still in existence). Any Gentiles found within the bounds of the court of Israel would be killed." *The NIV Study Bible* (Grand Rapids: The Zondervan Corporation, 1985), p. 1688.

the ark, the throne of *YAHveh.*

On one day of the year (*Yom Kippur*), the high priest would meet with *YAHveh,* who dwelled between the sculpted golden cherubim over the mercy seat of the ark (see Ex 25:22 and Nu 7:89). Enveloped in the Shekinah glory of the living God, the high priest would pour out the blood on the mercy seat for the forgiveness of his own sins and all the sins of the people.

Israel's salvation hung in the balance until her high priest returned from the Holy of Holies, aglow with the glory of *YAHveh.* Upon his return, he would stand in the presence of the penitent nation proclaiming *YAHveh's* name, His forgiveness, and His blessings for another year. "When the people heard this awesome utterance, they fell with faces to the ground exclaiming: '**BLESSED BE HIS NAME**, the glory of his Kingdom is forever and ever!' (Yoma 3:8)" (emphasis added)[3]

As we have seen, the earthly priests were a foreshadowing of *YAHshua,* who is our eternal High Priest.

> *But when Messiah appeared as a high priest ... He entered through the greater and more perfect tabernacle, not made with hands ... and not through the blood of goats and calves, but* THROUGH HIS OWN BLOOD, HE ENTERED THE HOLY PLACE ONCE FOR ALL, *having obtained eternal redemption. For if the blood of goats and bulls and the ashes of a heifer sprinkling those who have been defiled, sanctify for the cleansing of the flesh, how much more will the blood of Messiah ... cleanse your conscience from dead works to serve the living God?* (Heb 9:11-14)

When *YAHshua* was pierced and His body torn as a sacrifice for the sins of mankind, the heavy veil of the temple was also rent in two. At the exact moment of *YAHshua's* death, the veil dividing the Holy of Holies from the temple chambers was torn; *YAHveh's* throne room was opened for all redeemed Jews and Gentiles. All people were welcomed to enter as high priests into His divine presence through faith in His atoning blood.

Just as *YAHveh* put limits around His holy mountain, there are limits around His holy dwelling today. Although the way into the Most Holy Place was opened, there are righteous requirements to be met by the priesthood of believers in order to approach *YAHveh. Priests must not and CAN NOT force their way*

---

[3] Mitch and Zhava Glaser, *The Fall Feasts of Israel* (Chicago: Moody Press, 1987), p. 98.

into YAHveh's presence. They must be *consecrated and washed* by *YAHshua's* blood.

How precious is the atoning blood of *YAHshua,* the Lamb of *YAHveh!* The redeemed priests of God are to humble themselves before Him. The Scriptures tell us, *"If we confess our sins, He is faithful and righteous to forgive us our sins and to* CLEANSE *us from* ALL UNRIGHTEOUSNESS" (1Jn 1:9). Through the daily searching of their hearts and sincere repentance, the remnant will remain cleansed of sins and consecrated as priests that are *Holy to YAHveh.* Through His blood, *YAHshua's* righteousness becomes a holy, priestly garment to be worn by those who are sanctified for His service.

YAHveh is holy. No one who is uncircumcised in heart, no unconsecrated priest whether Jew, Gentile, or professing Christian, can enter His presence without first being cleansed. Many today are ignorant of His absolute requirement of purification. These cannot approach His Most Holy Place and see His Shekinah glory.

The multitudes of uncircumcised and unconsecrated professing believers spend much of their lives in the outer court of religion. Many in this outer court are worshiping God but they have never sincerely repented and been cleansed. They must worship at a distance from His true presence. Many others in this outer court are very busy with religious affairs; they are often consumed with empty rituals and traditions.

Just as the size of the courts of His temple decreased as one approached the Holy of Holies, there is a *diminishing number of sincere believers* who serve as priests in the Holy Place of His sanctuary. These dedicated servants give their lives selflessly as a sacrifice on His holy altar. This remnant is continually about the Father's business; they seek His glory rather than their own vain glory.

A very small remnant ascends the holy mountain to worship *YAHveh* in spirit and in truth. Very few redeemed priests stand enveloped in the presence of *YAHveh* and are transformed by His Shekinah glory. Messiah explained this principle to His disciples, telling them that few will make the pilgrimage on the *Highway of Holiness.*

And someone said to Him, "Lord [Master], ARE THERE JUST A FEW WHO ARE BEING SAVED?" *And He said to them, "*STRIVE TO ENTER BY THE NARROW DOOR; FOR MANY, I TELL YOU, WILL SEEK TO ENTER AND WILL NOT BE ABLE" (Lk 13:23-24). — *"Enter by* *the narrow gate; for the gate is wide, and the way is broad that leads to destruction, and many are those who enter by it. For the gate is* SMALL, *and the way is* NARROW *that leads to life, and* FEW ARE THOSE WHO FIND IT" (Mt 7:13-14). — *"Not everyone who says to Me, 'Lord, Lord [Master, Master],' will enter the kingdom of heaven;* BUT HE WHO DOES THE WILL OF MY FATHER WHO IS IN HEAVEN" (Mt 7:21).

Pious multitudes have warmed congregational pews; other multitudes have done great, even miraculous feats in the sight of men and in the name of God. Throughout history and around the globe, they have preached with eloquence from their pulpits and pedestals. *Yet many of these have neither known the living God nor come near His glorious presence.*

To the lukewarm masses in the religious outer court of the uncircumcised in heart, the Savior will say, *"I never knew you;* DEPART FROM ME, YOU WHO PRACTICE LAWLESSNESS" (Mt 7:23). In these last days, *YAHshua* is calling out to a remnant: *"Consecrate yourselves and be holy!"* (Lev 11:44; 20:7).

It is written, *"Blessed are those who wash their robes, that they may have the right to the tree of life, and may enter by the gates into the city"* (Rev 22:14). That city is the New *YAHrushalayim*, the throne of *YAHveh's* presence. It is the Holy of Holies, where only the cleansed, holy, and pure remnant—a righteous priesthood that is *Holy to YAHveh*—will dwell eternally.

Chapter 25
"The Ark that Is Called by the Name"

The ark of the covenant was built according to the Almighty's explicit design and instructions to Moses. The golden ark, called by His name, was the symbolic throne of *YAHveh's* divine presence amidst His chosen people. Ancient Israel was reverently aware that the nearness of the ark was somehow a comforting reality of the very nearness of the Most High's awesome Shekinah.

This golden container not only bore *YAHveh's* presence and name, it also housed His holy instructions to men. The Ten Commandments, written by *YAHveh* on stone tablets, were His expressed heartbeat to lead His people to righteous living. "The words on these tables were a kind of a spiritual portrait of the God of Israel, who could not be pictured in a bodily form."[1] He desired to have a people marked by Him as *Holy to YAHveh.* They were chosen to bring Him praise, honor, and glory among the Gentile nations.

As Israel's priests became less committed to His holy requirements, they became irreverent and negligent toward *"the ark that is called by the Name* [of *YAHveh*]*"* (1Ch 13:6 NIV — emphasis added). The Most High God has never tolerated half-hearted, double-minded priests. Biblical history gives the dramatic account of two priests who died for their irreverent treatment of the ark of the covenant, the symbolic dwelling place of *YAHveh.*

The priest Eli had two sons, Hophni and Phinehas, who were themselves rebellious, self-centered, greedy priests. Interested only in fattening themselves on the choice parts of every offering (see 1Sa 2:29), they also viewed the ark as a means of selfish gain. Rather than honoring the ark as *YAHveh's* throne, these corrupt priests took it into battle. They attempted to coerce and manipulate the Almighty by assuming that the presence of the ark would guarantee them victory.

Israel suffered dire consequences for the greed and irreverence of Hophni and Phinehas. The ark was lost to the Philistines, and both of the rebellious priests were killed. Upon

---

[1] *The International Standard Bible Encyclopaedia, Vol. 1,* s.v. "Ark of the Covenant."

hearing the report of their death and of the loss of the ark to the enemy, the wife of Phinehas died in childbirth, declaring with her last breath, *"The GLORY has departed from Israel, for the ark of God was taken"* (1Sa 4:22). She named the child to whom she gave birth *Ichabod*, which means *"the glory has departed"* (1Sa 4:21).

Like Phinehas and Hophni, many try to use various religious symbols, even *YAHveh's* holy name, as a superstitious "good luck charm." Some religious leaders even fatten themselves on the choice parts of the offerings made by the people of God. Like the sons of Eli, they use their influence and titles in an attempt to manipulate the Almighty and influence His people for selfish gain. Instead they should be offering themselves on the altar as a holy sacrifice to the Almighty, rather than dishonoring the One they call "Lord and Savior." These have "Ichabod" written across their foreheads and on their buildings rather than His seal reading *Holy to YAHveh.*

The Holy One's response to such an unrighteous modern-day priesthood is: *"'But I will raise up for Myself A FAITHFUL PRIEST WHO WILL DO ACCORDING TO WHAT IS IN MY HEART AND IN MY SOUL; and I will build him an enduring house, and he will walk before My anointed always'"* (1Sa 2:35).

The ark of the covenant was captured during Eli's carnal priesthood. Immediately upon David's ascension as king, he sent word far and wide to his brothers and the priests throughout the territories. He said to Israel what *YAHshua* is now saying to His redeemed remnant: *"come and join us. Let us bring the ark of our God back to us, for we DID NOT INQUIRE OF IT* [YAHveh's name and Shekinah glory] *during the reign of Saul"* (1Ch 13:2-3 NIV — emphasis added).

The name of *YAHveh* and His glorious indwelling presence has been neglected during the many centuries of the "Saul generation." *YAHshua,* the son of David, is urging His "David generation" to *inquire of and bring back YAHveh's memorial-name and presence* to His holy temple built of righteous living stones. *"The whole assembly* [the obedient 'David generation'] *agreed to do this, because it seemed right to all the people"* (1Ch 13:4 NIV — emphasis added).

The "David generation" will be of one mind and one spirit with *YAHshua,* who is bringing back the name and the glory of *YAHveh.* David humbly recognized the utmost significance of the ark of *YAHveh's* presence as the earthly throne of the God of Israel. As the true king under the Almighty's rule, he desired to acknowledge *YAHveh's* authority and sovereignty over himself and the people. Thus David restored the ark of *YAHveh's* glory to a place of prominence in the nation.

Now David again gathered all the chosen men of Israel ...
to bring the ark of God which is CALLED BY THE NAME, THE
VERY NAME OF YAHVEH OF HOST *who is enthroned above the*
cherubim. (2Sa 6:1-2)

When David brought the ark back to *YAHrushalayim*, he placed it inside the tent he had pitched for it, offered sacrifices before his God, and *"blessed the people* IN THE NAME OF YAHVEH*"* (1Ch 16:2). David appointed Levites as *"ministers before the ark of YAHveh, even to celebrate and to thank and praise YAHveh God of Israel"* (1Ch 16:4).

Then on that day
David first assigned Asaph and his relatives
to give thanks to YAHveh.
Oh give thanks to YAHveh,
CALL UPON HIS NAME ... GLORY IN HIS HOLY NAME;
Let the heart of those who seek YAHveh be glad. ...
Ascribe to YAHveh the GLORY DUE HIS NAME; ...
Worship YAHveh in holy array. ...
And let them say among the nations, "YAHVEH REIGNS.*"*
(1Ch 16:7-8, 10, 29, 31)

David wrote many more psalms to proclaim his love and adoration for *YAHveh's* name and glory.
Sing to God, SING PRAISES TO HIS NAME;
Cast up a highway for Him who rides through the deserts,
WHOSE NAME IS YAHVEH, *and exult before Him.*[2]
(Ps 68:4)

All nations whom Thou hast made
shall come and worship before Thee ...
And they shall GLORIFY THY NAME.
(Ps 86:9)

---

[2] see *New King James Version*, Ps 68:4, where the original *YAH* is retained.

Praise YAHveh [HalleluYAH]!
Praise, O servants of YAHveh.
PRAISE THE NAME OF YAHVEH.
BLESSED BE THE NAME OF YAHVEH
From this time forth and forever.
From the rising of the sun to its setting
THE NAME OF YAHVEH IS TO BE PRAISED.
(Ps 113:1-3)

PART SIX

Dedicated to the Tribe of Judah

Judah

"Praise YAHveh [HalleluYAH].

I will give thanks to YAHveh with all my heart,

In the company of the upright and in the assembly.

Great are the works of YAHveh ...

His righteousness endures forever. ...

All His precepts are sure. They are upheld forever and ever ...

He has sent redemption to His people;

He has ordained His covenant forever;

HOLY AND AWESOME IS HIS NAME."

(Ps 111:1-3, 7-9)

Chapter 26

"Holy and Awesome Is His Name"

YAHveh's name had been previously known and written in the Scriptures before Exodus, but never understood in the fullest meaning as the Redeemer of His chosen people. His divine name was not only to be glorified through His miraculous acts on behalf of Israel, but it was to be *remembered forever* as His *memorial-name* for all generations to come (Ex 3:15).

With His mighty outstretched arm, He delivered Israel to worship their God and bring Him the glory due His name. With that same outstretched arm, *YAHveh* proved Himself to be the protector and defender of His redeemed nation by bringing judgment on any people or nation who dared any attempt to thwart His purpose.

In *YAHveh's* sovereign plan, He ordained that the Gentile world would hear of His glorious name exemplified through His awesome acts. In extended mercy, He desired all foreigners to hear of the God of Israel so they too would worship and bring glory to His incomparable name.

"*YAHveh* Whose Name Is Jealous"

Moses desired *YAHveh's* presence to go with Israel wherever they went. He said to the Almighty:

"If Thy presence does not go with us, do not lead us up from here. For how then can it be known that I have found favor in Thy sight, I and Thy people? Is it not by Thy going with us, so that we, I and Thy people, may be distinguished from all the other people who are upon the face of the earth? ... "Then Moses said, "I pray Thee, SHOW ME THY GLORY!" And He said, "I Myself will make all My goodness pass before you, and will PROCLAIM THE NAME OF YAHVEH BEFORE YOU ..." (Ex 33:15-19)

And YAHveh descended in the cloud and stood there with him as he CALLED UPON THE NAME OF YAHVEH. Then YAHveh passed by in front of him and proclaimed, "YAHveh, YAHveh God, compassionate and gracious, ... abounding in lovingkindness and truth; who keeps lovingkindness for thousands, who forgives iniquity, transgression and sin; ..." (Ex 34:5-7)

Moses asked to see the Almighty's glory and YAHveh responded by proclaiming His name. YAHveh's name, presence, and glory are inseparably one. Remember the words spoken to Israel directly after Moses experienced His glory:

Watch yourself that you make no covenant with the inhabitants of the land [the world] *... lest it become a snare in your midst ... —for you shall not worship any other god* [including men's religious traditions], *for YAHveh, WHOSE NAME IS JEALOUS, is a jealous God—"* (Ex 34:12-14)

YAHveh is jealous of His *memorial-name*; He never intended for it to be dissolved in a sea of generic titles shared with pagan gods.[1] He gave an enticing promise to those who would faithfully reverence His name: *"where I cause MY NAME TO BE REMEMBERED, I will come to you* [personally], *and BLESS YOU"* (Ex 20:24).

"[He who is] ... the glory of Israel, will not lie or change his mind" (1Sa 15:29). His words to Israel after her deliverance from Egypt, are just as true for us, who have been delivered through YAHshua Messiah.

"YAHveh will establish you as a holy people to Himself, as He swore to you, IF YOU WILL KEEP THE COMMANDMENTS of YAHveh your God, and WALK IN HIS WAYS. So all the peoples of the earth shall see that YOU ARE CALLED BY THE NAME OF YAHVEH; and they shall be afraid of you." (Dt 28:9-10)

YAHveh's promises, whether blessings or curses, are always fulfilled according to the obedience or disobedience of His people.

"If you are not CAREFUL TO OBSERVE ALL THE WORDS of this law which are written in this book, to FEAR THIS HONORED AND AWESOME NAME, YAHVEH YOUR GOD, then YAHveh will bring extraordinary plagues on you and your descendants, even severe and lasting plagues, and miserable and chronic sicknesses." ... "YAHveh will give you a trembling heart, failing of eyes, and despair of soul." (Dt 28:58-59, 65)

---

[1] Baal was called *Lord*, causing Israel to forget *YAHveh's* name. See Chapter 2.

He Will Tolerate No Rivals

YAHveh, through Moses, gave Israel the pattern for the building of a holy dwelling place for His name and Shekinah glory. *YAHveh*, *"WHOSE NAME IS JEALOUS"* (Ex 34:14), would tolerate no rivals. He was very adamant that His name was to be remembered, revered and honored; it was to be the only name spoken on the lips of His redeemed nation and royal priesthood. The consequences for neglecting this mandate would bring severe curses upon His chosen people.

YAHveh said He would share His glory with no other. He commanded that the land be purified and stripped clean of all pagan gods, worship sites, and heathen customs before the dwelling for His glorious presence could be constructed. He warned His people: *"Now concerning everything which I have said to you, be on your guard; and do not mention the name of other gods, nor let them be heard from your mouth"* (Ex 23:13).

He would not tolerate the intermingling of His holy presence and name with the common, profane, and unholy. He told His people:

> *"These are the statutes and the judgments which you shall carefully observe in the land which YAHveh, the God of your fathers, has given you to possess ... You* SHALL UTTERLY DESTROY *all the places where the nations whom you shall dispossess serve their gods, ... you shall* OBLITERATE THEIR NAME *from that place. You shall not act like this* [in their pagan-rooted religious traditions] *toward YAHveh your God. But you shall seek YAHveh at the place which YAHveh your God shall choose ... To* ESTABLISH HIS NAME THERE FOR HIS DWELLING *..."* (Dt 12:1-5)

My People Forget My Name

YAHveh's dramatic manifestation upon Mount Sinai was the prelude to His Shekinah filling an earthly tabernacle. His glory, which illumined Mount Sinai, was now to dwell on earth in the midst of His redeemed nation. He declared to Moses and Israel that He would have a dwelling place for His name and glory.

Israel reverentially worshiped *YAHveh* and brought honor to His holy name and commandments for only a short time. Soon after Joshua's death, their hearts became compromised and evil. *And the people served YAHveh all the days of Joshua, and all the days of the elders who survived Joshua, who had seen all the great work of YAHveh which He had done for Israel. ... and there arose* ANOTHER GENERATION *after them* WHO DID NOT KNOW YAHVEH, NOR YET THE WORK WHICH HE HAD DONE FOR ISRAEL. *Then the sons of Israel did evil in the sight of YAHveh, and served the Baals, ... they provoked YAHveh to anger. So they forsook YAHveh* [forgetting His name] *and served Baal* [called 'the Lord'] ..." (Jdg 2:7, 10-13)

YAHveh's name was to be *remembered* forever (Ex 3:15). Israel turned to substitute gods, forsaking YAHveh and His name for the titles of "Lords."[2] & [3] This was most grievous and abominable in YAHveh's sight for it robbed Him of the praise, honor, and glory due His intimate, holy name.

The prophet Isaiah exhorts, *"there is* NO ONE WHO CALLS ON THY NAME, *Who arouses himself to take hold of Thee ..."* (Isa 64:7).

YAHveh's grief over the forgetting of His name is spoken through Jeremiah to the false prophets and apostate shepherds. *"[the prophets]* intend to make My people FORGET MY NAME *by their dreams which they relate to one another, just as their fathers* FORGOT MY NAME *because of Baal?"* (Jer 23:27).

The substituted title of "Lord" caused His people then and to this day to forget His original glorious and awesome name. "To forget the Lord's name is tantamount to forgetting Him."[4]

The apostasy of forgetting YAHveh's name through the worship of Baal was precisely why the prophet Elijah was sent to

---

[2] *"At first the name Baal (lord) was used by the Jews for their God without discrimination,* but as the struggle between the religions developed, the name Baal was given up in Judaism as a thing of shame" (emphasis added). *The Zondervan Pictorial Bible Dictionary,* s. v. "Baal."

[3] Footnote for Hosea 2:13. *"days of the Baals.* The whole period of the worship of Baal (the chief Canaanite deity) by Israel. Baal means "lord" or "owner" and was often used as a general term for god. Israel's worship of Baal developed in three stages: (1) placing the Canaanite gods in a secondary place to the LORD (Yahweh; see note on Gen 2:4); (2) considering Yahweh as a super- Baal; (3) Canaanizing or Baalizing Yahweh worship so that the people completely forsook Yahweh." *Ryrie Study Bible* (Chicago: Moody Press, 1995), p. 1377.

[4] Note on Jer 23:27. *The NIV Study Bible* (Grand Rapids: The Zondervan Corporation, 1985), p. 1162.

Israel and is now, as prophesied by Malachi, going forth at the close of the age. *EliYAHu* is sent to turn a remnant away from every generic title and compromised form of worship back to the pure worship of *YAHveh*.

A Temple for His Holy Name

The holy ark of *YAHveh* remained at Shiloh until it was captured during the priestly service of Eli's two rebellious sons. It was not inquired of during the rebellious reign of Saul. Through David's efforts, the ark, *YAHveh's* throne, was retrieved and *YAHveh's* name, presence, glory, and kingship were restored to Israel.

David had it in his heart, *"to build a house to the NAME OF YAHVEH My God"* (1Ch 22:7). He desired this dwelling to be an earthly temple more splendid than the one built at Shiloh. It was to be a holy and royal house for *YAHveh's* throne, the ark, where Israel could worship their King and praise His *memorial-name*.

The Almighty's reply to David's desire to build this royal house was:

"I will raise up YOUR DESCENDANT after you, who will come forth from you, and I will establish his kingdom. He SHALL BUILD A HOUSE FOR MY NAME, and I will establish the throne of his kingdom FOREVER. I WILL BE A FATHER TO HIM AND HE WILL BE A SON TO ME; ..." (2Sa 7:12-14)

This covenant with David finds its fulfillment in the eternal kingship of *YAHshua* Messiah who was born of David's lineage, the tribe of Judah. *YAHshua* is building the eternal house for *YAHveh* with living stones (Jews and Gentiles) who are redeemed and sanctified through His own sacrificial blood.

Solomon carried out David's desire for the building of this temple. He said,

"You know that David my Father was unable to build a house [temple] for the NAME of YAHveh his God because of the wars which surrounded him, ... I intend to build a house for the NAME of YAHveh my God, as YAHveh spoke to David my father, saying, 'YOUR SON [ultimately YAHshua], whom I will set on your throne in your place, he will BUILD [with holy, living stones] THE HOUSE FOR MY NAME.'" (1Ki 5:3-5)

When the temple was finished, during the Feast of Tabernacles (*Sukkot*) the ark of *YAHveh* was brought by the Zadok priests and Levites and placed in *"the most holy place, under the wings of the cherubim. ... when the priests came from the holy place, ... the cloud* [Shekinah] *filled the house of YAHveh* [this was like Mount Sinai when YAHveh's presence first descended]. ... *Then Solomon said, 'YAHveh has said that He would dwell in the thick cloud. I have surely built Thee a lofty house, A place for Thy dwelling forever'"* (1Ki 8:6-13).

YAHveh's name, His ark, His throne, and His covenant with Israel were inseparably one, and were to remain forever in the heart (Holy of Holies) of His temple. Likewise, in the heart of each believer who is a "living temple" redeemed by YAHshua's blood, YAHveh's presence, name, glory, and covenant promises to Israel are to be reverentially acknowledged and honored.

As the glory of YAHveh filled the temple, Solomon prayed not only for Israel, but also for the Gentile foreigners. He petitioned YAHveh that they too would learn of His holy name and be blessed to worship Him together with Israel.

"Also concerning the foreigner who is not from Thy people Israel, when he comes from a far country for Thy great NAME'S SAKE *... when they come and pray ... do according to all for which the foreigner calls to Thee, in order that all the peoples of the earth may* KNOW THY NAME, *and fear Thee, as do Thy people Israel, and that they* MAY KNOW THAT THIS HOUSE *which I have built* IS CALLED BY THY NAME." (2Ch 6:32-33)

The "David generation" is being called out and chosen to co-labor with the Master Builder, YAHshua, the "Son of David." Messiah's spirit is placing within the hearts of a remnant His ancient and holy passion to return YAHveh's name and glory back to its rightful place—the hearts of His holy remnant. Through living temples who bear His name, YAHveh will again receive the preeminence He intended for Himself.

YAHveh's name, like the ark, has been hidden in obscurity and has not been inquired of throughout the centuries of the compromised "Saul generation." Within the hearts of a chosen remnant, the Spirit of Truth will burn with a consuming desire, causing many to say as in David's day, *"let us bring back the ark of our God to us, for we did not seek it in the days of Saul"* (1Ch 13:3). The Almighty admonishes this upcoming "David generation," to do well and have this in your heart, to build a holy temple for YAHveh's name (see 1Ki 8:16 NIV). The "David generation" will be a royal remnant and a holy priesthood who carry back to prominence His name. He is consecrating a priesthood who will rejoice, as did David, in returning the ark, in restoring *YAHveh's* name, presence, and glory into His holy temple built of living stones. They agree with David as he proclaimed:

"O give thanks to YAHveh, ...

Then say, 'Save us, O God of our salvation,

And gather us and deliver us ...

To give thanks to Thy holy name, ...

Blessed be YAHveh, the God of Israel,

From everlasting even to everlasting. ..."

(1Ch 16:34-36)

"May His name endure forever;

May His name increase as long as the sun shines; ...

Blessed be YAHveh God, the God of Israel, ...

Blessed be His glorious name forever;

And may the whole earth

Be filled with His glory.

Amen, and Amen."

(Ps 72:17-19)

Chapter 27
Backdrop to *YAHshua's* Appearance

With the rebirth of Israel in 1948 came many dramatic archaeological discoveries. Because of the unearthing of the Dead Sea Scrolls and other findings, much of today's biblical scholarship is shifting its opinion to acknowledge that a large part of the original New Testament writings was in fact written by the Hebrew apostles in the Hebrew language.

The Jewish apostles may or may not have been fluent in Greek as many have argued. This, however, is not an issue in regard to the Almighty's *memorial-name*. While we can "transliterate" *YAHshua* letter for letter from Hebrew to English or whatever language we choose, His name was never to be *replaced* with Greek- or Latin-formed renderings.

Hebrew is the language chosen by the living God to communicate with and through His chosen people. Most of the Scriptures are known to have been written in Hebrew. Many other languages including Greek and Latin have their origins in pagan-rooted cultures.

The spreading of the Greek language and culture, called Hellenization, can be discerned in many ways as a strategy of the ancient Serpent in his diabolical obsession and perpetual quest to annihilate all that is of the holy Hebrew root. His crafty cunning has been aimed ultimately at keeping Messiah and His brethren separated. One of his major strategies was to hide and disguise *YAHshua's* true identity so the Jews would not recognize Him as their long-awaited Messiah.

In the inter-testament period, 432 to 5 B.C.E., sometimes called the "silent" years between the Old and New Testament writings, many events transpired that will help us understand the stage setting in the Jewish hearts and minds at the appearance of Messiah.

With Alexander the Great's acquisition of Palestine (332 B.C.E.), a new and more insidious threat to Israel emerged. Alexander was committed to the creation of a world united by Greek language and culture, a policy followed by his successors. This policy, called Hellenization, had a dramatic impact on the Jews.[1]

---

[1] *The NIV Study Bible* (Grand Rapids: The Zondervan Corporation, 1985), p. 1431.

"[Alexander] was convinced that Greek culture was the one force that could unify the world."[2] Alexander and the reign of the Ptolemies who followed were more or less "considerate towards the Jewish religious sensitivities ..."[3] However, following his reign came a true ambassador of the ancient Serpent. Once again on the stage of history the great Enemy of the Jews was rearing his ugly head and exposing his venomous fangs.

Satan's age-old strategies to eradicate the Hebrew people manifested through Antiochus IV Epiphanes (215-163 B.C.E.) with a furious hatred and an intolerance towards the Jewish people, religion, and customs, and a commitment to the radical Hellenization of the world.

While a segment of the Jewish aristocracy had already adopted Greek ways, the majority of Jews were outraged. Antiochus' atrocities were aimed at the eradication of Jewish religion. He prohibited some of the central elements of Jewish practice, attempted to destroy all copies of the Torah, and required offerings to the Greek god Zeus. His crowning outrage was the erection of a statue of Zeus and the sacrificing of a pig in the Jerusalem temple itself.[4]

This appalling desecration of *YAHveh's* temple, according to many commentators, was done on December 25th in celebration of the Solstice and the birthday of the sun deity, named Zeus in pagan mythology. Added to these abominations was his blatant attempt to nullify the Sabbath which was to be a *"perpetual covenant"* (Ex 31:16) between *YAHveh* and His people.

It is interesting to note that Antiochus Epiphanes, whose name means "God made manifest," attempted to *manifest the Greek god Zeus and to obliterate the God of the Hebrews, YAHveh.* The psalmist pleaded with an anguished heart,

Remember the people [Jews] you purchased of old, the tribe of your inheritance, whom you redeemed—Mount Zion, where you dwelt. Turn your steps toward these everlasting ruins, all this destruction the enemy has brought on the sanctuary. Your foes roared in the place where you met with us; they set up their standards [pagan-rooted traditions] as signs. They behaved like

---

[2] Ibid., p. 1430.

[3] Ibid., p. 1431.

[4] Ibid., p. 1431.

men wielding axes ... THEY DEFILED THE DWELLING PLACE OF YOUR NAME. They said in their hearts, "We will crush them completely!" (Ps 74:2-8 NIV — emphasis added)

"How long, O God, WILL THE ADVERSARY REVILE, AND THE ENEMY SPURN THY NAME FOREVER? ... Remember this, O YAHveh, that the enemy has reviled; And a FOOLISH PEOPLE HAS SPURNED THY NAME." (Ps 74:10, 18)

Years prior to Antiochus Epiphanes, the angel Michael prophesied to Daniel of this exact desecrating of *YAHveh's* temple and attack against of the holy Hebraic root. Michael said,

"And he will speak out against the Most High and wear down the saints ... and he will intend TO MAKE ALTERATIONS IN TIMES [Hebrew memorial feasts and the Sabbath day] *AND IN LAW* [*Torah* and the Ten Commandments]; ..." (Da 7:25)

"the PRINCE OF GREECE [possibly Antiochus Epiphanes] *will come; but first I will tell you what is written in the Book of Truth."* (Da 10:20-21 NIV — emphasis added)

"his heart will be set AGAINST THE HOLY [Hebrew] *COVENANT. ... And forces from him will arise, DESECRATE THE SANCTUARY fortress, and do away with the regular sacrifice* [the daily sacrifice placed on the holy altar of *YAHveh* was replaced with a mandatory sacrifice of abhorrent swine]. *And they will set up THE ABOMINATION OF DESOLATION."* (Da 11:28, 31)

The angel Michael's words held dual prophetic meaning; this was fulfilled through Antiochus Epiphanes as he set up the altar to the Greek god Zeus causing the desecration of *YAHveh's* holy temple. This event was also a prefiguring of a similar abomination that Messiah predicted would be set up to desecrate *YAHveh's* holy house.

YAHshua, in reference to Daniel's prophecy, was pointing to the future when the abomination similar to Antiochus' would occur again. *"Therefore when you see THE ABOMINATION OF DESOLATION ... standing in the holy place (LET THE READER UNDERSTAND) ..."* (Mt 24:15).

Messiah was saying that the reader should seek to understand what this abomination is in *YAHveh's* sight that causes His sanctuary to be *desolate of His holy presence and Shekinah glory.* Many theologians believe this to be the "Man of

Sin," the anti-Messiah who would desecrate the temple in *YAHrushalayim* by placing himself there to be worshiped (see 2Th 2:3-5). In a similar vein believers are to beware continually of the desecrating influences of all that is carnal and unholy, including the traditions and customs of the pagan world. We are to learn to distinguish the holy from the common in order to avoid any abominations entering our hearts or religious systems that could cause desolation—the departure of *YAHveh's* divine presence.

Cleansing the Temple

The Serpent's strategies were insidiously perpetuated through the early Christian church fathers who began fusing their familiar pagan customs with the new messianic faith. Most assuredly, Satan's eggs were laid and hatched in the fertile bed of ignorance in Gentiles who did not understand *YAHveh* or His holy requirements. Many Christians unknowingly harbored the ancient Serpent's venom of anti-Semitism.

At the close of the Gentile age, many professing believers stand in jeopardy of *YAHveh's forthcoming righteous judgments* because their bodies, redeemed to be holy temples, are desecrated by abominations in *YAHveh's* sight. As in the days of Antiochus' defeat, *our temples*—hearts, mind and body—*must be cleansed and purified of all fleshly, worldly and pagan influence.*

Chanukah is the Feast of Dedication, symbolized by the *Menorah* (the sacred candelabra that lights the holy temple). This winter feast took place three years to the exact day after the desecrating of the temple.[5] This biblical feast, observed by Messiah, commemorates the cleansing of *YAHveh's* temple from Antiochus Epiphanes' Grecian and pagan abominations (see John 10:22).

May the light of *YAHshua's* countenance begin to shine brightly as the *Menorah*, burning in the living temples of our hearts. May we be willing for the light of *YAHshua* to expose any darkness in our hearts and thoroughly cleanse us with His blood of any pagan defilement. And may Messiah *dedicate us to His Father* as living temples and consecrated priests—*Holy to YAHveh.*

---

[5] *The Works of Josephus* (Peabody, Massachusetts: Hendrickson Publishers, 1987), p. 328.

Chapter 28
"Ask for the Ancient Paths"

The world and much of Christianity's religious system have been inundated with the glory of pagan-rooted traditions while the true glory and holiness of *YAHveh* has departed. *YAHshua* warned the pious religious leaders, *"YOU INVALIDATED THE WORD OF YAHVEH FOR THE SAKE OF YOUR TRADITION"* (Mt 15:6).

The redeemed Gentiles, through the Holy Spirit, were to provoke the Jews to jealousy by exceeding them in their faith, holy living and wholehearted worship and obedience to the Mighty One of Israel.

Instead, by the unbiblical mixing and superimposing of pagan anti-Jewish customs in place of the pure holy Hebrew root, the Jews have been rightfully *appalled and repulsed* by much of historical Christianity. The majority of *YAHshua's* brethren have run from the God and Savior of Christianity. Too often, Messiah has been disfiguratively conveyed through the errors of men's doctrines and traditions.

YAHshua Messiah continues to weep over the slain of Jacob and over the lost sheep of the House of Israel. Added to this unceasing anguish is His nauseating disgust and indignation over the *"trampling of My courts"* (Isa 1:12). For centuries, His sacred courts have been thoroughfares for the indiscriminate and unholy religious activities that drag pagan-rooted traditions in and out of sanctuaries, individual lives, and congregations, which were to be dedicated to the awesome reverence and pure worship of the holy King of Kings.

Coupled with this, the pervasive ignorance of the full meaning of Messiah's sacrificial blood to create *one new man* has caused the trampling under foot of His precious blood (see Heb 10:28) by the multitudes who do not understand His love and plan for Israel.

YAHveh's promises, blessings, curses, and judgments are always in His divine order—first to the Jews, *then* to the Gentiles. Ignorance and arrogance have caused much of corporate Christianity to greedily grab and appropriate Israel's blessings as primarily for "the church." Yet, when it comes to the righteous judgments prophesied to fall on the rebellious, the church is oftentimes quick to apply these solely to Israel. The apostle Paul emphasizes:

> There will be tribulation and distress for every soul of man who does evil, of the Jew first and also of the Greek, BUT GLORY AND HONOR AND PEACE TO EVERY MAN WHO DOES GOOD, TO THE JEW FIRST AND ALSO TO THE GREEK. For there is no partiality with YAHveh. (Ro 2:9-11)

> YAHveh God of hosts, the Mighty One of Israel, declares, "Ah, I will be relieved of My adversaries ... I will also turn My hand against you, and will SMELT [purge or separate] AWAY YOUR DROSS ... and WILL REMOVE ALL YOUR ALLOY [impurities]. Then I will RESTORE your judges AS AT THE FIRST, And your counselors as at the beginning; After that you will be called the city of RIGHTEOUSNESS, A faithful city." (Isa 1:24-26)

> Thus says YAHveh, "Stand by the ways [the crossroads] and see and ASK FOR THE ANCIENT PATHS, where the good way is, and walk in it ... I set watchmen over you, saying, LISTEN TO THE SOUND OF THE TRUMPET! ..." (Jer 6:16-17)

A Righteous Remnant for a Righteous Kingdom

The Spirit of Truth will circumcise the hearts of a remnant. YAHveh will separate His people from all that is impure, pagan-rooted and abominable in His sight. Messiah said, *"BLESSED ARE THE PURE IN HEART, FOR THEY SHALL SEE YAHVEH"* (Mt 5:8).

The *Ruach HaKodesh* (Holy Spirit) desires to separate a people from every vestige of deceit. Much religious deception is a by-product of Satan's strategies to replace the holy Hebrew root with pagan-rooted traditions. As we approach the *Highway of Holiness, the road becomes narrower, the remnant becomes smaller, the cost becomes higher, and the requirements become greater.*

Those redeemed by the blood of *YAHshua* have been given the divine gift of the priesthood. Only the consecrated priests, who are pure in heart, can approach *YAHveh* and stand in His presence to be transformed in His Shekinah glory. The New *YAHrushalayim* will be the eternal home of *YAHveh's* righteousness, inhabited only by His righteous priesthood.

The King of the Jews is reminding a remnant that those

with uncircumcised, impure hearts will never again trample His sanctuary. The religious majority will never bring man-invented traditions in and out of His eternal Holy of Holies, the New *YAHrushalayim.*

When the age of the Gentiles is eternally over, all generic substitutes for the holy name and all traditions linked with pagan gods and man-made customs will find no place in the righteous home of *YAHshua*, the heir of David, the King of Israel.

The New *YAHrushalayim* (the city of *YAH*), whose physical dimensions form a perfect square, is the magnification of the square dimensions of the earthly Holy of Holies. The Most Holy Place, containing the ark of the covenant which bore *YAHveh's* name, measured fifteen feet square. It was a foreshadowing of the eternal Holy City. The New *YAHrushalayim* will be the eternal Holy of Holies, housing *YAHveh's* throne, name, and Shekinah glory as the divine focal point of its holy priests.

Only the smallest remnant of Israel, the Levitical priesthood, could enter the holy sanctuary. An even smaller remnant, one man on one day a year, could enter the Holy of Holies. Much preparation for purification and consecration was required before the high priest with awesome reverence, fear and trembling, entered into *YAHveh's* presence.

YAHveh is preparing His redeemed priests to move from the Holy Place of service into the Most Holy Place of intimate fellowship and worship. Ultimately He is preparing this remnant, a *royal priesthood*, to enter His eternal Holy of Holies, the New *YAHrushalayim.*

Wheat or Weeds

Messiah told his disciples: *"Do not think that I came to bring peace on the earth; I did not come to bring peace, but a sword* [that divides]. ... A MAN'S ENEMIES WILL BE THE MEMBERS OF HIS HOUSEHOLD" (Mt 10:34, 36).

It is sad but true that the issue of *YAHshua's* most holy name will inevitably divide physical as well as spiritual households. At the close of the Gentile age, Messiah's sword is sharper than ever and it will cut away that which is man-made from that which is *YAH*-made. He will winnow the religious from the righteous.

The issue of Israel is ordained as a threshing sledge in

YAHveh's hand. The Almighty spoke to Israel through Isaiah the prophet:

"Behold, I have made you [Israel] a new, sharp THRESHING SLEDGE with double edges; You will thresh the mountains [man's national and political pride against Israel], and pulverize them, And will make the hills [religious apostasy and pride] like chaff. You will winnow them, and the wind will carry them away, And the storm will scatter them; but you will rejoice in YAHveh, You will glory in the Holy One of Israel." (Isa 41:15-16)

The sharp point on YAHveh's threshing instrument, as well as the point on YAHshua's sword, is the issue of His eternal love for Israel and jealousy for His holy and awesome name. As this age closes, His sovereign threshing sledge is destined to go through the harvest fields to distinguish and separate the weeds from the wheat. Those seeds sown by the Enemy through the doctrines of men, will be separated from those seeds sown by the Son of Man through the Spirit of Truth.

Messiah said the wheat and the weeds would grow as indistinguishable from one another, side by side until the harvest or the end of the age (see Mt 13:24-30, 37-42). Now, we are at that critical time when the threshing and winnowing must take place in order for YAHshua to have a pure harvest of righteousness for His name's sake. YAHveh magnifies this issue through the prophet Micah:

"And now many nations have been assembled against you [Israel] Who say, 'Let her be polluted, And let our eyes gloat over Zion.' But they [many Gentile rulers and spiritual leaders] DO NOT KNOW THE THOUGHTS OF YAHVEH, AND THEY DO NOT UNDERSTAND HIS PURPOSE; FOR HE HAS GATHERED THEM LIKE SHEAVES TO THE THRESHING FLOOR. Arise and thresh, daughter of Zion, For your horn I will make iron and your hoofs I will make bronze, That you may pulverize many peoples [nations]. ... " (Mic 4:11-13)

Through the Narrow Sheep Gate

The chosen remnant will recognize their Shepherd's voice. His little flock of obedient sheep will follow their shepherd wherever He goes. As the night is upon us, He is leading His flock from the outer court of religion through that narrow sheep gate into the pasture of refuge and safety in the Holy of Holies and ultimately the New *YAHrushalayim*. Not one of His sheep will be lost.

The prophet Micah foretold that out of Bethlehem One would go forth as the Great Shepherd:

"... to be ruler in Israel.

His goings forth are from long ago, From the days of eternity."

"He will arise and SHEPHERD HIS FLOCK

in the strength of YAHveh,

in the majesty of THE NAME OF *YAHveh*

His God. ... "

(Mic 5:2, 4)

YAHshua the Shepherd says:

"And I have other sheep [Gentiles],

which are not of this fold [the Jews];

I must bring them also, and they shall hear My voice;

and they shall become one flock with one shepherd."

"My sheep HEAR MY VOICE *and I know them,*

and THEY FOLLOW ME.*"*

(Jn 10:16, 27)

Chapter 29
"Give Him the Name *YAHshua*"

"Behold, a virgin will be with child and bear a son, and she will call His name Immanuel [meaning 'God with us']" (Isa 7:14). — *"And the Word became flesh, and* DWELT AMONG US *..." (Jn 1:14).*

The angel Gabriel appeared to the prophesied Jewish virgin, *Miryam* (Mary), proclaiming that she would bear the One who would tabernacle (dwell) among men.

"YOU SHALL NAME HIM YAHSHUA. He will be great, and will be called the Son Of The Most High; and the Lord [Master] *YAHveh will give Him the* THRONE OF HIS FATHER DAVID; *and He will* REIGN OVER THE HOUSE OF JACOB *forever, and His Kingdom will have no end." (Lk 1:31-33)*

YAHveh, the Holy One of Israel, became flesh and blood and dwelt on earth to bring salvation to Israel and all Gentiles later to be joined with her. In Hebrew, the word for salvation or saves is *SHUA*. That is why the angel told Joseph, *"she will bear a Son; and you shall call His name YahSHUA, for it is He who will save His people from their sins"* (Mt 1:21).

The psalmist, in announcing Israel's redemption, exclaimed: *"O Israel, hope in YAHveh; ... with Him is abundant redemption. And He* [through YAHshua] *will redeem Israel From all his iniquities"* (Ps 130:7-8).

In the prophetic foreknowledge of the coming Hebrew Messiah, Isaiah proclaimed: *"Then you* [Israel] *will say on that day, ... 'Behold, God is my salvation, I will trust and not be afraid; For YAH, YAHveh is my strength and song, And* HE HAS BECOME MY SALVATION'" *(Isa 12:1-2).*[1] YAH has become my *SHUA*, called YAH-SHUA—YAHshua, the Savior!

And in that day you will say, "Give thanks to YAHveh, CALL ON HIS NAME. ... *Make them remember that HIS NAME IS EXALTED." ... "Cry aloud and shout for joy, O inhabitant of Zion* [and all Gentiles joined with you], *For great in your midst is the Holy One of Israel* [who tabernacles among men]." (Isa 12:4, 6)

With reverential joy, the Hebrew virgin proclaimed the

[1] Isa 12:2 affirms the use of both *YAH* and *YAHveh* in this quote.

faithfulness of the Almighty to His chosen people. *"He has given help to Israel His servant, In* REMEMBRANCE *of His* MERCY, *As He spoke to our fathers, To Abraham and his offspring* FOREVER*"* (Lk 1:54-55).

The infant Messiah's Hebrew parents, *Yosef* and *Miryam* were very careful to follow the *Torah* (the Law). *"And when eight days were completed before His circumcision, His name was then called YAHshua, the* NAME GIVEN BY THE ANGEL *before He was conceived in the womb"* (Lk 2:21).

Following His circumcision, the baby was taken to Jerusalem to be presented to the God of Israel in obedience to the law: *"*EVERY first-born *MALE THAT OPENS THE WOMB SHALL BE CALLED HOLY TO YAHVEH"* (Lk 2:23).

The Divine Name Divides

Many are hesitant to leave the familiar holy place of service and cross over the threshold into the Most Holy Place of His Shekinah glory. His unfamiliar, yet original and divine name, is a stumbling block which will sadly hinder many from entering the fullness of His glorious presence.

Since *His divine name divides,* we must realize the pendulum is swinging from the religious system of the Jews in Messiah's day to the religious system of the Gentiles in these last days. As stated, through the Serpent's strategies, the name of *YAHveh* was first hidden by Jewish leaders and later dissolved by the Christian leaders. These historically influential church pillars, through ignorance and deception, allowed Satan's anti-Jewish purposes to perpetuate.

The Jews suffered an agonizing and appalling assault through Satan's strategy of Hellenization. Antiochus IV Epiphanes' raping and ravaging of the Hebrew temple was a blatant attempt to "Gentilize" the world and obliterate the holy Hebrew root. The anti-Semitic atrocities aimed at replacing *YAHveh,* the God of the Jews, with Zeus, the God of the Greeks, is a core issue in the battle between Satan and the Almighty.

The Jews in Messiah's day were stunned by the atrocities of their recent past. "... it was obvious that to a loyal Jew, anything

---

[2] C.G. Montefiore and H. Loewe, *A Rabbinic Anthology* (Philadelphia: The Jewish Publication Society of America, 1960), p. 145.

Greek was, *eo ipso*, anti-Jewish. Hellenization stood for apostasy."[2]
It is recorded in the sacred writings of the Jews (*Talmud*), "Cursed
be a man who rears pigs and cursed be a man who teaches his son
Greek wisdom."[3]

To further emphasize the Jewish mind set towards the
Greeks, we note the account in Acts 21. Paul enters the temple
with four Greek converts:

*"the Jews from Asia, upon seeing him in the temple,
began to stir up all the multitude and laid hands on him,
crying out, 'Men of Israel, come to our aid! This is the man
who preaches to all men everywhere against our people,
and the Law, and this place; and besides he has EVEN
BROUGHT GREEKS INTO THE TEMPLE AND HAS DEFILED THIS HOLY
PLACE.'"* (Ac 21:27-28)

Greek men, Greek idols and Greek names were an offense
and strictly forbidden in the homes of the Jews and the temple of
the God of the Jews. Archaeological findings verify the fact that no
Greeks were allowed in the temple courts upon penalty of death.[4]

A Substitute for the Original

When Messiah was first named by the angel, and later given that
name at His circumcision, a Greek name would never have been
permitted. Jews were vitally concerned with pedigrees. According
to Jewish biblical tradition, the name of the offspring was always
given with the name of the father. It was completely unacceptable
for a Jew to take a Gentile name.

With this in mind, the Almighty appeals to our common
sense and spiritual wisdom and asks us, *"WHAT IS HIS NAME, AND*

---

[3] Rabbi B.D. Klien, trans., Rabbi Dr. I. Epstein, ed., *The Babylonian Talmud*
(New York: M.P. Press, 1983), *Sotah* p. 49b.

[4] Footnote Ac 21:28: "*brought Greeks into the Temple area.* Explicitly forbidden
according to inscribed stone markers [still in existence]. Any Gentiles found
within the bounds of the court of Israel would be killed. But there is no evidence
that Paul had brought anyone other than Jews into the area." (emphasis added).
The NIV Study Bible (Grand Rapids: The Zondervan Corporation, 1985). Author's
note: It should be noted that indeed Paul **never** transgressed the righteousness
of *YAHveh's* decrees by bringing a *Greek name* for the Hebrew Messiah into the
temple of the Holy One of Israel.

THE NAME OF HIS SON? *Tell me if you know!"* (Pr 30:4).

YAHshua, the name above all names, became the name *beneath all names as a result of Satan's schemes.* The Father of Lies, working through the doctrines of men, once again turned things upside down. He cunningly assaulted *YAHveh,* His holy name, His Jewish people, and His eternal plan in and through Israel.

The true and holy name of Messiah was *incorrectly rendered* by early writers in Greek as *Iesous* (Ίησους). This word does translate into Engilsh as "Jesus"; however *Gentile scholars began substituting YAHshua's true name with the Greek replacement.* Transliterating the Hebrew would have maintained the integrity of the holy name.

The pure word Messiah (Hebrew, *Mashiach* or *Mashiah*) is correctly translated as the "Anointed One of *YAH* (*MashiYah*)." *YAHshua HaMashiach,* never heard Himself called "Jesus Christ." He was the "anointed of *YAH*" and bore His Father's name in order to bring *YAHveh* the glory. The epithet or title "Christ" is the Greek translation (replacement) for Messiah.

The liberally used label of *Christian* is a man-made Gentile tradition stemming from the word "Christ." Many scholars concur that its first use was in a spirit of reproach rather than respect for the true righteous followers of *YAHshua* Messiah.

> ... in Acts 11:26, we have the inspired record of the Antiochians coining the word *Christian.* Antiochians were witty, worldly, and rather wicked. There is no reason to believe that they were being complimentary when they used the term *Christian* to describe followers of Jesus. It was no doubt... a term of reproach, which became a badge of honor.[5]

The early believers were never *respectfully* referred to by the name "Christian." They were messianic believers and disciples of *YAHshua* and often known as *"Followers of the Way"* (Ac 22:4).

This may be a difficult juncture for many of you traveling on the *Highway of Holiness.* The cutting away of religious and traditional foreskin is a painful but most glorious operation. Messiah exhorted His disciples that they must *count the cost.* They must be willing to *forsake everything* including their honored traditions, in order to keep in step with the One they call "Lord and Master."

---

[5] *The New Open Bible — NASB Study Edition* (Nashville: Thomas Nelson Publishers, 1990), p. 6.

At the climax of this age, as the scroll of His ancient biblical truths is unsealed and opened, may your hearts likewise be opened to the full counsel of Messiah. May His *Ruach HaKodesh* make you willing to pay the price to walk in the greater light given through *YAHshua's* true name and Hebrew identity. He is "A LIGHT OF REVELATION TO THE GENTILES, and ... THE GLORY of Thy people ISRAEL" (Lk 2:32).

Chapter 30
Divine Dividends

Darkness is upon us; the Enemy has hidden the holy name and deflected the radiant glory of the Holy One of Israel. The prophet Isaiah exclaimed, *"NO ONE CALLS ON YOUR NAME or strives to lay hold of you; ..."* (Isa 64:7 NIV — emphasis added).

Throughout the ages, most of us, including the historical multitudes, have addressed the Savior by the Greek-formed name "Jesus," and addressed the heavenly Father by the generic titles "God" and "Lord." The redeemed have walked in the only light available. Man's Greek rendering of the Messiah's name was all that was commonly known and wholeheartedly accepted. For those who believed in Him, the Savior responded to our heart's cry and saved us. We must, however heed the words of Paul regarding man's ignorance of *YAHveh's* holy decrees.

"THEREFORE HAVING OVERLOOKED THE TIMES OF IGNORANCE, YAHveh is now declaring to men that ALL EVERYWHERE SHOULD REPENT, because He has fixed a day in which HE WILL JUDGE THE WORLD IN RIGHTEOUSNESS through a Man [YAHshua] whom He has appointed, ..." (Ac 17:30-31)

Hear the words of *YAHveh* as spoken through the prophet Isaiah:

"I have kept silent for a long time, I have kept still and restrained Myself. Now ... I will lead the blind by a WAY THEY DO NOT KNOW, IN PATHS THEY DO NOT KNOW I will guide them. I will make DARKNESS INTO LIGHT before them and rugged places into plains ..." (Isa 42:14-16)

Now *YAHveh* is calling a chosen people to depart from the familiar, yet dimly lit, crooked paths of religion to make a pilgrimage on the *Highway of Holiness* illuminated by the full truth and light of *YAHshua* the Son.

Let those who seek the full light of *YAHshua* join the psalmist in proclaiming, *"O send out Thy LIGHT and Thy TRUTH, let them lead me; LET THEM BRING ME TO THY HOLY HILL, AND TO THY DWELLING PLACES [the Holy of Holies]"* (Ps 43:3).

When *YAHshua* first dwelled among men, He was called *" the Sunrise from on high ... TO SHINE UPON THOSE WHO SIT IN DARKNESS AND THE SHADOW OF DEATH, ..."* (Lk 1:78-79). Indeed for a brief time the full countenance of the *"root and the offspring of David, the* bright morning star ..." (Rev 22:16) brought the full intensity of YAHveh's divine radiance. John said: "In Him was life, and the life was the light of men" (Jn 1:4).

However, "men loved the darkness rather than the light; ..." (Jn 3:19). YAHshua understood the propensity of human nature to prefer the darkness of traditions over His bright light of truth. YAHveh inspired Paul to pen these words:

... the god of this world has blinded the minds of the unbelieving, that they might not see the light of the gospel [the Good News[1]] of the glory of Messiah, who is the image of YAHveh. ... For God, who said, "Light shall shine out of darkness," is the One who has shone in our hearts to give the light of the knowledge of the glory of YAHveh in the face of [YAHshua] Messiah." (2Co 4:4-6)

John adds, "And the light shines in the darkness, and the darkness did not comprehend it" (Jn 1:5). He continues, stating that YAHshua is "the true light which, coming into the world, enlightens every man. ... as many as received Him, to them He gave the right to become children of YAHveh, even to those who BELIEVE IN HIS NAME" (Jn 1:9-12).

YAHshua, emphasizing His oneness with YAHveh, states: "he who does not believe has been judged already, because he has not BELIEVED IN THE NAME of the only begotten Son of YAHveh. And this is the judgment, that the light is come into the world, and men loved the darkness [including faulty traditions] rather than the light [truth]; for their deeds were evil. For everyone who does evil hates the light, and does not come to the light, lest his deeds should be exposed. "BUT HE WHO PRACTICES THE TRUTH COMES TO THE LIGHT, ..." (Jn 3:18-21)

Messiah prophesied that His departure would bring the waning of His light on earth. Before His return to the Father, YAHshua admonished His disciples:

"For a little while longer the light is among you. Walk while you have the light, that darkness may not overtake you; he who walks in the darkness does not know where he goes. While you have the light, believe in the light, in order that you may become sons of light." (Jn 12:35-36)

Not long after the ascension to His Father, that supreme

---

[1] The word gospel, as commonly known in New Testament Gentile translations, was originally referred to by early believers as the "Good News."

brightness of the full "Son light" began to be hidden by the doctrines and traditions of men. Just as the moon eclipses the full light of the sun, so have many untrue traditions eclipsed the light of the "Son." Consequently, throughout the centuries, the majority of those who truly sought the Savior did so by the "light of the moon" and walked in sincerity of heart by the dimness of that light. *YAHveh* is now bringing to light all that was hidden, calling us to return to the "ancient paths" brightly lit through *YAHshua*, the true light of revelation.

Hear the heart cry of Isaiah as he grieved over the sins of Israel. May the fear of *YAHveh* lead us to join with the prophet in godly sorrow accompanied by true repentance over the Gentiles' similar transgressions of His righteous commands.

> WE HOPE FOR LIGHT, BUT BEHOLD, DARKNESS; *For brightness, but we WALK IN GLOOM. We grope along the wall like blind men, We grope like those who have no eyes; We stumble at midday as in the twilight,* ... FOR OUR TRANSGRESSIONS ARE MULTIPLIED BEFORE THEE, *And our sins testify against us; For our transgressions are with us, And* WE KNOW OUR INIQUITIES: *Transgressing and denying YAHveh, And* TURNING AWAY FROM OUR GOD, *Speaking oppression* [against the Jews] *and revolt,* CONCEIVING IN AND UTTERING FROM THE HEART LYING WORDS [including doctrines and traditions of men]. ... AND RIGHTEOUSNESS STANDS FAR AWAY; FOR TRUTH HAS STUMBLED IN THE STREET, and uprightness cannot enter. YES, TRUTH IS LACKING; ... *Now YAHVEH SAW, AND IT WAS DISPLEASING IN HIS SIGHT* ... *He put on garments of vengeance for clothing, And wrapped Himself with zeal as a mantle. According to their deeds, so He will repay,* ... SO THEY WILL FEAR THE NAME OF YAHVEH *from the west And His glory from the rising of the sun,* ... (Isa 59:9-19)

Now at the close of the Gentile age, *YAHveh* is stripping away the results of Satan's massive Gentilization program. The true Hebraic root and *YAHveh's* ancient seeds of truth are being unearthed from under the centuries of men's compromises and faulty teachings. The psalmist spoke prophetically of the time when *YAHveh's* favor would shift back to His Jewish people.

> *Thou wilt arise and have compassion on Zion; For it is time to be gracious to her,* FOR THE APPOINTED TIME HAS COME. ... *the nations will* FEAR THE NAME OF YAHVEH, ... *that men may tell of the* NAME OF YAHVEH IN ZION, *And His praise in Jerusalem; When the peoples are* GATHERED TOGETHER, ... *To* SERVE YAHVEH. (Ps 102:13-15, 21-22)

The psalmist was prophesying of the distant day when *YAHveh's* holy name would be feared and worshiped by the Gentiles. When the redeemed Gentiles from many nations assemble to worship *YAHveh*, the God of Israel, then Israel will truly be provoked to jealousy. As the Jews hear the *ineffable name* of their God proclaimed from the righteous lips of *one new man*, then a remnant of Jews will be mercifully drawn from darkness to the light and truly again worship *YAHveh*, the Father, as they embrace *YAHshua*, the Son.

The Gentilization process has been a stumbling block to YAHveh's purposes. He has mercifully tolerated this for it has not been discerned, *even by the elect*, as a tare of the Enemy. With the bright morning star rising to give full light on this blighted harvest field, a holy remnant will discern Satan's strategies (fruitless tares) and his stumbling blocks to the Almighty's sovereign purposes. They will worship the Son of Righteousness in spirit and truth.

Sowing toward Success

There is a double issue regarding the Jews and the God of the Jews, resulting from the Greek rendering of Messiah's name, "Jesus Christ." As stated earlier, the majority of the non-Hellenistic Jews vehemently shunned anything of Greek origin. To add to this offense has been hundreds of years of Christian history riddled with Satan's odious trail, spewing venom against the Jews in the name of Jesus Christ. Messiah *YAHshua* weeps over the slain of His people and grieves that the majority of redeemed Gentiles have neglected His mandate to mercifully and lovingly draw His Jewish brethren to their Messiah.

Over many centuries, eternal life has come to masses of Gentiles and even a remnant of Jews in the name of Jesus Christ. Grievously, however, this name has been a banner under which millions of Jews have been hated, tortured, killed, and continually persecuted. The Greek substitute for Messiah's true name has not, by and large, brought salvation or blessings to the Jews but rather alienation, death, and destruction.

Messiah said, *"Greater love has no one than this, that one lay down his life for his friends"* (Jn 15:13). He is calling out a remnant who will lay aside their own religious agendas and self-interests that the full truth flowing from the holy Hebraic root and love of *YAHshua* will be manifested on earth in His biblical order, *to the Jew first.*

Zechariah foresaw a symbolic ratio of Gentiles following redeemed Jews. *"... 'In those days ten men from all the nations of every language will grasp the garment of a Jew saying, "Let us go with you, for we have heard that God is with you"'"* (Zec 8:23). This serves as an inspiration for those who long for the great ingathering of Jewish and Gentile souls.

The beloved John wrote: *"By this we know that we are in Him; the one who says he abides in Him ought himself to walk in the same manner as He walked"* (1Jn 2:5-6). Those who are faithfully co-laboring with *YAHshua* in the harvest field of men's souls will wholeheartedly desire to follow in the footsteps of the Great Harvester. *YAHshua's* path and method for sowing and reaping of the eternal harvest of a righteous remnant had a divine order; the wise will follow their Master's ways to reap OPTIMUM BOUNTY.

Messiah came *to the Jews first* to manifest *YAHveh's* name, glory, and salvation. Through this remnant of redeemed Jews who believed, salvation spread to multitudes of Gentiles. Paul said, *"For I am not ashamed of the gospel* [Good News], *for it is the power of YAHveh for salvation to every one who believes to the Jew first and also to the Greek"* (Ro 1:16).

Going in *YAHveh's* order of salvation to the Jew first requires and releases the fullest measure of truth embodying the holy Hebrew root and its nourishing sap. When we have the full power and light of *YAHshua* in the magnitude of His Jewish identity and heartbeat we will have a truth so pure that it will draw a remnant of Jews to their Messiah with a potency so great as to attract many Gentiles. As we have seen, a religious system going in man's order to the Gentiles first and foremost has been stripped of this full power. It has not drawn many Jews and appeals to fewer and fewer Gentiles of this day and age. *To the Jew first* releases the power of salvation but *it does not imply the neglect of Gentiles to search out the Jews.*

Messiah's proven method for harvesting souls is beyond compare. *YAHshua* and His disciples sowed and reaped going *to the Jews first* in the name of *YAHveh*, the Father, and *YAHshua*, the Son.

"Ten Gentiles per Jew," as prophesied by Zechariah, is a worthy harvest to the glory of the Almighty! *Such are divine dividends!*

Chapter 31
"Salvation Is from the Jews"

The Savior of the world came first to His own brethren, the children of Israel. He was the Jew of all Jews and walked in absolute obedience to the Law of Moses. His appearance was extremely and distinctly Jewish in obedience to the biblical instructions recorded in the *Torah* (Lev 19:27). He had a Hebrew name, spoke the Hebrew language, and walked and ministered, with few exceptions, only among His Jewish brethren.

With the modern discovery of the Dead Sea Scrolls and the advancement of knowledge concerning the language of Messiah, it is becoming increasingly obvious to many seekers of truth that pure Hebrew was most likely the language of *YAHshua* and His disciples.[1]

In the book of Matthew we read of *YAHshua's* commission to His disciples: "*And having summoned His twelve disciples, ... These twelve YAHshua sent out after instructing them, saying, 'Do not go in the way of the Gentiles, and do not enter any city of the Samaritans; BUT RATHER GO TO THE LOST SHEEP OF THE HOUSE OF ISRAEL'*" (Mt 10:1, 5-6).

---

[1] "'The spoken languages among the Jews of that period were Hebrew, Aramaic, and to an extent Greek. Until recently, it was believed by numerous scholars that the language spoken by Jesus' disciples was Aramaic. It is possible that Jesus did, from time to time, make use of the Aramaic language. But during that period Hebrew was both the daily language and the language of study. The gospel of Mark contains a few Aramaic words, and this was what misled scholars. Today, after the discovery of the Hebrew Ben Sira (Ecclesiasticus) [a book of the Apocrypha], of the Dead Sea Scrolls, and of the Bar Kokhba Letters, and in the light of more profound studies of the language of the Jewish Sages, it is accepted that most people were fluent in Hebrew. The Pentateuch was translated into Aramaic for the benefit of the lower strata of the population. The parables in the Rabbinic literature, on the other hand, were delivered in Hebrew in all periods. There is thus no ground for assuming that Jesus did not speak Hebrew; and when we are told (Acts 21:40) that Paul spoke Hebrew, we should take this piece of information at face value.' (*Jewish Sources in Early Christianity*, POB 7103, Tel Aviv 61070: MOD Books, 1989)" David H. Stern, *Jewish New Testament Commentary* (Clarksville, MD: Jewish New Testament Publications, 1992).

YAHshua is faithful to the Abrahamic covenant to BLESS THOSE Gentiles WHO BLESS ISRAEL. The exceptionally few Gentiles to whom He ministered were specific examples of foreigners who had a reverence and love for the Jewish people and the God of Israel. Luke, most probably a Gentile convert to Judaism, gives the account of the centurion, one of the few Gentiles who received directly from the Messiah of Israel.

And when he [the centurion] heard about YAHshua, he sent some Jewish elders asking Him to come and save the life of his slave. And when they had come to YAHshua, they earnestly entreated Him, saying, "He is worthy for You to grant this to him; FOR HE LOVES OUR [Jewish] NATION, and it was he who built us our synagogue." Now YAHshua started on His way with them; ... (Lk 7:3-6)

Matthew gives the account of a Canaanite woman who humbly acknowledged her alien position. She came to Messiah

... and began to cry out, saying, "Have mercy on me, O Lord [master], Son of David; ..." But He did not answer her a word [because she was a Gentile outcast]. And His disciples came to Him and kept asking Him, saying, "Send her away, ..." But He answered and said, "I WAS SENT ONLY TO THE LOST SHEEP OF THE HOUSE OF ISRAEL." But she came and began to bow down before Him, saying, "Lord, help me!" And He answered and said, "It is not good to take the children's [Jew's] bread and throw it to the dogs [Gentiles]." But she said, "Yes, Lord; but even the dogs feed on the crumbs which fall from their master's table." (Mt 15:22-27)

This Gentile outcast received from *YAHshua* the crumbs that had the same divine power as the full loaf given first to the children of Israel.

Cornelius and his family were the first Gentiles to receive salvation. He was *"a righteous and God-fearing man WELL SPOKEN OF BY THE ENTIRE NATION OF THE JEWS, ..."* (Ac 10:22). This Gentile reverenced the God of Israel, honored and obeyed His laws, and blessed so many Jews that he was the recipient of the Abrahamic covenant's ultimate promised blessing—"YAH's salvation," *YAHshua.* Although Messiah had ordered His disciples not to go to the Gentiles or Samaritans, He made another exception by exhorting the Samaritan woman at the well:

"You worship that which you do not know;

WE WORSHIP THAT WHICH WE KNOW;

for

SALVATION IS FROM THE JEWS.*"*

(Jn 4:22)

Chapter 32
"I Have Come in My Father's Name"

To reemphasize, because of the extreme caution of the ancient Jewish leadership, the most sacred name, *Yod Hey Vav Hey* or *YAHveh*, was thought as too holy for any man, especially Gentiles to utter. This resulted in the tradition which allowed only the high priest to speak the sacred name on the day of *Yom Kippur*. This was a blatant transgression of *YAHveh*'s command. *"THIS IS MY NAME FOREVER, AND THIS IS MY MEMORIAL-NAME TO ALL GENERATIONS"* (Ex 3:15).

YAHshua said: *"thus you INVALIDATED THE WORD OF YAHVEH FOR THE SAKE OF YOUR TRADITION. 'You hypocrites ... IN VAIN DO THEY WORSHIP ME, TEACHING AS THEIR DOCTRINES THE PRECEPTS OF MEN'"* (Mt 15:6-9).

Messiah despised the traditions of men which turned things upside down; He came to turn things right-side up by first declaring His Father's name which had been hidden by Jewish doctrine. *YAHshua* reiterated the words of His forerunner Moses and His forefather David saying: *"I WILL TELL OF THY NAME TO MY BRETHREN; ..."* (Ps 22:22 — cf. Heb 2:12).

The tendency of human nature is to guard fiercely our customs and religious practices. The self-righteous Jewish religious leaders vehemently guarded the status quo of their man-favored traditions and positions and seized the opportunity to accuse *YAHshua* of blasphemy.

YAHshua declared *YAHveh*'s name and claimed to be one with the Father. In several accounts this is dramatically illustrated. *YAHshua* said, *"Truly, truly, I say to you, before Abraham was born, I AM"* (Jn 8:58). Here He was expressing the eternality of His being and the oneness with the Father whose very name, *YAHveh*, comes from the root verb *HAYAH* which means "I am."

When *YAHshua* asserted His oneness with *YAHveh*, *" they* [Jewish religious leaders] *picked up stones to throw at Him; ..."* (Jn 8:59). Because He, a common carpenter and not a high priest, had declared the holy name, He was considered a blasphemer worthy of death.

On another occasion, He was questioned by the high priest: *"Are You the Messiah, the Son of the Blessed One?"* Notice how the high priest avoids using the name of *YAHveh*. *YAHshua* responds, *"I am ...' And tearing his clothes, the high priest said, '... You have heard the blasphemy; ...' And they all* [the religious leaders] *condemned Him to be deserving of death"* (Mk 14:61-64). For this very reason YAHshua said, *"I HAVE COME IN MY FATHER'S NAME* [YAHveh], *and you do not receive Me; if another shall come in his own name* [or a man-made name], *you will receive him"* (Jn 5:43).

The divine name is the embodiment of YAHveh's very divinity—His being. Messiah said, *"IF YOU HAD KNOWN ME* [and accepted My name and oneness with YAHveh], *YOU WOULD HAVE KNOWN MY FATHER ALSO;* ... [and would have accepted His name]" (Jn 14:7).

Messiah warned His disciples: *"But all these things they will do to you FOR MY NAME'S SAKE, because they do not know the One who sent Me. ... He who hates Me* [and My true name] *hates My Father* [and His true name] *also"* (Jn 15:21-23).

Like the Jewish religious leaders of old, many of the Gentile religious leaders of today will also reject the One who comes in His Father's true name. However, just as there were many humble believers in Israel who received YAHshua, so too there will be a humble remnant today who recognize the truth of the Father and the Son as fully embodied in the divine names.

YAHshua came to His Jewish brethren and revealed the name of YAHveh and manifested the *power in that name.* He was opposed by the vehement religious leaders and their traditions, which substituted YAHveh's *memorial-name* with common titles. His name is to be exalted and proclaimed as He again reveals it to this end-time generation to whom He says, *"Until now you have asked for nothing IN MY NAME; ask, and you will receive, that your joy may be made full"* (Jn 16:24).

Using YAHshua's true name brings glory to the name of YAHveh the Father. *"And WHATEVER YOU ASK IN MY NAME, that will I do, that the Father may be glorified in the Son* [and His name]. *If you ask Me anything in MY NAME, I will do it"* (Jn 14:13-14).

Messiah said, *"For where two or three have GATHERED IN MY NAME, there I AM in their midst"* (Mt 18:20). He was reemphasizing His Father's words to Israel through Moses: *"in every place where I cause MY NAME TO BE REMEMBERED, I will come to you and bless you"* (Ex 20:24).

But we must be aware of the shrewd Serpent's schemes; the Adversary of all men's souls strategized with great success to prevent the *name above all names* from going forth to bring infinite blessings to *YAHveh's* redeemed children. This is why *YAHshua* warned that the Enemy would come behind and sow tares of men's doctrines and distorted traditions in the harvest field where *YAHshua* had planted the good wheat of truth (see Mt 13:24-27).

Because we are at the close of the Gentile age, *YAHshua* is separating His wheat from the Enemy's tares. His seeds of truth and righteousness are being separated from the weed seeds of falsehood sown by the Enemy. *YAHveh*, the Great Harvester, will have for Himself a pure harvest to His eternal glory.

The Father and the Son Are One

YAHVEH (THE FATHER)
YAHSHUA (THE SON)

The reality of the Father *YAHveh* and the Son *YAHshua* being *One* is easily seen in the sharing of *YAHveh's* name with the Son's name. The remnant has been redeemed to be witnesses that *YAHveh* is the eternal holy God and Redeemer through *YAHshua* the Messiah.

The essence of the *ONENESS* of the Almighty is deeply ingrained in the heart of every child of Israel. Almost every Jew from ancient times until now has learned and recited this sacred Scripture-prayer and affirmation of their Jewish heritage called in Hebrew, *Shema*. Since the hiding of the *memorial-name*, Jews have recited the *Shema* with "Adonai" or "Lord." *"Shema Israel! Adonai Eloheinu, Adonai 'echad!"* — *"Hear O Israel! The LORD is our God, the LORD is one!"* (Dt 6:4). However this great declaration was originally recited by Moses and Israel in proclaiming *YAHveh's* memorial-name. *"Shema Israel! YAHveh Eloheinu, YAHveh 'echad."* — *"Hear, O Israel! YAHveh is our God, YAHveh is One!"*[1]

---

[1] The word "God," *Elohim*, is actually the *plural* of the *singular* form *El*; e.g., in Exodus 20:3 the word "gods" is *Elohim*. The Hebrew word for "one" *Continued on next page*

210

The Most High, the great I AM, emphasizes this eternal oneness through the prophet Isaiah:

*"For **I am** YAHveh your God, THE HOLY ONE OF ISRAEL, YOUR SAVIOR; ... I, even I, am YAHveh; and THERE IS NO SAVIOR BESIDES ME. It is I who have declared and saved and proclaimed, ... you are My witnesses,"* declares YAHveh, *"And **I am** God. Even from eternity **I am** He; ..."* (Isa 43:3, 11-13)[2]

*"Thus says YAHveh, the King of Israel and his Redeemer, YAHveh of hosts: '**I AM** THE FIRST AND **I AM** THE LAST, And there is no God besides Me."* (Isa 44:6)

Note the striking similarity of *YAHveh's* proclamation through Isaiah to *YAHshua's* words recorded by John in the book of Revelation: *"**I AM** THE FIRST AND THE LAST"* (Rev 1:17 and 22:13). By this proclamation, it is established beyond doubt, that *YAHveh* and *YAHshua* are ONE.

The undermining of this vital truth is magnified as we look at two important foundational New Testament Scriptures. The most beloved confession of faith for those who seek salvation has undergone a noteworthy change by replacing *YAHveh's* name with the Greek translation of the title "Lord" (*kyrios*). Over the centuries of Gentile Christianity, it has been rendered, *"That if you confess with your mouth, 'Jesus is Lord,' and believe in your heart that God raised him from the dead, you will be saved"* (Ro 10:9 NIV). In truth, however, the original was the confession that **"YAHshua is YAHveh."**

An equally well-known Scripture that has undergone the same change reads: *"no one can say, 'Jesus is Lord,' except by the Holy Spirit"* (1Co 12:3 NIV[3]). In the original, "Jesus is Lord" again

---

Continued from previous page   is `echad. The word literally means "united" or "unity." This word does not necessarily mean singular, but is also used to express a compound unity such as in Genesis 2:24, where Moses wrote regarding Adam and Eve becoming "one flesh." Thus, "God," in the *Shema*, is spoken of as a *compound unity* or as *unity of Being*—the "Oneness" of "God" shown in His Name, *YAHveh.*

[2] Note *HAYAH*, the Hebrew root verb for **I AM**, is the root of the divine name **YAH**veh.

[3] *The NIV Study Bible* (Grand Rapids: The Zondervan Corporation, 1985), p. 1750. Footnote for 1Co 12:3: "... *Jesus is Lord* ... The Greek word for 'Lord' here is used in the Greek translation of the OT (the Septuagint) to translate the Hebrew name *Yahweh* ('the LORD')."

reads "*YAHshua* is *YAHveh.*" The words of Scripture are crystal clear; it is the Holy Spirit Who enables and compels both Gentiles and Jews alike to proclaim that *YAHshua* is *YAHveh* and they are One.

One of the Serpent's main strategies to keep Jews from recognizing their Messiah was to break apart the Father and the Son into two separate names as incorrectly rendered in the Greek. The restoration of the ONENESS of the Father and Son's true name thwarts this anti-Semitic device. By removing this stumbling block it becomes more apparent to the Jews that indeed *their God* and *their Messiah* are one. The righteous remnant proclaims with one heart and voice to Israel that *YAHveh* their God *IS ONE* with *YAHshua*, their Messiah.

The name "Jesus" was never heard by the Messiah, His disciples, nor the Jews or Gentiles of His day. The Greek rendering of the Savior's true name has its origins with Gentile men and a pagan-rooted language. It has become a dreaded and cursed name to the Jews, predominantly because of Gentile attitudes and resulting historical anti-Jewish atrocities performed in the "name of Jesus."

That pseudo-name distorts the essence of ONENESS of the Mighty One of Israel and His Son, the Messiah, making it a repulsion to Jews. With this in mind, let us remember the biblical mandate to the Gentiles to lovingly and mercifully provoke the Jews to worship *YAHveh* their God through *YAHshua* their Messiah. "*You* [Gentiles] *who bring good tidings to Zion, go up on a high mountain. … LIFT UP YOUR VOICE WITH A SHOUT, LIFT IT UP, DO NOT BE AFRAID; say to the towns of Judah* [and to all Jews], '*HERE IS YOUR GOD* [YAHveh]!'" (Isa 40:9 NIV — emphasis added).

The Most Important ONE

One of the scribes … asked YAHshua, "What commandment is the foremost of all?" YAHshua answered [quoting the sacred *Shema*], "*The foremost is, 'HEAR, O*

ISRAEL; YAHVEH OUR GOD IS ONE LORD [Master]; *AND YOU SHALL LOVE YAHVEH YOUR GOD WITH ALL YOUR HEART, AND WITH ALL YOUR SOUL, AND WITH ALL YOUR MIND, AND WITH ALL YOUR STRENGTH.' "The second is this, 'YOU SHALL LOVE YOUR NEIGHBOR AS YOURSELF.' There is no other commandment greater than these."* (Mk 12:28-31)

By reciting the sacred *Shema*, *YAHshua* was reminding Israel of the oneness of her God with whom *He is One*. Messiah was also referring to Moses' words in Deuteronomy, *"YAHveh your God will* CIRCUMCISE YOUR HEART *and the heart of your descendants,* TO LOVE YAHVEH YOUR GOD WITH ALL YOUR HEART AND WITH ALL YOUR SOUL, IN ORDER THAT YOU MAY LIVE*"* (Dt 30:6).

There are those who believe that because of the grace of the New Testament, the believer is no longer subject to the Law. Messiah Himself said that the Law could be summarized and reduced to the essence of these two most vital commandments.

The Son of the Most High implies that all of *YAHveh's* commandments are naturally upheld by a remnant circumcised in heart, who love *YAHveh* with every fiber of their being. His wholehearted disciples do not swerve to the right or left of their heavenly Father's plumb line of truth. With reverential awe this remnant will proclaim with the psalmist:

I have chosen the faithful way; I have placed Thine ordinances before me. I cleave to Thy testimonies; O YAHveh, do not put me to shame! I shall run the way of Thy commandments, For Thou wilt enlarge my heart. Teach me, O YAHveh, the way of Thy statutes, And I shall observe it to the end. (Ps 119:30-33)

The righteous remnant does not hesitate to purify themselves *"from all defilement of flesh and spirit,* PERFECTING HOLINESS IN THE FEAR OF YAHVEH*"* (2Co 7:1). They walk in reverential fear and humble awe of His holiness; they are faithful disciples who have counted the cost and are worthy to be called priests *Holy to YAHveh.*

In obedience to His commandments, Messiah's disciples will love their neighbors as themselves. With tender hearts, the circumcised remnant will also grieve with *YAHshua* over the lack of love demonstrated throughout Christian history towards His brethren. As this small but holy group understands the oneness of *YAHveh* with *YAHshua*, they will attempt to demolish every argument and tradition obscuring the importance of the *name above all names.* They will testify in the words of John:

> *Beloved, if our heart does not condemn us, we have confidence before YAHveh, and whatever we ask we receive from Him, because we keep His commandments and do the things that are pleasing in His sight. AND THIS IS HIS COMMANDMENT, THAT WE BELIEVE IN THE NAME OF HIS SON, YAHSHUA MESSIAH, AND LOVE ONE ANOTHER, ... the one who keeps His commandments abides in Him, and He in him.* ... (1Jn 3:21-24)

> *For this is the love of YAHveh, THAT WE KEEP HIS COMMANDMENTS; AND HIS COMMANDMENTS ARE NOT BURDENSOME."* (1Jn 5:3)

The Shout of the Living Stones

When the Son of David made his triumphal entry into Jerusalem,

> *... the whole multitude of the disciples began to praise YAHveh joyfully with a loud voice ... saying, "BLESSED IS THE KING WHO COMES IN THE NAME OF YAHVEH; ..."* ... *some of the Pharisees in the multitude said to Him, "Teacher* [Rabbi], *rebuke Your disciples* [the arrogant religious leaders did not want this crowd calling on the ineffable name of the Almighty]." *And He answered and said, "I tell you if these become silent, THE STONES WILL CRY OUT!"* (Lk 19:37-40)

There always will be arrogant spiritual leaders and misdirected religious masses who would like to silence the mouths of those who proclaim His true and holy name. Regardless of the persecution, the *redeemed living stones*—the "David generation"—will cry out, *"Hosanna! BLESSED IS HE* [YAHshua] *WHO COMES IN THE NAME OF YAHVEH, even the King of Israel"* (Jn 12:13). They will glorify His name; the living stones will cry out; they will praise His holy name. *They will not be silent!*

Even in the midst of the "Saul generation's" pharisaical pride and flying spears, the *living stones* will be as *YAHshua,* the Son of David, before His fatal piercing at Calvary.

> *"Now My soul has become troubled;*
>
> *and what shall I say,*

214

'Father, save Me from this hour'?
But for this purpose I came to this hour.
Father, GLORIFY THY NAME."
There came therefore a voice out of heaven:
"I HAVE BOTH GLORIFIED IT,
AND WILL GLORIFY IT AGAIN."

(Jn 12:27-28)

Chapter 33

The Name above All Names

The disciples asked the Master, *"Teach us to pray"* (Lk 11:1). In response, *YAHshua* instructed them: *"Pray, then, in this way: 'Our Father who art in heaven, HALLOWED BE THY NAME'"* (Mt 6:9 — cf. Lk 11:2). *YAHshua* was teaching that His Father's name was to be kept distinctly separate and revered above all other names and titles. The psalmist declares, *"you have EXALTED ABOVE ALL THINGS YOUR NAME AND YOUR WORD"* (Ps 138:2 NIV — emphasis added).

Wherever the holy Scriptures have been accepted throughout the world, the universal proclamation *"HalleluYAH!"* (praise be to *YAHveh*) has been accepted and integrated into that national dialect. Therefore, His name and His Word have been exalted in spite of Satan's schemes. As hard as the crafty Serpent tries to obliterate His name and the glory due it, he did not AND WILL NOT totally succeed—*HALLELU-YAH(veh)*!

Power and Protection in His Name

When Messiah prayed for His beloved disciples and those who would follow, He said, *"I MANIFESTED THY NAME to the men whom Thou gavest Me out of the world; ... and THEY HAVE KEPT THY WORD"* (Jn 17:6). The psalmist David wrote, *"May YAHveh answer you in the day of trouble! May the NAME of the God of Jacob set you securely on high!"* (Ps 20:1) and again, *"Spread your PROTECTION over them, that those WHO LOVE YOUR NAME may rejoice in you"* (Ps 5:11 NIV — emphasis added). And Solomon added, *"THE NAME OF YAHVEH is a strong tower; The righteous runs into it and is safe"* (Pr 18:10).

Messiah understood the power of protection in His Father's name; when He prayed concerning His beloved disciples, He said, *"Holy Father, PROTECT THEM BY THE POWER OF YOUR NAME—THE NAME YOU GAVE ME—so that they may be one as we are one. While I was with them, I PROTECTED THEM AND KEPT THEM SAFE BY THAT NAME YOU GAVE ME ..."* (Jn 17:11-12 NIV — emphasis added). *YAHshua* continued, *"Father, I desire that they also, whom Thou hast given Me, ... behold My glory, which Thou hast given Me; ..."* (Jn 17:24).

When Moses asked to see the Almighty's glory, *YAHveh*

proclaimed His name two times. Could these two proclamations of His glorious name be symbolic? The first proclamation was of His deliverance of Israel through Moses; the second was of His ultimate deliverance of both Jews and Gentiles through *YAHshua*, the One who comes in His name. His *name* and His *glory* are inseparably ONE, just as *YAHveh* and *YAHshua* are inseparably one.

YAHshua ended His High Priestly Prayer in this manner: *"O righteous Father, ... I HAVE MADE THY NAME KNOWN to them, and WILL MAKE IT KNOWN; that the love wherewith Thou didst love Me may be in them, and I in them"* (Jn 17:25-26). *YAHshua's* prayer is still being answered as He continues to reveal the Father's *memorial-name* to a remnant He is preparing to bear it with honor.

The Father and the Son grieve over the loss of His holy *memorial-name*. The Holy Spirit also laments over the substituting of the divine name with common titles shared with other deities and objects of worship. His holy name must be exalted in order for His glory to pour out upon individual lives and flow as a river of life upon the earth. *YAHveh* says, *"I AM YAHVEH; THAT IS MY NAME; I WILL NOT GIVE MY GLORY TO ANOTHER* [or another name], ..." (Isa 42:8).

Because of the Serpent's shifty strategies working in history through the doctrines of Jewish and Gentile men, His name has not been exalted as the *name above all names*. It has been hidden, suppressed and substituted rather than proclaimed and glorified as He sovereignly ordained. *"For nothing is hidden that shall not become evident, nor anything secret that shall not be known and come to light. Therefore take care how you listen; ..."* (Lk 8:17-18).

"The Falling and Rising of Many"

YAHshua was cruelly opposed by the religious segments in Israel; likewise, He will be opposed again as He comes to proclaim His Father's name, especially to the religious masses within Gentile Christendom.

The pendulum always swings; *YAHshua's* revealing the Father's name to Israel and her rejection of His name directly preceded the beginning of salvation in the name of *YAHshua* going to the Gentiles. As this Gentile age terminates, the *Ruach HaKodesh* is again declaring the Father's and the Son's holy names. As in Messiah's day, the traditionally religious multitudes will reject the One who comes in His Father's *memorial-name*.

Perhaps this rejection by Christendom will precede the prophesied calling out by the Jews. *"BLESSED IS HE [YAHshua] WHO COMES IN THE NAME OF YAHVEH; ..."* (Mt 21:9)[1]

YAHshua's initial appearance in His Father's name caused *"the falling and rising of many in Israel, ..."* (Lk 2:34 NIV). Now, in the truth of His holy name, He is destined *"for the falling and rising of many"* in Christendom. As Paul said, *"So, if you think your are standing firm, be careful that you don't fall!"* (1Co 10:12 NIV).

True Light in the True Name

YAHshua, *"... the true light which, coming into the world, enlightens every man ... He came to His own, ..."* (Jn 1:9-11); and said, *"I HAVE COME IN MY FATHER'S NAME, AND YOU DO NOT RECEIVE ME; ..."* (Jn 5:43); and *"He who does not honor the Son [and His name] does not honor the Father [and His name] ..."* (Jn 5:23); *"But as many as received Him, to them He gave the right to become children of YAHveh, even to those who BELIEVE IN HIS NAME ..."* (Jn 1:12). *"... that* repentance for forgiveness of sins would be *PROCLAIMED IN HIS NAME* to all the nations, beginning from Jerusalem." (LK 24:47)

To the disciples who believed in His name, He gave the Great Commission: *"Go therefore and make disciples of all nations, baptizing* [immersing[2]] *them IN THE NAME of the Father [YAHveh] and the Son [YAHshua] and the Holy Spirit [Ruach HaKodesh], TEACHING THEM TO OBSERVE ALL THAT I COMMANDED YOU; and lo, I am with you always, even to the end of the age"* (Mt 28:19-20).

This small band of close followers were to be ambassadors of reconciliation between sinful man and *YAHveh*, the holy God.

---

[1] *"Blessed is He who comes in the name of YAHveh"* in Hebrew is *"Ba-rukh ha-ba ba-shem YAHveh."*

[2] *Immersing*, from "immersion" stemming from John (*YAHchanan*) the Baptist originally called "the Immerser." "But John's washing was different enough that he came to be called 'the immerser,' 'the baptizer.' ... a unique seal that marked those who repented as belonging to the renewed people of God, prepared for God's intervention in the world." *Jesus and His Times* (Pleasantville, NY: The Reader Digest Association, Inc., 1987), p. 200.

As faithful disciples they were to continue with *YAHshua's* work of proclaiming His Father's name to others who would, in turn, worship *YAHveh* and glorify His *memorial-name.*

As we approach the very end of the age, He continues to proclaim His Father's name. His Spirit asks you to receive the *true light* that comes in His *true name.* Will you deny His name, His power, and the fullness of the light of His countenance because you prefer to walk in the dim light of the doctrines of men that have eclipsed *YAHshua?*

> *How blessed are the people that know the joyful sound! O*
> *YAHveh, they walk in the light of Thy countenance. IN THY*
> NAME THEY REJOICE ALL THE DAY, *And by Thy righteousness*
> *they are exalted.* (Ps 89:15-16)

Praise be to *YAHveh* who gives light to those who have walked in the dim light of men's doctrines and traditions. He gives us a choice; as prophesied, the spirit of Elijah (*EliYAHu*) is come asking the professing religious masses, "HOW LONG WILL YOU HESITATE BETWEEN TWO OPINIONS?" (1Ki 18:21).

Since *YAHveh* **IS** the Father and *YAHshua* **IS** the Son, and their holy names **ARE** from eternity's thresholds, *spoken* by the mouth of the Almighty, *proclaimed* by the angel Gabriel, and *declared* by the Messiah, then why not worship Him—*THE NAME ABOVE ALL NAMES*—in spirit *and* truth?—*HALLELU-YAH(veh)!*

> *Let those who love Thy salvation*
>
> *say continually,*
>
> "YAHVEH BE MAGNIFIED!"
>
> (Ps 40:16)

> *... your name and renown*
>
> *are the desire of our hearts.*
>
> ... YOUR NAME ALONE
>
> DO WE HONOR.
>
> (Isa 26:8, 13 NIV)

Chapter 34
The Apostle to the Jews

The Apostle Peter (*Kefa*) was sent to the Jews to proclaim *YAHveh's* name and salvation to Israel through *YAHshua* Messiah. On the day of *Shavuout* (Pentecost), all Jews, including Gentile converts to Judaism, were gathered in Jerusalem. Peter stood up with the eleven Jewish disciples and addressed his fellow Israelites. He explained to their amazement the outpouring of the *Ruach HaKodesh*, resulting in their speaking in other tongues, was the partial fulfillment of the prophecy of Joel. He ends by proclaiming the prophet's words: *"AND IT SHALL BE, THAT EVERYONE WHO CALLS ON THE NAME OF YAHVEH SHALL BE SAVED"* (Ac 2:21).[1]

As the apostle continued, many Jews were *"pierced to the heart"* (circumcised) and asked Peter and the other Jewish apostles, *"Brethren, what shall we do?" And Peter said to them, "REPENT, and let each of you be BAPTIZED* [immersed[2]] *IN THE NAME OF YAHSHUA Messiah for the forgiveness of your sins, ..."* (Ac 2:37-38). Peter spoke and ministered only in the name of *YAHshua*.

The Greek name for the Savior had not yet been rendered or spoken at that time. There are many dramatic accounts of miracles, signs, and wonders which testified then and throughout eternity of the *power in the name of YAHshua*. Peter spoke to the amazed Jewish crowds, *"The God of Abraham, Isaac, and Jacob, the God of our fathers, has glorified His servant YAHshua, ..."* (Ac 3:13).

---

[1] The Apostle Peter, in quoting Joel 2:32, was using *YAHveh's* name. Most New Testament translators have changed Peter's quote of Joel's from "LORD" [*YAHveh*] to "Lord," thereby obscuring the obvious connection to the *memorial-name*.

[2] The word *baptism* is from the Greek root word, *baptizo* (βαπτίζω). This Greek term is used for the Hebrew-rooted word meaning "purification" and "cleansing"—*immerse* or *immersion*. "βαπτίζω — ... *dip, immerse, ... wash ...* of Jewish ritual washings ... The Law of Purification ..." William F. Arndt and F. Wilbur Gingrich, *A Greek-English Lexicon of the New Testament and Other Early Christian Literature* (Chicago: The University of Chicago Press, 1957), s. v., "βαπτίζω.] It is the author's desire to emphasize the original Hebraic root of this Hellinized term, not to suggest a particular or exclusive *mode* of the sacrament of baptism about which there is variance among Christian groups.

"Now Peter and John were going up to the temple at the ninth hour, the hour of prayer. And a certain man who had been lame from his mother's womb was being carried along, whom they used to set down every day at the gate of the temple ... in order to beg alms ..." (Ac 3:1-2)

This man who was begging for money received a greater blessing through the Jewish apostle who said, *"IN THE NAME OF YAHSHUA MESSIAH the Nazarene—walk!"* (Ac 3:6). Peter then addressed the astonished Jews who had witnessed this miracle: *"And on the basis OF FAITH IN HIS NAME, IT IS THE NAME OF YAHSHUA which has strengthened this man ..."* (Ac 3:16).

Peter reminded them of Moses' words which foretold of a future prophet; he was pointing to the coming Messiah. *"YAHVEH GOD SHALL RAISE UP FOR YOU A PROPHET LIKE ME FROM YOUR BRETHREN; TO HIM YOU SHALL GIVE HEED IN EVERYTHING HE SAYS TO YOU"* (Ac 3:22).

Peter is quoting directly *YAHveh's* words of warning from Deuteronomy: *"If anyone does not listen to my words that the prophet SPEAKS IN MY NAME, I myself will call him to account"* (Dt 18:19 NIV — emphasis added). The apostle was emphasizing that this prophet, spoken of by Moses, was indeed *YAHshua* who came and spoke in *YAHveh's* name.

The day after the cripple was healed, the Jewish rulers and elders met in Jerusalem with the high priest,

And when they had placed them [Peter and John] *in the center, they began to inquire, "By what power, or in what name have you done this?" Then Peter, filled with the Holy Spirit, said to them, "... let it be made known to all of you, and to all the people of Israel, that by the NAME OF YAHSHUA MESSIAH THE NAZARENE, ... this man stands here before you in good health. ... And there is salvation in no one else;* for THERE IS NO OTHER NAME *under heaven that has been* GIVEN AMONG MEN, *by which we must be saved."* (Ac 4:7-12)

This statement was spoken to his Jewish brethren long before the Greek rendering of *YAHshua's* name. There have been multitudes who have been redeemed in the only name they knew which was Jesus Christ. *YAHveh*, the merciful One, extends His grace to such as this; He is the searcher of men's hearts. At issue now, however, is *how do we respond once He has revealed His holy, awesome, memorial-name to our hearts?*

The disciples did not refrain from proclaiming the name of *YAHshua* regardless of men's threats. The self-righteous religious leaders, with unrighteous indignation, conferred with each other and decided, *"in order that it may not spread any further among the people, let us warn them to speak no more to any man IN THIS NAME." ... they commanded them not to speak or teach at all in the NAME OF YAHSHUA"* (Ac 4:17-18).

The cripple rejoiced and the self-righteous raged. May YAHveh almighty who blesses those who honor His name cause you to rejoice in His and His Son's true names.

In the Name of *YAHshua*

Peter and the disciples continued to pray, *"And now, YAHveh, take note of their threats, and grant that Thy bond-servants may speak Thy word with all confidence, while Thou dost extend Thy hand to heal, and signs and wonders take place through THE NAME OF THY HOLY SERVANT YAHSHUA"* (Ac 4:29-30). After they prayed and agreed they would boldly proclaim and minister in the name of YAHshua regardless of the persecution, *"the place where they had gathered together was shaken, and they were all filled with the Holy Spirit, and began to speak the word of YAHveh with boldness"* (Ac 4:31).

Through the power of the *Ruach HaKodesh*, in the name of YAHshua Messiah, *"at the hands of the apostles many signs and wonders were taking place among the people; ..."* (Ac 5:12). *"But the high priest rose up, along with all his associates ... and they were filled with jealousy* [typical mentality of the 'Saul generation'] *..."* (Ac 5:17).

They brought in the apostles to be questioned by the high priest. *"We gave you STRICT ORDERS NOT TO CONTINUE TEACHING IN THIS NAME, ..."* But Peter and the apostles answered and said, *"WE MUST OBEY YAHVEH RATHER THAN MEN* [truly the mentality of the 'David generation']*"* (Ac 5:28-29).

These Jewish men, servants to Messiah, remembered the admonition from *YAHshua*:

"... that slave who KNEW HIS MASTER'S WILL and did not get ready or ACT IN ACCORD WITH HIS WILL, shall receive many lashes, but the one who did not know it, and committed deeds worthy of flogging, will receive but few. AND FROM EVERYONE WHO HAS BEEN GIVEN MUCH SHALL MUCH BE REQUIRED; and to whom they entrusted much, of him they will ask all the more." (Lk 12:47-48)

These men had been privileged and entrusted to bear the name of *YAHveh* the Father through *YAHshua* their Master. Peter had already felt the agonizing pain and despair of denying Him. With boldness and courage they would proclaim and minister in the *name above all names* regardless of the hostility and threats flung through self-righteous men.

The murderous fury of the religious leaders was halted by a Pharisee named Gamaliel. In wisdom he addressed them:

"Men of Israel, take care what you purpose to do with these men. ... stay away from these men and let them alone, FOR IF THIS PLAN OR ACTION SHOULD BE OF MEN, IT WILL BE OVERTHROWN; but if it is of God, you will not be able to overthrow them; or else you may even be found FIGHTING AGAINST GOD." (Ac 5:35, 38-39)

Gamaliel, being a rabbi, may have been reflecting on *YAHveh's* words of warning through Jeremiah.

Therefore thus says YAHveh concerning the men ... who seek your life, saying, "DO NOT PROPHESY IN THE NAME OF YAHVEH, that you might not die at our hand"; therefore, thus says YAHveh of hosts, "Behold, I am about to punish them! ..." (Jer 11:21-22)

"And they took his advice; and after calling the apostles in, they flogged them and. ORDERED THEM TO SPEAK NO MORE IN THE NAME OF YAHSHUA, and then released them" (Ac 5:40). — *"So they went on their way from the presence of the Council, REJOICING THAT THEY HAD BEEN CONSIDERED WORTHY TO SUFFER SHAME FOR HIS NAME"* (Ac 5:41). — *"For they went out FOR THE SAKE OF THE NAME ..."* (3Jn v. 7).

The wisdom of Gamaliel continues to speak to those who oppose the use of His divine name. *"for if this plan or action should be of men, it will be overthrown; BUT IF IT IS OF YAHVEH, YOU WILL NOT BE ABLE TO OVERTHROW THEM;* [the 'David generation' of these last days]; *OR ELSE YOU MAY EVEN BE FOUND FIGHTING AGAINST GOD"* (Ac 5:38-39).

Upon their release, Peter and John went to their brethren to relay all that had transpired with the religious leaders. When they heard this report,

... they lifted their voices to YAHveh with one accord and said, "O YAHVEH, IT IS THOU ... who by the Holy Spirit, through the mouth of our father David Thy servant, didst say, 'WHY DID THE GENTILES RAGE, AND THE PEOPLES

DEVISE FUTILE THINGS? THE KINGS OF THE EARTH ... AND THE RULERS WERE GATHERED TOGETHER AGAINST YAHVEH, AND AGAINST HIS MESSIAH.'" (Ac 4:24-26)

The Adversary hates *YAHveh's* name, His people, and His eternal purposes for Israel. His devious strategies employed through the proud and traditionally religious, have always caused a furious opposition and vehement rejection of the *name above all names.*

The pendulum is swinging from the religious system in Messiah's day to the religious systems of our day. As *YAHshua's* name is proclaimed at the close of this age, many will warn the "David generation" not to speak or teach in His true name.

Over the many centuries of Christianity, multitudes have received salvation through a pure faith and have been "born again" in the only name they knew which was Jesus Christ. *If you embraced with a humble heart the truth that came through the name of Jesus, what would keep your heart from embracing the full light and truth of YAHveh's and YAHshua's memorial-names, and the holy Hebrew root of our faith?*

Through Isaiah the prophet and King David come these challenging words:

> *WHO IS AMONG YOU THAT FEARS YAHVEH,*
>
> *THAT OBEYS THE VOICE OF HIS SERVANT?*
>
> *THAT WALKS IN DARKNESS, AND HAS NO LIGHT?*
>
> *LET HIM TRUST IN THE NAME OF YAHVEH*
>
> *and rely on his God.*
>
> (Isa 50:10)

> *LET THOSE ALSO WHO LOVE YOUR NAME*
>
> *BE JOYFUL IN YOU.*
>
> (Ps 5:11 NKJV — emphasis added)

Chapter 35

First Century Dilemma

Could a Gentile receive salvation from the Jewish Messiah? This issue was truly a dilemma for the thousands of Jews who first believed in *YAHshua* the Messiah. The issue of the Gentiles had been clearly spelled out by *YAHveh* through the Old Testament mandates; the Jews, *YAHveh's* chosen people, could not have fellowship with a Gentile. The obedience to the Holy One on this issue was vital in keeping Israel pure and undefiled by pagan contact.

Through the sacrificial death of *YAHshua*, His blood opened the door for Gentiles to be joined with the Jews. This reality was made clear to Peter through a vision. *YAHveh's* voice clarified the meaning of this vision; He said, "WHAT YAHVEH HAS CLEANSED NO LONGER CONSIDER UNHOLY" (Ac 10:15). Upon hearing this, Peter was released to bring salvation to the first "*righteous and God-fearing man* [Gentile, Cornelius], ... *who* [was] *respected by all the Jewish people*" (Ac 10:22 NIV — emphasis added).

In the Hebrew apostle's great joy over this revelation from above, he exclaimed,

"*I most certainly understand now that YAHVEH IS NOT ONE TO SHOW PARTIALITY, but in every nation the man who FEARS HIM and DOES WHAT IS RIGHT, is welcome to Him. ... Of Him all the prophets bear witness that THROUGH HIS NAME EVERYONE WHO BELIEVES IN HIM RECEIVES FORGIVENESS OF SINS.*" (Ac 10:34-35, 43)

The Humble Will Call on His Name

At a council meeting in Jerusalem, the Jewish apostles and elders met to consider the question of Gentiles coming to salvation. After much discussion, Peter addressed them:

"*Brethren, you know that in the early days YAHveh made a choice among you, that by my mouth the Gentiles should hear the word of the gospel and believe. AND YAHVEH, WHO KNOWS THE HEART, BORE WITNESS TO THEM, GIVING THEM THE HOLY SPIRIT, JUST AS HE ALSO DID TO US; ...*" (Ac 15:7-8)

*"Simon had related how YAHveh first concerned Himself about taking from AMONG THE GENTILES A PEOPLE FOR HIS NAME. And with this the words of the Prophets agree, ... 'AFTER THESE THINGS I WILL RETURN, AND I WILL REBUILD THE TABERNACLE OF DAVID WHICH HAS FALLEN, AND I WILL REBUILD ITS RUINS, AND I WILL RESTORE IT, IN ORDER THAT THE REST OF MANKIND MAY SEEK YAHVEH, **AND ALL THE GENTILES WHO ARE CALLED BY MY NAME**,' SAYS YAHVEH, WHO MAKES THESE THINGS KNOWN FROM OF OLD."* (Ac 15:14-18)[1]

The Mighty One has a way of humbling all men. *To call on the name of YAHveh the Father through YAHshua the Son, was humbling for both Jews and Gentiles.* For the Jews, it was against their man-made tradition for any man to utter the most holy name. For the Gentiles, it meant humbly walking through anti-Semitic barriers to call upon a Jewish Messiah with a very Hebrew name.

The Holy One does not show partiality. He is calling all men everywhere to repentance, to receive forgiveness of sins through the blood and in the name of *YAHshua* the Messiah. A remnant of both Jews and Gentiles, the humble "David generation," will cry out in unison with King David's words,

"MAKE ME KNOW THY WAYS, O YAHVEH; Teach me Thy paths. LEAD ME IN THY TRUTH AND TEACH ME, For Thou art the God of my salvation; ... He leads the humble in justice, And He teaches the humble His way. FOR THY NAME'S SAKE, O YAHveh, Pardon my iniquity [and the sin of the forefathers of my religion], for it is great." (Ps 25:4-5, 9, 11)

Again His words speak to the "Saul generation"—both those who are Jews and those who are Gentiles—who justify man's ways at the expense of *YAHveh's* holy decrees. *"Has YAHveh as much delight in burnt offerings and sacrifices* [and your religious traditions, rituals, and doctrines] *As in OBEYING THE VOICE OF YAHVEH? BEHOLD, TO OBEY IS BETTER THAN SACRIFICE, ..."* (1Sa 15:22).

---

[1] Cf. Amos 9:12: "... 'And all the Gentiles are called by My name,' says *YAHveh* [literal translation] who does this thing." Peter is quoting Amos who prophesied this event years before Messiah's birth.

In the words of *YAHshua*, the Son of David, *"IF YOU LOVE ME YOU WILL KEEP MY COMMANDMENTS"* (Jn 14:15). *"For whoever does the will of My Father who is in heaven, he is My brother and sister and mother"* (Mt 12:50).

The humble and righteous "David generation" will join the psalmist in overflowing gratitude.

> *"What shall I render to YAHveh*
>
> *For all His benefits toward me?"*
>
> *I shall lift up the cup of salvation* [through *YAHshua*],
>
> *And CALL UPON THE NAME OF YAHVEH. ...*
>
> *To Thee I shall offer a sacrifice of thanksgiving,*
>
> *And CALL UPON THE NAME OF YAHVEH."*

(Ps 116:12-13, 17)

Chapter 36
The Apostle to the Gentiles

Paul was the great apostle to the Gentiles. Out of respect for this very Jewish man and his love and reverence for his Hebrew roots, this author will employ the use of his original Hebrew name, *Sha'ul*. *Sha'ul* was the embodiment of self-righteousness and religious pride that often accompanies those whose lives have been totally committed to a religious system altered by tradition. He obsessively persecuted messianic believers whose faith in *YAHshua* seemed contrary to the doctrines he wholeheartedly studied and embraced since his youth.

Sha'ul, a Pharisee and a son of Pharisees (Ac 23:6), was on a path of destruction as he pompously marched down the Damascus road. This zealous Jew was consumed with indignation and Satan's fury against his brethren who dared to call upon the name of *YAHveh* through *YAHshua* Messiah.

This headstrong but learned Hebrew was obsessed with protecting the purity of the traditional Judaism of his day. He was convinced persecution of the messianic Jews was in defense of "God's" (*Elohim's*) righteousness. Scales covered the eyes of *Sha'ul* which kept him from beholding *YAHshua*, the Messiah of Israel.

In grace and mercy from the very One he persecuted, he was suddenly stopped in his tracks from continuing his fight against *YAHshua*. A blinding light from heaven forced this zealous Pharisee to bow before the Mighty One; he fell to the ground and *"heard a voice saying ... in the HEBREW DIALECT, 'Sha'ul, Sha'ul, why are you persecuting Me?'... And I [Sha'ul] said, 'Who art Thou, Lord [Master]?' And Messiah answered, 'I AM YAHSHUA, whom you are persecuting'"* (Ac 26:14-15).

Sha'ul's physical eyes were blinded through this experience in order that his spiritual eyes would be opened. For three days he sat in darkness as the Holy Spirit prepared him for his commissioning. *YAHshua* sent a man named Annanias to him: *"Go, for he is a chosen instrument of Mine, to BEAR MY NAME before the Gentiles and kings* [and religious leaders] *and the sons of Israel; for I will show him how much HE MUST SUFFER FOR MY NAME'S SAKE"* (Ac 9:15-16). The humbled Pharisee was

"... filled with the Holy Spirit." And immediately there fell from his eyes something like scales, and he regained his

228

sight, and he arose and was baptized [immersed]; ... *immediately he began to proclaim YAHshua in the synagogues, saying, "HE IS THE SON OF YAHVEH." And all those hearing him continued to be amazed, and were saying, "Is this not he who in Jerusalem destroyed those WHO CALLED ON THIS NAME, ... when he had come to Jerusalem, ... he had spoken out boldly IN THE NAME OF YAHSHUA."* (Ac 9:17- 27)

Sha'ul, the persecutor of those who called on this name, became the anointed apostle to carry *YAHshua's* name to the Gentiles. But although he was the appointed ambassador to the Gentiles, *Sha'ul* never forsook *YAHveh's* directive to take the Good News *"to the Jews first."* Every town he entered he went into the Jewish synagogue (see Ac 13:5, 14; 14:1; 18:4; 18:19). Only when the door was closed by the Jews of the town would he then go to the Gentiles.

It should also be noted that *Sha'ul* never ceased in his passionate reverence for his ancient Hebrew roots or weakened in his faithful obedience to the *Torah* (the Law). On the contrary, like all Jews who come to faith in *YAHshua*, the apostle became *completed* as a redeemed righteous Jew and *not converted from* Judaism. *It has been a continual ploy of the Adversary to imply that faith in Messiah necessitates the abandoning of one's Jewish identity* and forsaking *YAHveh's* biblical mandates to His Jewish people.

Many thousands of Jews believed in the name *YAHshua*, yet were concerned about false reports in regards to *Sha'ul's* ministry.

"You see, brother [Sha'ul], *how many THOUSANDS there are AMONG THE JEWS of those who have BELIEVED, and they are ALL ZEALOUS FOR THE LAW* [Torah]; *and they have been told about you, that you are teaching all the Jews who are among the Gentiles to forsake Moses, telling them not to circumcise their children nor to walk according to the customs."* (Ac 21:20-21)

A few of the elders at Jerusalem advised *Sha'ul* to take a Nazarite vow along with four other men. *Sha'ul* was to pay the expenses for all five of them to have their heads shaved to fulfill this biblical vow. In doing so the brothers told the apostle, *"all will know that there is nothing to the things which they have been told about you, but that you yourself also walk orderly, keeping the Law* [Torah]*"* (Ac 21:24). *Sha'ul* readily complied in order to prove to the Jews that *neither he nor they should forsake their Jewish roots, the Torah, or their biblically ordained customs.*

Even after this purification and Nazarite vow, Satan stirred up more lies. A crowd shouted, *"Men of Israel, come to our aid! THIS IS THE MAN WHO PREACHES TO ALL MEN EVERYWHERE AGAINST OUR PEOPLE, AND THE LAW, AND THIS PLACE; and besides he has even brought Greeks into the temple and has defiled this holy place"* (Ac 21:28). This was a lie of the Enemy to keep the Jews from their Messiah. There are many quotes of this great apostle which Satan has twisted through *insidious attempts to misrepresent Sha'ul as an anti-Semitic propagator of an anti-Semitic gospel.* What a grief this would be to the one who would forfeit his own salvation in order to save his Jewish brethren (Ro 9:3).

Unfortunately these lies have continued throughout New Testament history causing both Jews and Gentiles to distort and misunderstand this great apostle by stripping him of his Jewish heart and Hebrew identity. Toward the end of *Sha'ul's* ministry, as he was bidding farewell to the Ephesians, he said:

"... I testify to you this day, that I am innocent of the blood of all men. For I DID NOT SHRINK FROM DECLARING TO YOU THE WHOLE PURPOSE OF YAHVEH [including mandates to Gentiles regarding the Jews]. *... I know that after my departure savage wolves will come in among you, not sparing the flock; and FROM AMONG YOUR OWN SELVES MEN WILL ARISE* [some to become church pillars], *SPEAKING PERVERSE THINGS, to draw away disciples after them. THEREFORE BE ON THE ALERT, ..."* (Ac 20:26-31)

Sha'ul knew the divine commission to carry *YAHshua's* name to the Gentiles was also a call to suffer and ultimately to die for the name of *YAHveh* and his Messiah *YAHshua.* Regarding his suffering and impending death, the faithful *Sha'ul* said, *"I am ready not only to be bound, but even TO DIE AT JERUSALEM FOR THE NAME OF THE LORD* [Master] *YAHSHUA"* (Ac 21:13).

The apostle reminds the redeemed to be holy because *YAHveh* is a holy God. *Sha'ul* said: *"Nevertheless, the firm foundation of YAHveh stands, having this seal, 'YAHveh KNOWS THOSE WHO ARE HIS,' and, 'LET EVERY ONE WHO NAMES THE NAME OF YAHVEH* [and *YAHshua*] *abstain from wickedness'"* (2Ti 2:19).

He prayed for the elect *"that He may establish your hearts unblamable in holiness before our God and Father at the coming of our Lord YAHshua with all His saints"* (1Th 3:13).

So then do not be foolish, BUT UNDERSTAND WHAT THE WILL OF

YAHVEH IS. ... always giving thanks for all things in THE NAME OF OUR LORD [Master] *YAHshua Messiah to YAHveh, even the Father;* (Eph 5:17-20)

The one who was willing to die for the name of *YAHshua* said:

... YAHveh highly exalted Him, and bestowed on Him THE NAME WHICH IS ABOVE EVERY NAME, that at THE NAME of YAHshua EVERY KNEE SHOULD BOW, of those who are in heaven, and on earth, and under the earth, and that every tongue should confess THAT YAHSHUA MESSIAH IS YAHVEH[1] TO THE GLORY OF YAHVEH THE FATHER. (Php 2:9-11)

From Stumbling Stone to Capstone

YAHshua and His name, which manifests the Father's holy name, have been the *stumbling stone* for the religious spirits throughout His sojourn on earth up to this day. He is the *"stone the builders* [Jews and Gentiles] *rejected"* which *"has become the capstone"* (Ps 118:22). *YAHshua*, and all that His name embodies in regard to *YAHveh's* salvation including His love and purpose for Israel, is the *chief cornerstone* of His eternal holy temple.

Let us join in praise with selected verses from the 118th Psalm.

YAHveh is my strength and song, and HE HAS BECOME MY SALVATION. ... Open to me the gates of righteousness; I shall enter through them, I shall give thanks to YAHveh. ... I shall give thanks to Thee, for Thou hast answered me; And Thou [YAHveh] hast become [YAHshua] my salvation. The stone which the builders rejected Has become the chief corner stone. This is YAHveh's doing; It is marvelous in our eyes. ... O YAHveh, DO SAVE, we beseech Thee; ... BLESSED IS THE ONE WHO COMES IN THE NAME OF YAHVEH; ... YAHVEH IS GOD, and HE HAS GIVEN US LIGHT; ... Give thanks to YAHveh, for He is good; for His lovingkindness is everlasting. (Ps 118:14, 19, 21-23, 25-27, 29)

---

[1] Modern translations incorrectly render this as "Jesus Christ is LORD [Master]." "He is God (Yahveh of the OT). Obviously this cannot mean personal Lord and Master of one's life, since those 'under the earth' (v. 10) could not acknowledge this." Footnote to Php 2:11, *Ryrie Study Bible* (Chicago: Moody Press, 1995), p. 1890.

Now, let us pause for this fervent prayer to go forth on the reader's behalf.

Heavenly Father: *May Your Holy Spirit be merciful to each reader who is ensnared and blinded by the doctrines of men and religious pride. Your Word says we will need no man to teach us because the Ruach HaKodesh will separate us from all falsehood and lead us into all truth. May the name of YAHveh the Father and YAHshua the Son not be a stone upon which Your remnant stumbles. I pray You'll open the blind eyes and the deaf ears that they may see You and hear Your voice. Declare Your name to a chosen remnant as you did to Sha'ul on his self-righteous and indignant religious path where You stopped him and said in the HEBREW DIALECT, "Saul, Saul [Sha'ul, Sha'ul], why are you persecuting me? ... I AM YAHSHUA ..."[1]*

YAHveh, in Your mercy please blind the eyes of human understanding of the reader and remove the shackles of spiritual sight. May You lead a remnant to wholeheartedly accept Your Son as He is both in name and essence YAHshua the Son of YAHveh, the Messiah of Israel. Enable the reader to reverence the blood of your Son with awe. Bring together Jews and Gentiles united as one new man through YAHshua's blood sacrifice. By the power of Your Spirit of Truth, bring forth a royal priesthood who will embrace You and Your holy memorial-name. Amen.

---

[1] Ref. Ac 26:14. From this Scripture, we must infer that the Savior identified Himself in the Hebrew name, *YAHshua.*

PART SEVEN

Dedicated to the Tribes of Joseph (Ephraim and Manasseh) and Benjamin

Joseph

(*Manasseh, Ephraim*)

Benjamin

THE WAY OF THE RIGHTEOUS IS SMOOTH;
O Upright One, make the path of the righteous level.
Indeed, while following the way of Thy judgments, O YAHveh,
We have waited for Thee eagerly;
THY NAME, EVEN THY MEMORY,
is the desire of our souls. ...
FOR WHEN THE EARTH EXPERIENCES THY JUDGMENTS,
THE INHABITANTS OF THE WORLD LEARN RIGHTEOUSNESS.
THOUGH THE WICKED IS SHOWN FAVOR,
HE DOES NOT LEARN RIGHTEOUSNESS; ...
O YAHveh our God,
other masters than Thou have ruled us;
But through Thee alone
WE CONFESS THY NAME.
(Isa 26:7-13)

Chapter 37
Merciful Warning from the Mercy Seat

YAHveh came to earth and dwelled among men in the person of His Son *YAHshua*. Messiah came to Israel at a time when His people were embroiled in a complex religious system intricately riddled with traditions. In the centuries prior to His appearance, "... the rabbis had built upon the Law of Moses an immense superstructure of ethical comments and minute injunctions, ..."[1]

Although the *Torah* was pure and holy and given by *YAHveh* through Moses to direct the people in righteousness, there were laws added by scribes (rabbis) that were handed down from generation to generation. The pious religious leaders' absolute obedience to the oral laws[2 & 3] of men became more important than absolute obedience to *YAHveh's* words.

> "SCRIBES, ... A class of learned men who made the systematic study of the law and its exposition their professional occupation. The majority of the scribes belonged to the Pharisee party which recognized the legal interpretations of the scribes. They were professional students who devoted themselves to the preservation, transcription, and exposition of the law. When during the Hellenistic period the upper priests became largely tainted with paganism, the scribes became the zealous defenders of the law and the true teachers of the common people. By NT times they held undisputed sway as the recognized exponents of the law and the revered representatives of Judaism. They received the deep respect of

---

[1] F.B. Meyer, Lance Wubbels, ed. *The Life of Paul*, (Lynnwood, WA: Emerald Books, 1995), p. 20.

[2] The oral law began during the intertestamental period from Malachi to Matthew. "... during this period there was created that mass of tradition, comment, and interpretation, known as *Mishna, Gemara* (forming the *Talmud*), *Midrashim,* and *Kabbala*, that was so superimposed upon the law that obedience was transferred from the law itself to traditional interpretations." *Study Bible, New International Version* (New York: Oxford University Press, 1967), p. 964.

[3] The oral law, "... a vast legal tradition, was not committed to writing but instead to memory by 'scribes.' It was carefully transmitted orally from rabbi to student from generation to generation ... The decentralization and dispersion of Jews to different parts of the world, and the *Continued on next page*

the people, as indicated in the honorable term *rabbi*, meaning 'my master, or teacher.' ... Accepting the law as the basis for the regulation of all of life, they made it their primary task to study, interpret, and expound that law as the rule for daily life. The lack of details in the law they filled up through the gradual development of an extensive and complicated system of teaching intended to safeguard the sanctity of the law. By their practice of making 'a fence about the law' they added to its actual requirements, thus loading the people with 'burdens grievous to be borne' (Luke 11:46; Matt. 23:4). ... This vast and complicated mass of scribal teaching, known as 'the tradition of the elders' (Matt. 15:2-6; Mark 7:1-13), was orally transmitted and required prolonged study to master. In their desire to know the law the common people readily turned to the legal experts as teachers. They taught in the synagogues, and trained their pupils in their scribal lore. All higher instruction, if not all instruction of the day, was in their hands. ... They constituted an important element in the membership of the Sanhedrin. ... Not all scribes were wholly bad, for Nicodemus and Gamaliel were scribes, but as a whole they were marked by spiritual corruption ..."[4]

YAHshua's displeasure with the distorted religious system of His day was not an issue over the purity of the *Torah* but over the traditions of men nullifying *YAHveh's* Word. The Son of *YAHveh* was righteously jealous and indignant over any transgression of the holy commands of His Father. Any doctrines

---

Continued from previous page overwhelming amount of material that had accumulated as part of the oral tradition by the third century, contributed to the growing fear that aspects of that tradition would become distorted or forgotten. It was these conditions that finally prompted Rabbi Yehudah ha-Nasi (Judah the Prince) of Palestine to commit a skeletal outline of the oral tradition to writing (circa 250 c.e.). The *Mishnah,* meaning 'teachings,' as it came to be known, was written entirely in Hebrew. It is a concise commentary on the Tanakh, or written tradition, and was transmitted orally from generation to generation until finally written down in the third century. ... The Mishnah, therefore, codifies the meaning and intent of the Torah in light of the generations-old oral tradition. The Misnah, along with its commentary, the Gemara, are together referred to as the *Talmud."* Rabbi Yechiel Eckstein, *What You Should Know About Jews and Judaism* (Chicago: International Fellowship of Christians and Jews, 1994), pp. 37, 39.

[4] *The Zondervan Pictorial Bible Dictionary*, s. v. "Scribes."

or traditions superimposed upon these were an offense when they produced self-righteous worshipers rather than those who worshiped Him in spirit and truth. YAHehua adamantly spoke out:

> *"Do not think that I came to abolish the Law or the Prophets; I did not come to abolish, but to fulfill. For truly I say to you, until heaven and earth pass away, not the smallest letter or stroke shall pass away from the Law, until all is accomplished."* (Mt 5:17-18)

He had strong words for their self-righteous adherence to the oral laws of men:

> *"... you nullify the word of God for the sake of your tradition. You hypocrites! Isaiah was right when he prophesied about you: 'These people honor me with their lips, but their hearts are far from me. They worship me in vain; their teachings are but rules taught by men.'"* (Mt 15:6-9 NIV.[5]

The religious system, with the Sanhedrin[6] as the central core, was composed of two conflicting groups, the Pharisees[7] [& 8] and the Sadducees.[9] [& 10]

> "each strove to promote its influence in civic matters and to establish its religious views as a true standard of

---

[5] Notes on Mt 15:2 "*the tradition of the elders.* After the Babylonian captivity, the Jewish rabbis began to make meticulous rules and regulations governing the daily life of the people. These were interpretations and applications of the law of Moses, handed down from generation to generation. In Jesus' day this 'tradition of the elders' was in oral form. It was not until A.D. 200 that it was put into writing in the Mishnah." *The NIV Study Bible*, (Grand Rapids: The Zondervan Corporation, 1985), p. 1464.

[6] "The supreme council which governed Jewish religious matters was the Sanhedrin. ... At times its decisions influenced Judaism all over the world. On other occasions its pronouncements were taken seriously only by the people living in Judea. ... Both Sadducees and Pharisees were represented in the council, its membership comprised of high priests, former high priests, members of the high priests' families, and heads of families or tribes called elders and scribes (legal authorities). A total of 70 to 71 made up the body ..." William L. Coleman, *Today's Handbook of Bible Times & Customs* (Minneapolis: Bethany House Publishers, 1984), p. 210.

[7] "A party bearing the name of Pharisee is first mentioned during the reign of John Hyrcanus (134-104 B.C.) ... The word **Pharisee** means 'separated one,' and the name probably meant, in the first instance, one who *Continued on next page*

Continued from previous page had separated himself from the corrupting influence of Hellenism in his zeal for the biblical Law. ... With a sincere desire to make the Law workable within the changing culture of the Greco-Roman world, the Pharisees developed systems of tradition which sought to apply the Law to a variety of circumstances. ... Tradition, in Pharisaic thought, began as a commentary on the Law, but it was ultimately raised to the level of Law itself. To justify this teaching, it was maintained that the 'oral law' was given by God to Moses on Mount Sinai along with the 'written law' or **Torah**. ... The ultimate in this development is reached when the **Mishna** states that oral law must be observed with greater stringency than the written law ... As in many worthy movements, the early piety of those who had separated themselves from impurity at great cost was exchanged for an attitude of pride in the observance of legal precepts. ... Pharisaism began well, and its perversion is a constant reminder that self-complacency and spiritual pride are temptations to which the pious are particularly susceptible." *The Open Bible, NKJV* (Nashville: Thomas Nelson Publishers, 1985), pp. 1344-1345.

8 "[The Pharisees] joined in the enthusiasm for the coming Messiah. Unfortunately, they were so confident in their own preconceptions that they could not recognize the Messiah when He came. ... As protectors they felt responsible to define the boundaries which would allow Jews to live safely before God. Thus their teachers built fences which would corral believers snugly within the borders of biblically acceptable behavior. ... Repeatedly they insisted on improving on God's laws. They thought obedience to God consisted mostly in details and not in love. ... Not every Pharisee fit into this distorted mold. Some vigorously complained about these petty practices and refused to keep the multiplicity of laws." William L. Coleman, op. cit., pp. 209-210.

9 "[The Sadducees] emerged from the turmoil of war with a firm grip on some important parts of Jewish life. First, they controlled the temple, the heart of the Jewish faith on earth. As its guardians they exercised tremendous power over its religious practices. ... after a series of corrupt transactions, they were able to purchase the office of high priest. For years they were able to hold the position by the sheer power of money. ... they managed to secure the leadership of the ruling Sanhedrin through their monopoly on the office of high priest. The people of this group held to rigid biblical interpretations, which included the denial of parts of the Old Testament because they were non-Mosaic. Therefore, there were certain widely held doctrines they could not accept. Generally, they denied the likelihood that God was concerned with their daily lives. ... They refused any doctrine of a physical resurrection (Matt. 22:23; Mark 12:18; Luke 20:27). They felt because the doctrine was not declared in the books of Moses, it was unacceptable. ... Their theology led them in a deistic position which saw God as a great Creator and Lawgiver who virtually divested himself of interest in this world." Ibid., p. 207. *Continued on next page*

devout Judaism. At the same time, other sects proliferated, ranging from those who withdrew into solitary asceticism devoted to spiritual life on one extreme to those who were committed to violent action on behalf of their beliefs on the other."[11] (also see — [12, 13, 14, 15, 16, & 17])

This cacophony of religious mind sets and dogmas created a whirlwind of spiritual fervor to which Messiah posed a threat to many of its stiff necked constituents.

Much of the priesthood of that time was no longer *Holy to YAHveh.* Most of the priests did not have *YAHveh's* favor resting

---

Continued from previous page [10] "The Sadducees were the party of the **Jerusalem aristocracy** and **high priesthood**. ... The Pharisaic attempts at applying the Law to new situations were rejected by the Sadducees, who restricted their concept of authority to the Torah, or Mosaic Law. They did not believe in resurrection, spirits, or angels ... With the destruction of the Temple in A.D. 70, the Sadducean party came to an end. Modern Judiasm traces its roots to the Pharisees." *The Open Bible, NKJV,* op. cit., p. 1345.

[11] Kaari Ward, ed., *Jesus and His Times* (Pleasantville, NY: The Reader's Digest Association, Inc., 1987), pp. 203-204.

[12] "Zealots. A few religious groups were deeply entrenched in their beliefs and were willing to both kill and die for them. The Zealots fit this category. Their name comes from the Hebrew words for 'zeal' and 'jealous.' They refused to tolerate the foreign societies which polluted their religion and controlled their government. Zealots willingly risked their lives in combat to serve their God and restore their nation." William L. Coleman, op. cit., p. 202.

[13] "Essenes. The Essenes felt just as strongly as the Zealots about the adulteration of their religion. As purists they longed for the 'good old days' which they imagined to be better and truer to God's laws. ... The Essenes believed that withdrawal and seclusion, not violent confrontation, were the best relief from an oppressive, pagan society." Ibid., p. 204.

[14] "Essenes and Pharisees both trace their roots to the orthodox leader of Maccabean times, who stood their ground against Hellenism. ... They maintained their separation from defilement, but not from the Jewish community itself. ... They seem to have lived for the most part in **monastic communities** such as the one which maintained headquarters at Qumran, near the northwest corner of Dead Sea." *The Open Bible, NKJV,* op. cit., p. 1345.

[15] "The meaning of the name [Essenes] is much debated; possibly it denotes 'holy ones.' ... The Essenes have come into public attention in late years because of the study of the Dead Sea scrolls, and the excavation of the monastery called Khirbet Qumran where the scrolls were written. ... The *Continued on next page*

upon them. Many were self-appointed and had political influence and/or financial inroads, buying their way into the priesthood and becoming functionaries along with the scribes, elders,[18] and rulers[19] (see Acts 4:5-8). The high priests outwardly were clothed in vestments of ceremonial purity and splendor; but their hearts were defiled with selfish ambition, self-righteousness, compromise, pride, and men-pleasing spirits.

The central core and focus of the religious system was the great temple built by Herod, an embellished replica of the previous holy temple erected by Solomon then rebuilt by Ezra. This grandiose edifice was one of the wonders of the world, and was the pride of the entire Jewish nation. Beauty, however, is in the eyes of the beholder. To the penetrating eyes of *YAHveh* dwelling in the person of *YAHshua*, Herod's masterpiece of

---

Continued from previous page literature reveals that the people of Qumran Community were avid students of Jewish Scriptures. Many scholars believe them to be the Essenes; ..." *The Zondervan Pictorial Bible Dictionary*, s. v. "Essenes."

[16] "The New Testament mentions **Herodians** (Mark 3:6; Matt 22:16) ... The Herodians appear to have been Jews of influence and standing who were well disposed to the Herodian rule and, as a result, to the Romans who supported the Herods." *The Open Bible*, NKJV, op. cit., p. 1346.

[17] "Herodians. A party mentioned only three times (Matt 22:16; Mark 12:13; 3:6) as joining with the Pharisees to oppose Jesus. Nothing more is known about them than what the Gospels state. It appears that they were neither a religious sect nor a political party, but Jews who supported the dynasty of Herod, and therefore the rule of Rome." *The Zondervan Pictorial Bible Dictionary*, s. v. "Herodians."

[18] "... the 'tradition of the elders' had definitely multiplied. ... until life became a veritable slavery. ... any breach of the rules was counted a heinous sin, to be punished by excommunication. This was the charge these Scribes and Pharisees brought against the disciples (Mk 7:1-8) ... They had committed the monstrous crime of breaking one of the multitudinous trumpery rules with which Rabbinism had burdened and encumbered human life." J.D. Jones, *Commentary on Mark* (Grand Rapids: Kregel Publications, 1992), p. 213.

[19] "... In the first three Gospels and in Acts there are numerous references to priests, elders, and rulers as functionaries within the communal and religious life of Judaism. Generally, they are mentioned together with one or more of the others ... Their primary duty was judicial. They were the custodians of the Law and its traditional interpretations ... and were charged with both its enforcement and the punishment of offenders." *Baker Encyclopedia of the Bible, Vol. 1.* s. v. "elders."

creativity and wealth was an abomination representing man's spiritual poverty, hypocrisy, and defilement.

Although Herod's temple may have been more glorious to behold than the former temples, *it was devoid of the divine presence of the eternal King.* The Holy of Holies, *YAHveh's* throne room, was vacant. There was no ark of the covenant, no mercy seat, no Shekinah glory—*YAHveh's* Spirit had departed. In essence, "Ichabod" was written by the finger of the Master Designer over this man-made wonder of the ancient world. *YAHveh* was giving warning that this was CONDEMNED PROPERTY.

Messiah did not come to bring *religion;* He came rather to bring *reconciliation* between sinful man and the Holy One of Israel. The Son of the Most High came to the religious masses in Israel and later for the Gentiles to purchase a righteous remnant for *YAHveh's* name, honor, and glory. *YAHshua* came to tear down all that was built by man on an erroneous foundation. He came to rebuild on the ancient foundations based on *YAHveh's* plumb line of truth.

When the Hebrew disciples marveled over the magnificent buildings and massive stones of the temple, *YAHshua* responded, *"... Not one stone shall be left upon another which will not be torn down"* (Mk 13:2). So it will be at the end of this age, when He destroys everything built by man contrary to His immutable decrees and purposes.

Herod's temple was built of earthly stones and erected to embrace man's religious traditions. As David's heir, *YAHshua* came to earth to purchase living stones for a holy temple in which His Father could dwell. He came to fulfill His forefather's passionate desire to build a temple for the ark bearing the name and glory of *YAHveh*, the Mighty One of Israel.

YAHveh's Dwelling among Men

In His desire to dwell among men, the Holy One had purposed through Moses that Israel should clear the land He had given them of all pagan defilement and customs. Anything unholy must be completely destroyed, it was to *"remain a ruin forever, never to be rebuilt."* YAHveh warned, *"None of those condemned things should be found in your hands, ..."* (Dt 13:16-17). Israel rebelled. Instead of cleansing the land of pagan influences and customs, she continued to embrace that which was abominable in His sight, mixing the profane with the pure worship of YAHveh.

Likewise, YAHshua was sent to purify the land of men's hearts with His sacrificial blood that they could become the dwelling place for the King of Glory. The hearts of redeemed men were to become the Holy of Holies housing YAHveh's throne and Shekinah presence.

No longer would a physical golden ark or a magnificent temple of massive stones be the location of YAHveh's dwelling among men. Through YAHshua's blood and by the power of His Spirit, only purified hearts would be suitable to house His divine presence.

The golden ark called by the name of YAHveh was not inquired of during the "Saul generation." Today, the "Saul generation" is likened to the compromised rule of many religious systems, where there is a grievous absence of YAHveh's glorious, life-changing presence.

In contrast, David retrieved the ark and restored YAHveh's name and glory to its ordained prominence among the people. Today, the "David generation" is a remnant who wholeheartedly loves the Most High God. This remnant, like David, desires to bring forth YAHveh's name from a place of obscurity beneath men's doctrines, to a place of eminence and reverential awe within the hearts of a holy people. This generation seeks to co-labor with YAHshua, the Son of David, in building a temple of living stones for the memorial-name and Shekinah glory of YAHveh.

Where Is the Ark?

What happened to the earthly throne of YAHveh's Shekinah? Where is the ark? In the present time, there is a great fervor in the modern-day nation of Israel concerning the rebuilding of the temple and the necessity of locating the missing original ark of the covenant to place in the Holy of Holies.

There is considerable controversy over when the ark actually disappeared and varying opinions as to where it may still be hidden. According to some scholars, the ark disappeared when Israel went into Babylonian captivity because of her rebellion against YAHveh's commandments.

Could it be that the ark, the throne of *YAHveh*, is living in the reality of *YAHshua* Who bears *YAHveh's* name and Shekinah glory?

YAHshua is the ark that bears *YAHveh's* name, the throne of *YAHveh's* presence and glory. He is the manna and the budding rod of the true priesthood; He is the Living Word of *YAHveh*. *YAHshua* is the sacrificial Lamb—the *Yom Kippur* sacrifice—who atones for the sins of all who repent for their transgressions of the Ten Commandments guarded within the ark.

The "David generation" will joyfully embrace and restore the divine name. This consecrated priesthood will radiate *YAHveh's* glory, having been cleansed and made holy by the blood of the lamb. With David, the remnant will say: *"Let us bring the ark of our God back to us, for we did not inquire of it during the reign of Saul"* (1Ch 13:3 NIV).

We will not find *YAHveh* in a magnificent golden structure built by men's hands. A holy priesthood will find the ark in the reality of *YAHshua* the Messiah. Although the original golden ark of the Old Testament may one day be found, it will no longer be the throne of *YAHveh's* Shekinah glory. *YAHshua* is the ark of the New Testament dwelling in the purified hearts of living temples. Truly this latter house of living stones and ultimately the New *YAHrushalayim* will be filled with more glory than all the former dwelling places of *YAHveh*.

The Holy One proclaimed this day to Jeremiah saying: *"... THEY SHALL SAY NO MORE, 'THE ARK OF THE COVENANT OF YAHVEH,' And it shall not come to mind, nor shall they remember it, NOR SHALL THEY MISS IT, NOR SHALL IT BE MADE AGAIN. At that time they shall call Jerusalem 'The Throne of YAHveh,' and all nations will be gathered to it, to Jerusalem [YAHrushalayim], FOR THE NAME OF YAHVEH; ..."* (Jer 3:16-17)

Requirements for Handling the Ark

To acknowledge the reality of *YAHshua* as the sacred ark is not enough. Israel recognized with awe that the divine presence over the ark brought victory over their enemies. They discovered however, through a major defeat to the Philistines when the ark was captured, that selfish motives and impure manipulations of the ark brought *YAHveh's* judgments rather than His grace and mercy.

When it was returned by the Philistines, many Israelites touched the ark with curiosity and died. The people, in dread of *YAHveh's* righteous judgments said, *"Who is able to stand before YAHveh, this holy God? And to whom shall He* [and the ark] *go up from us?"* (1Sa 6:20).

Likewise, David's first and zealous attempt to bring back the ark proved disastrous. He did not seek *YAHveh's* explicit instructions for handling it. Through negligence, David had allowed the mixing of the holy with a pagan custom of honoring deities. Following the method of the Philistines, David placed the ark on a wooden cart pulled by oxen. The oxen stumbled and Uzzah the priest reached out to steady the ark. This seemingly innocent move brought the joyous processional to a dramatic halt. *YAHveh* struck Uzzah dead for His irreverent touching of the ark.

"So David was afraid of YAHveh that day; and he said, 'How CAN THE ARK OF YAHVEH COME TO ME?'" (2Sa 6:9). David was learning the reality of *YAHveh's* word spoken through Moses: *"... 'By those who come near Me I WILL BE TREATED AS HOLY, ...'"* (Lev 10:3).

After this, David sought *YAHveh's* righteous requirements for handling the throne of His name and presence. He employed the "six-step-stop-sacrifice" method (2Sa 6:13) with awesome fear and wholehearted obedience and joyously brought the ark into Jerusalem.

As the ark was entering the City of David, Michal, daughter of Saul, watched from a window. Refusing to join this jubilant processional, she sat perched in her ivory tower, wrapped in self-righteous pride and indignation. She despised David as she saw him clothed in humble righteous garments, dancing and worshiping before the throne of *YAHveh*. Because of her contempt, the Almighty judged her with a barren womb (2Sa 6:23).

There will be many from the religious "Saul generation" who will be as Michal. With self-importance and unrighteous indignation, they will observe from a lofty distance, refusing to join the joyous processional at the return of *YAHveh's* name through *YAHshua*, the ark. But sadly, and also like Michal, they will bear no spiritual offspring for *YAHveh's* honor because they disdain rather than participate in the bringing back of *YAHveh's* name and glory.

"You Shall Not Misuse the Name"

True disciples bearing the name of *YAHveh* through *YAHshua* have NOT been given a key to success in appropriating their fleshy desires and selfish ambitions. Through Messiah's blood, we have been redeemed as priests whose obedient lives bring honor to the name we confess.

YAHshua spoke to His disciples of the *power and blessings of praying in His name.* He made it clear that prayers are not for selfish motives but for His Father's will and glory. Those who proclaim His name through *YAHshua* are to be separate from the world's systems and traditions. His name is to be spoken from clean lips by a priesthood separated from sin's defilement. *YAHshua's* name is a gift to the priesthood who have been given the privilege of proclaiming blessings and prayers in *YAHveh's* divine name (Nu 6:22-27).

YAHshua told His disciples that *"whatever you ASK IN MY NAME, that will I do, that the Father* [and His name] *may be glorified in the Son* [and His Name]. *If you ASK ME IN MY NAME, I will do it. IF YOU LOVE ME, YOU WILL KEEP MY COMMANDMENTS"* (Jn 14:13-15).

The power in the divine names of the Father and the Son brings greater responsibility, *greater blessings,* and *greater judgments* depending on how these holy names are used. According to His commandment, *"You shall not take the name of YAHveh your God in vain, for YAHveh will not leave him unpunished who takes His name in vain"* (Dt 5:11).

The name above all names WAS NOT and still IS NOT to be changed, hidden, or used in vain. That commandment must be acknowledged in order for a righteous remnant to walk in obedience before the Almighty.

At Risk of Trampling His Blood

Counting the cost is a continual process for the true follower of Messiah; working out our "*salvation with fear and trembling*" (Php 2:12) must not be underestimated. The blood of the only begotten Son of *YAHveh* must be focused upon and reverenced with wholehearted devotion.

YAHshua, the Passover Lamb—the *Yom Kippur* sacrifice— willingly shed His divine blood to cover the heavenly mercy seat.

He provided a way of redemption for a remnant who truly counts the cost to forsake the seductions of the world, carnal desires, and Satan's lies. *YAHshua's* sacrificial blood demolished the dividing wall between Jew and Gentile, making *one new man* for His Father's glory.

Through His atoning blood, a royal priesthood is redeemed, consecrated, and ushered into the eternal Holy of Holies; there in *YAHveh's* presence we find refuge from the coming righteous judgments soon to fall on the whole earth. Unless the priests are separate from all that is common and defiling, they cannot stand in His holy presence which is a consuming fire. The "religious majority" has little regard for the Almighty's righteous requirements. The *"fear of YAHveh is the beginning of wisdom"* (Ps 111:10; Pr 9:10 — cf. Pr 4:7), a wisdom sorely missing from the sectarian masses who call him "God" and "Lord."

The *Ruach HaKodesh* admonishes through both the apostle Paul and Moses:

"I urge you therefore, brethren, by the mercies of YAHveh, TO PRESENT YOUR BODIES A LIVING AND HOLY SACRIFICE, ACCEPTABLE TO YAHVEH, WHICH IS YOUR SPIRITUAL SERVICE OF WORSHIP. AND DO NOT BE CONFORMED to this world [including its man-tainted religious systems], BUT BE TRANSFORMED by the renewing of your mind [through the full counsel of YAHveh's Word], ..." (Ro 12:1-2). — "... 'YOU SHALL BE HOLY, FOR I YAHVEH YOUR GOD AM HOLY'" (Lev 19:2).

The prophet Malachi speaks of compromised priests who neither revere *YAHveh's* holy name nor honor His righteous requirements. In their hearts they say, *"... 'It is vain to serve God;* AND WHAT PROFIT IS IT THAT WE HAVE KEPT HIS CHARGE, AND THAT WE HAVE WALKED IN MOURNING BEFORE YAHVEH OF HOSTS? So now we call the arrogant blessed; not only are the doers of wickedness built up, but they also test God and escape'" (Mal 3:14-15).

Synagogues and churches are filled with multitudes who have no desire to live separated, righteous lives. Shallow confessions of faith are illustrated through their mixing of the common and the holy. The eternal King responds to this compromised priesthood:

Listen, O heavens, and hear, O earth; For YAHveh speaks, "SONS I HAVE REARED AND BROUGHT UP [to be Holy to YAHveh], BUT THEY HAVE REVOLTED AGAINST ME." ... THEY HAVE ABANDONED YAHVEH, THEY HAVE DESPISED THE HOLY ONE OF ISRAEL, THEY HAVE TURNED AWAY FROM HIM. ... HEAR THE WORD

OF YAHVEH, ... "WHAT ARE YOUR MULTIPLIED SACRIFICES [religious traditions and rituals] *TO ME?" Says YAHveh. ... "When you come to appear before Me, Who requires of you THIS TRAMPLING OF MY COURTS? Bring your worthless offerings* [the mixtures of the holy and the common] *no longer,* [Your] *Incense* [prayer] *is an abomination to Me. ... I am weary of bearing them. So when you spread out your hands in prayer, I will hide My eyes from you, Yes, even though you multiply prayers, I will not listen. Your hands are covered with blood. WASH YOURSELVES, MAKE YOURSELVES CLEAN; Remove the evil of your deeds from My sight. CEASE TO DO EVIL, LEARN TO DO GOOD; ... If you consent and obey, You will eat the best of the land; But if you refuse and rebel, you will be devoured ..." TRULY, THE MOUTH OF YAHVEH HAS SPOKEN.* (Isa 1:2-20)

The apostle Paul warned of the trampling underfoot of the atoning blood of *YAHshua.*

For if we go on sinning willfully after receiving the knowledge of the truth, there no longer remains a sacrifice for sins, but a certain terrifying expectation of judgment, and THE FURY OF A FIRE WHICH WILL CONSUME THE ADVERSARIES. Anyone who has set aside the Law of Moses dies without mercy ... HOW MUCH SEVERER PUNISHMENT DO YOU THINK HE WILL DESERVE WHO HAS TRAMPLED UNDERFOOT THE SON OF YAHVEH, AND HAS REGARDED AS UNCLEAN THE BLOOD of the covenant by which he was sanctified [through *YAHshua*], *and has INSULTED THE SPIRIT OF GRACE? ... "YAHVEH WILL JUDGE HIS PEOPLE." IT IS A TERRIFYING THING TO FALL INTO THE HANDS OF THE LIVING GOD.* (Heb 10:26-31)

The Most High has extended infinite mercy and grace to all who will receive it with humble hearts. *Through this grace, however, we do not have a license to transgress His righteous and immutable commands.* On the contrary, through His grace, mercy, and the cleansing by *YAHshua's* blood, His spirit empowers a separated priesthood to *uphold His righteous decrees.*

WARNING: Anyone who treats His *memorial-name* and His atoning blood with a hardened heart of irreverence, compromise, or selfish motives is at risk of trampling underfoot His precious blood. Anyone who calls Him "Lord and Savior," yet has contempt

246

for His holy requirements, is also at risk. Messiah said that not everyone who called Him "Lord, Lord" would enter His eternal kingdom (Mt 7:21).

May a humble remnant join the psalmist in praying:

Help us, [YAHveh] O God of our salvation

FOR THE GLORY OF THY NAME,

And deliver us,

and forgive our sins,

FOR THY NAME'S SAKE.

(Ps 79:9)

Chapter 38
Judgments from the Throne Room

His *memorial-name* is no longer to be hidden, for *YAHveh* will soon arise from His heavenly throne room and will make His name known in power, glory, and awesome judgments. Isaiah foresaw this day and said, "BEHOLD, THE NAME OF YAHVEH COMES FROM A REMOTE PLACE [from afar]; BURNING IS HIS ANGER, ..." (Isa 30:27).

"... *YAHveh abides forever; He has established His throne for judgment, And He will judge the world in righteousness;* ... THOSE WHO KNOW THY NAME WILL PUT THEIR TRUST IN THEE; *For Thou, O YAHveh, hast not forsaken those who seek Thee*" (Ps 9:7-10). — "*The voice of YAHveh will call* ... AND IT IS SOUND WISDOM TO FEAR THY NAME: ..." (Mic 6:9). — "*And it will come about that* WHOEVER CALLS ON THE NAME OF YAHVEH WILL BE DELIVERED; ..." (Joel 2:32).

All His name embodies will be magnified in His vengeance against those who have transgressed His righteous commandments and violated His statutes. The Holy One of Israel, whose name is the embodiment of His character as Israel's deliverer and redeemer, will be dramatically manifested when His name *"comes from afar"* (see Isa 30:27 NIV) to all who have mocked His decrees concerning His chosen people. *YAHveh* says concerning Israel's enemies:

"... *My sword is satiated in heaven, Behold it shall descend for judgment upon Edom* [symbolic of Israel's enemies], ... *for YAHveh has a sacrifice* ... *a great slaughter in the land of Edom.* ... A YEAR OF RECOMPENSE FOR THE CAUSE OF ZION. ... *He shall stretch over it the line of desolation And the plumb line of emptiness*" (Isa 34:5-11). — *Who is this who comes from Edom,* ... *This One who is majestic in His apparel, Marching in the greatness of His strength?* "IT IS I [YAHSHUA] WHO SPEAK IN RIGHTEOUSNESS, MIGHTY TO SAVE" (Isa 63:1). — "*For he who avenges blood* REMEMBERS; ..." (Ps 9:12 NIV).

Merciful Grace to Righteous Judgment

John the revelator, who had witnessed the onset of the age of grace, was given a panoramic vision of its cataclysmic end. He was shown the heavens opening up revealing the tabernacle with YAHveh's ark. The ark, YAHveh's throne and mercy seat, had now become a place of judgment.

> "AND THE TEMPLE OF YAHVEH WHICH IS IN HEAVEN WAS OPENED; AND THE ARK OF HIS COVENANT APPEARED IN HIS TEMPLE, and there were flashes of lightning and sounds and peals of thunder and an earthquake and a great hailstorm" (Rev 11:19). — "... the temple of the tabernacle of testimony in heaven was opened, and the seven angels who had the seven plagues came out of the temple, ... one of the four living creatures gave to the seven angels seven golden bowls full of the wrath of YAHveh, ... and no one was able to enter the temple until the seven plagues of the seven angels were finished" (Rev 15:5-8).

The age of grace and mercy through which Jews and Gentiles could approach the throne of YAHveh, had come to an end. The dramatic display at the giving of the Ten Commandments at Mount Sinai was now surpassed by the awesome display of YAHveh's forthcoming wrath from His ark. His commandments within the ark, His plumb line of truth, would now become a plumb line of flashing judgments stretched out over the defiled earth and the disobedient hearts of men.

The righteousness of His name which brought mercy and deliverance will bring the power of His righteous indignation and divine judgments. At this time, no one will be able to approach YAHveh's mercy seat, the ark; for in His sovereignty, He will cleanse the earth of all defilement in order to establish His eternal, righteous kingdom. This is the hope for those who faithfully obey YAHveh's commandments and hold fast to the testimony of YAHshua. Isaiah prophesied of this most sorrowful day:

> "The earth is also polluted by its inhabitants, FOR THEY TRANSGRESSED LAWS, VIOLATED STATUTES, BROKE THE EVERLASTING COVENANT... . Therefore, the inhabitants of the earth are burned, and few men are left." (Isa 24:5-6)

YAHveh's mercy will find ultimate fulfillment in cleansing the earth of everyone who has trampled the Lamb's blood under foot. The ark which had been the seat of the Lamb's mercy and forgiveness will become the seat of the Lion of the Tribe of Judah's vengeance and wrath.

YAHveh's sovereign judgments will pour out upon the whole earth, including the outer court of man's tainted religious systems. Many professing, lukewarm believers in the Almighty will encounter the "Wrathful Lion" and not the "Loving Lamb" as He comes forth in fury to uphold the glory and honor of YAHveh's holy *memorial-name* and righteous commandments.

> *For it is time for judgment to begin with the household of God; and if it begins with us first, what will be the outcome for those who do not obey the gospel of YAHveh? AND IF IT IS WITH DIFFICULTY THAT THE RIGHTEOUS IS SAVED, WHAT WILL BECOME OF THE GODLESS MAN AND THE SINNER? Therefore, let those also who suffer according to the will of God entrust their souls to a faithful Creator in doing what is right.* (1Pe 4:17-19)

It is time to avenge; He will repay.

"THEREFORE HAVING OVERLOOKED THE TIMES OF IGNORANCE, YAHVEH IS NOW DECLARING TO MEN THAT ALL EVERYWHERE SHOULD REPENT, because He has fixed a day in which HE WILL JUDGE THE WORLD IN RIGHTEOUSNESS through a Man [YAHshua] whom He has appointed, ..." (Ac 17:30-31)

"The Day Is Coming"

Directly preceding John's great revelation of the temple and ark in heaven, he heard a great holy proclamation:

> *"We give Thee thanks, O YAHveh God, the Almighty, who art and who wast, ... the nations were enraged, and Thy wrath came, and the time came for the dead to be judged, and the time to give their reward to Thy bond-servants the prophets and to the saints and to those who FEAR THY NAME, ..."* (Rev 11:17-18)

John saw and heard a heavenly throng singing the song of Moses originally sung and recorded in Deuteronomy 32. This song emphasizes YAHveh's *memorial-name* and all it embodies. It was a prophetic overview proclaimed to Israel in regards to YAHveh's sovereignty on her behalf. At the close of the age, His awesome name is being magnified into all eternity from the lips of a holy remnant. *"GREAT AND MARVELOUS ARE THY WORKS, ... RIGHTEOUS*

AND TRUE ARE THY WAYS, THOU KING OF THE NATIONS. WHO WILL NOT FEAR, O YAHVEH, AND GLORIFY THY NAME?..." (Rev 15:3-4).

The plagues of the angels sent forth from the tabernacle in heaven are the ultimate fulfillment of the curses spoken to His people in the plains of Moab before entering the Promised Land.

"IF YOU ARE NOT CAREFUL TO OBSERVE all the words of this law which are written in this book, TO FEAR THIS HONORED AND AWESOME NAME, YAHVEH YOUR GOD, then YAHveh will bring extraordinary plagues on you and your descendants, ... you shall be left few in number, ... because you did not obey YAHveh your God." (Dt 28:58-62)

The apostle Paul (*Sha'ul*) reminded the Gentiles that judgments as well as blessings are always first to the Jew and then to the Gentiles.

"... in the day of wrath and revelation of the righteous judgment of YAHveh, who WILL RENDER TO EVERY MAN ACCORDING TO HIS DEEDS: ... There will be tribulation and distress for every soul of man who does evil, of the Jew first and also of the Greek [Gentile], *BUT GLORY AND HONOR AND PEACE TO EVERY MAN WHO DOES GOOD, TO THE JEW FIRST AND ALSO TO THE GREEK. ... for not the hearers of the Law are just before YAHveh, but THE DOERS OF THE LAW WILL BE JUSTIFIED."* (Ro 2:5-13)

The heavenly Father speaks words of comfort and hope to His children, the remnant who are cleansed in His Son's blood and walk in wholehearted obedience to His commandments. Concerning the dreadful day of *YAHveh's* judgments, His word says, "SAY TO THE RIGHTEOUS THAT IT WILL GO WELL WITH THEM, ..." (Isa 3:10). — "*Because he has loved Me, therefore I will deliver him; I will set him securely on high, because he has KNOWN MY NAME*" (Ps 91:14).

Again, YAHveh encourages the remnant through Malachi's words,

... those who feared YAHveh spoke to one another, and YAHveh gave attention and heard it, and a BOOK OF REMEMBRANCE was written before Him for THOSE WHO FEAR YAHveh and WHO ESTEEM HIS NAME. "And they will be Mine," says YAHveh of hosts, "on the day that I prepare My own possession, and I WILL SPARE THEM as a man spares his own son who serves him." SO YOU WILL AGAIN DISTINGUISH BETWEEN THE RIGHTEOUS AND THE WICKED, between one who serves God and one who does not serve Him. (Mal 3:16-18)

251

"When I select an appointed time, It is I who judge with equity." (Psa 75:2)

"FOR BEHOLD, THE DAY IS COMING, BURNING LIKE A FURNACE; and all the arrogant and every evildoer will be chaff; ..." says YAHveh of hosts, *"so that it will leave them neither root nor branch* [a warning to any arrogant natural-Jewish and wild-Gentile olive tree branches]. *But for you who FEAR MY NAME the sun of righteousness will rise with healing in its wings; ..."* (Mal 4:1-2)

Isaiah prophesied the righteous will sing at the time of YAHveh's decreed destructions.

They raise their voices, they shout for joy. They cry out from the west concerning the majesty of YAHveh. THEREFORE GLORIFY YAHVEH in the east, THE NAME OF YAHVEH, THE GOD OF ISRAEL In the coastlands of the sea. From the ends of the earth we hear songs, "Glory to the Righteous One," ... THE EARTH REELS TO AND FRO LIKE A DRUNKARD, ... FOR ITS TRANSGRESSION IS HEAVY UPON IT, AND IT WILL FALL, NEVER TO RISE AGAIN. ... O YAHveh, Thou art my God; I will exalt Thee, I WILL GIVE THANKS TO THY NAME; For Thou hast worked wonders, ... For Thou hast made a city into a heap, A fortified city into a ruin; ... Therefore a strong people [a "David generation"] *will glorify Thee; ... And it will be said in that day, "Behold, this is our God for whom we have waited that He might save us. THIS IS YAHVEH FOR WHOM WE HAVE WAITED; LET US REJOICE AND BE GLAD IN HIS SALVATION."* (Isa 24:14-16, 20; 25:1-3, 9)

The holy priesthood secure within the Holy of Holies will proclaim,

Pour out Thy wrath

upon the nations which do not know Thee,

And upon the kingdoms which do not CALL UPON THY NAME. ...
(Ps 79:6)

We give thanks to Thee, O God,

WE GIVE THANKS, FOR THY NAME IS NEAR; ...

I will sing praises to the God of Jacob.
(Ps 75:1, 9)

For our heart rejoices in Him,
BECAUSE WE TRUST IN HIS HOLY NAME.
(Ps 33:21)

There is none like Thee, O YAHveh;
Thou art great,
and GREAT IS THY NAME IN MIGHT.
Who will not fear Thee, O King of the nations?
Indeed it is Thy due! ...
(Jer 10:6-7)

Chapter 39
"The Holiness of My Great Name"

As stated in the beginning of this book, biblical names were a vital embodiment of the nature and character of a person or deity. The Mighty One of Israel's name is likewise the very manifestation and embodiment of His character as first explained in Exodus 6:

> *God spoke further to Moses and said to him, "I AM YAHVEH;*
> *and I appeared to Abraham, Isaac, and Jacob, as God*
> *Almighty [El Shaddai in Hebrew[1]], but by My Name,*
> *YAHveh, I did not make Myself known to them. ... I have*
> *remembered My covenant. "Say, therefore, to the sons of*
> *Israel, 'I AM YAHVEH, and I WILL BRING YOU OUT ... I WILL*
> *DELIVER YOU ... I WILL ALSO REDEEM YOU with an outstretched*
> *arm and with great judgments. Then I WILL TAKE YOU FOR MY*
> *PEOPLE, AND I WILL BE YOUR GOD; and YOU SHALL KNOW THAT I*
> *AM YAHVEH YOUR GOD, ... And I WILL BRING YOU TO THE LAND*
> *WHICH I SWORE to give to Abraham, Isaac, and Jacob, and I*
> *will give it to you for a possession; I AM YAHVEH.'"* (Ex 6:2-
> 8)

At the close of the Gentile age, the Holy One of Israel is proving the sovereignty of His *memorial-name* and will accomplish *all* that His name *YAHveh* embodies:

"I WILL BRING YOU OUT" — He is regathering a remnant of Israel from Gentile nations where they have been dispersed.

"I WILL FREE YOU" — He will deliver Israel from her enemies.

"I WILL REDEEM YOU" — A remnant of Israel will embrace Messiah and be redeemed through faith in His atoning blood.

"I WILL BE YOUR GOD" — The surviving remnant of Israel will be His everlasting people with *YAHveh* dwelling in their midst.

"I WILL BRING YOU TO THE LAND I SWORE" — He will restore to Israel the ancient boundaries of *all* the land He promised her.

---

[1] *El Shaddai* IS NOT A NAME. The meaning "describes" *YAHveh* as a God who is "Almighty," "All-Sufficient," or the "All-Bountiful One." See Genesis 49:24-25.

254

YAHveh's name signifies He is the covenant-keeping God of Israel; He is also the covenant-keeping God of the redeemed remnant of Gentiles joined together with the remnant of Israel through Messiah's blood.

Through Ezekiel He said, "AND MY HOLY NAME I SHALL MAKE KNOWN IN THE MIDST OF MY PEOPLE ISRAEL; AND I SHALL NOT LET MY HOLY NAME BE PROFANED [dissolved] ANYMORE. AND THE NATIONS WILL KNOW THAT I AM YAHVEH, THE HOLY ONE IN ISRAEL. BEHOLD, IT IS COMING and it shall be done," declares the Lord YAHveh. "THAT IS THE DAY OF WHICH I HAVE SPOKEN." (Eze 39:7-8)

The Righteous One will complete His purpose for Israel; His sovereign promise to bring His chosen people into the eternal promised land will be mightily fulfilled.

"Therefore, say to the house of Israel, 'Thus says YAHveh God, "It is not for your sake, O house of Israel, that I am about to act, but FOR MY HOLY NAME, ... I WILL VINDICATE THE HOLINESS OF MY GREAT NAME WHICH HAS BEEN PROFANED [dissolved] AMONG THE NATIONS, ... THEN THE NATIONS WILL KNOW THAT I AM YAHVEH, ... when I prove Myself holy among you in their sight."'" (Eze 36:22-23)

"... I will take the sons of Israel from among the nations where they have gone, and I will gather them from every side and bring them into their own land; AND I WILL MAKE THEM ONE NATION IN THE LAND, ON THE MOUNTAINS OF ISRAEL; AND ONE KING WILL BE KING FOR ALL OF THEM; ... AND MY SERVANT DAVID [YAHshua, the Son of David] WILL BE KING OVER THEM, AND THEY WILL ALL HAVE ONE SHEPHERD; AND THEY WILL WALK IN MY ORDINANCES, AND KEEP MY STATUTES, AND OBSERVE THEM. ... they will live on the land ... they, and their sons, ... forever; and David My servant shall be their prince forever. ... and I ... WILL SET MY SANCTUARY IN THEIR MIDST FOREVER. My dwelling place also will be with them; ... And the nations will know that I am YAHveh who sanctifies Israel, when My sanctuary is in their midst forever."'" (Eze 37:21-28)

YAHveh's division of the land of Israel during the messianic kingdom is sovereignly ordained to be divided among the twelve tribes of Israel. With this divine allotment of the Promised Land comes a beautiful prophetic picture of the inclusion of Gentiles to be given a place with Israel as native-born Israelites.

"You are to distribute this land among yourselves according to the tribes of Israel. You are to allot it as an inheritance for yourselves and for the ALIENS [Gentiles] who have settled among you ... YOU ARE TO CONSIDER THEM AS NATIVE-BORN ISRAELITES; ALONG WITH YOU THEY ARE TO BE ALLOTTED AN INHERITANCE AMONG THE TRIBES OF ISRAEL." (Eze 47:21-22 NIV — emphasis added)

He Will Vindicate His Name

The mighty hand that brings redemption for Israel will also bring judgment upon all her enemies. Truly the name of *YAHveh* comes from afar with burning and wrath. Before the establishment of His eternal kingdom, He must cleanse the earth of every desecrating influence. All that is unholy, common, and man-made will not survive the sweeping hand of the Almighty when He comes to vindicate His holy name and fulfill His prophetic promises.

Many of the prophets foresaw the day when all the nations of the earth would be inflamed with the ancient Serpent's venom toward Israel.

"And it will come about in all the land," Declares YAHveh, "That two parts in it will be cut off and perish; But the third [a remnant] will be left in it. ... I will ... Refine them as silver is refined, And test them as gold is tested. THEY WILL CALL ON MY NAME, and I will answer them; I will say, 'They are My people,' And they will say, 'YAHveh is my God.'" "For I will gather all the nations against Jerusalem to battle, ... Then YAHveh will go forth and fight against those nations, as when He fights on a day of battle." (Zec 13:8-9; 14:2-3)

This will be the ultimate showdown between the Mighty One of Israel and Satan. In the climactic battle of Armageddon, *YAHshua*, as a mighty warrior, will stand on the Mount of Olives as the triumphant Commander in Chief of heaven's army. At last the ancient Serpent and all his anti-Jewish venom will be crushed under the feet of the eternal King of the Jews.

"And it will come about in that day that living waters will flow out of Jerusalem, ... YAHveh will be king over all the earth; in that day YAHveh will be the only one, and HIS NAME THE ONLY ONE" (Zec 14:8-9). — *"Thus says YAHveh of*

hosts, 'I am exceedingly jealous for Zion; ... I will return to Zion and will dwell in the midst of Jerusalem. Then Jerusalem [YAHrushalayim] will be called the CITY OF TRUTH, ...'" (Zec 8:2-3). — "... and the name of the city from that day shall be, 'YAHVEH IS THERE [YAHveh Shammah]'" (Eze 48:35).[2]

"'... Then Jerusalem [YAHrushalayim] will be called the CITY OF TRUTH, and the mountain of YAHveh of hosts will be called the HOLY MOUNTAIN.' ... Thus says YAHveh of hosts, 'Behold, I am going to save My people [the remnant of Israel] ... and I will bring them back, ... they will be My people and I will be their God in truth and righteousness.' Thus says YAHveh of hosts, 'Let your hands be strong, YOU WHO ARE LISTENING IN THESE DAYS TO THESE WORDS FROM THE MOUTH OF THE PROPHETS, ... I will not treat the remnant of this people as in the former days,' declares YAHveh of hosts." (Zec 8:3-11)

And YAHveh their God will save them [the Jews] in that day As the flock of His people; For they are as the stones of a crown, Sparkling in His land. (Zec 9:16)

"... I WILL SURELY GATHER THE REMNANT OF ISRAEL. I will put them together like sheep in the fold; ... So their king goes on before them, And YAHveh at their head." (Mic 2:12-13)

"... And I shall bring them back, Because I HAVE HAD COMPASSION ON THEM; And they will be AS THOUGH I HAD NOT REJECTED THEM, For I am YAHveh their God, and I will answer them. ... I WILL WHISTLE FOR THEM[3] TO GATHER THEM TOGETHER, For I have redeemed them; And they will be as

---

[2] The NIV Study Bible (Grand Rapids: The Zondervan Corporation, 1985), p. 1297 (footnote on Eze 48:35). "THE LORD IS THERE. The great decisive word concerning the holy city; in Hebrew, Yahweh-Shammah, a possible wordplay on Yerushalayim [more accurately, YAHrushalayim in reference to His name]" (emphasis added).

[3] YAHveh will whistle for His chosen people through various instruments. The hearts and mouths of the engrafted Gentiles have been ordained to be one of His most selected conduits through which this whistle will sound.

*numerous as they were before. ... And I shall strengthen
them in YAHveh, AND IN HIS NAME THEY WILL WALK," declares
YAHveh.* (Zec 10:6-12)

YAHveh proclaimed through the prophet, Zephaniah:
*"FOR THEN I WILL GIVE TO THE PEOPLES PURIFIED LIPS,[4] THAT ALL
OF THEM* [redeemed Jews and Gentiles] *MAY CALL ON THE
NAME OF YAHVEH, To serve Him shoulder to shoulder. ... I
will remove from your midst Your proud, exulting ones,
And you will never again be haughty On My holy
mountain. But I will leave among you A humble and lowly
people, And they will TAKE REFUGE IN THE NAME OF YAHVEH."*
(Zep 3:9-12)

Let the hearts of the redeemed "David generation" sing his
psalm, *"Let heaven and earth praise Him, ... For YAHveh will save
Zion ... AND THOSE WHO LOVE HIS NAME WILL DWELL IN IT"* (Ps 69:34-36).

Behold the Tabernacle of *YAHveh*

John saw the ending of the age under the wrath of *YAHveh* and
the beginning of the eternal kingdom built on His righteousness:
*"... THE TABERNACLE OF YAHVEH IS AMONG MEN, AND HE SHALL
DWELL AMONG THEM, ..." ... He who sits on the throne said,
"Behold, I am making all things new." ... "He who
overcomes shall inherit these things, and I will be his God
and he will be My son. ..."* (Rev 21:3-7)

*And he carried me away in the Spirit ... and showed me
the holy city, Jerusalem [YAHrushalayim], ... having the
glory of YAHveh. ... It had a great and high wall
[separating the holy from the common], WITH TWELVE GATES,
... and names were written on them, which are those of
the TWELVE TRIBES OF THE SONS OF ISRAEL. ... And the wall of
the city had TWELVE FOUNDATION STONES, and on them were
the twelve names of the TWELVE [Jewish] APOSTLES of the
Lamb. ... And the city is laid out as a square [as the Holy
of Holies], ... I saw no temple in it, for YAHveh God, the
Almighty, and the Lamb, are its temple. ... NOTHING UNCLEAN*

---

[4] Consecrated lips that speak according to His plumb line of truth—lips that
have been purified of all foreign substitutes and titles for His *memorial-name.*

AND NO ONE WHO PRACTICES ABOMINATION AND LYING [distortions of truth], SHALL EVER COME INTO IT, ... (Rev 21:10-27)

... *the throne of YAHveh and of the Lamb ... shall be in it, and His bond-servants* [the holy priesthood] *shall serve Him; and they shall see His face, and* HIS NAME SHALL BE ON THEIR FOREHEADS [like the diadem reading *Holy to YAHveh*]. (Rev 22:3-4)

And he said to me, "Do not seal up the words of the prophecy of this book, for the time is near. "LET THE ONE WHO DOES WRONG, STILL DO WRONG; *and let the one who is filthy, still be filthy; and let the one who is righteous, still practice righteousness;* AND LET THE ONE WHO IS HOLY, STILL KEEP HIMSELF HOLY." (Rev 22:10-11)

"Behold, I am coming quickly, and My reward is with Me, to render to every man according to what he has done. I AM ... *the first and the last* [the *Aleph* and the *Tav*[5]], *the beginning and the end. Blessed are those who wash their robes* [in the Lamb's blood], *that they may have the right to the tree of life, and may* ENTER BY THE GATES [of the twelve tribes of Israel] *into the city."* (Rev 22:12-14)

"I, YAHSHUA, HAVE SENT MY ANGEL TO TESTIFY TO YOU THESE THINGS ... I AM THE ROOT AND THE OFFSPRING OF DAVID, THE BRIGHT MORNING STAR." *He who testifies to these things says, "Yes, I am coming quickly."* ... (Rev 22:16, 20)

This book has been dedicated to the regathering of a remnant from the twelve tribes of Israel and a remnant of Gentiles to be joined with her, to become a priesthood made *Holy to YAHveh*. *YAHshua* is clarifying once and for all, in the conclusion of the holy Scriptures as well as the end of this book, that His soon-coming, eternal kingdom will be focused around *YAHveh* and a holy people. This priesthood will reverently serve Him and bear His *memorial-name* on their foreheads. He gives a clear picture that His messianic kingdom will be inextricably linked to His people, the twelve tribes of Israel, whose very names will be upon the entry gates into the heavenly Holy of Holies.

The priests of old were dressed in vestments of purity; they were also adorned with an ephod and a breastplate embellished with twelve gemstones representing the twelve tribes of Israel. The priests of today, like the original priesthood, are still reminded of

---

[5] The *Aleph* and *Tav* are the first and last letters of the Hebrew alphabet.

their responsibility to bear the twelve tribes upon their heart, bringing them in loving prayer and supplication before the God of Israel.

YAHshua, in the last paragraphs of the Scripture, is admonishing that a remnant must wash their robes in His blood of all that defiles including anti-Semitic attitudes (in the Gentiles), and anti-Messiah attitudes (in the Jews). Gentiles cannot go through the twelve gates of Israel bearing anti-Semitism in their hearts, for hypocrisy and disobedience will keep them from entering through those memorial gates. Likewise the Jews must humbly receive and reverence their Messiah with uncompromised obedience in order to go through their tribal gates into the eternal Promised Land. As *YAHshua* said, *"Behold, I am coming quickly,"* both Jews and Gentiles must consecrate themselves to become holy priests who can stand in His eternal presence.

Many truths have been revealed and magnified. May both Jew and Gentile hearken to *YAHshua* who gave His life that they might live in the New *YAHrusalayim* united as *one new man* before *YAHveh* the King of Glory.

Chapter 40
YAHveh's Resounding Heart Cry

Through the pages of *Holy to YAHveh, YAHshua's* Spirit has unsealed and opened much of His ancient scroll, magnifying many hidden truths. The bright light of His countenance is illuminating *YAHveh's* eternal words and inscribing them on humble hearts.

> "... 'He who has an ear, let him hear what the Spirit says ...'" "... He who is holy, who is true, who has the key of David, who opens and no one will shut, and who shuts and no one opens, says this: 'I know your deeds. Behold, I have put before you an open door [into My presence] which no one can shut, because you [the contrite and meek] have a little power, and have kept My word [without compromise], and have not DENIED MY NAME. ... Because you have kept the word of My perseverance, I also will keep you from the hour of testing, that hour WHICH IS ABOUT TO COME UPON THE WHOLE WORLD, to test those who dwell upon the earth. I am coming quickly; hold fast what you have [the full measure of truth], in order that no one take your crown. He who overcomes, I will make him a pillar in the temple of My God, and he will not go out from it anymore; and I will write upon him the NAME OF MY GOD, and the name of the city of My God, the new Jerusalem [YAHrushalayim] ...'" (Rev. 3:6-12)

Those who have willingly submitted to the pain of His flint knife by which He has cut away the foreskin of fleshly traditions and lusts, are ready to be consecrated as priests who are *Holy to YAHveh.* His precious blood is on the atonement cover of the heavenly ark, mercifully available for the cleansing of all who humbly request it.

This remnant has heard and heeded the heart cry of *EliYAHu.* They will no longer *"hesitate between two opinions"* (1Ki 18:21). In their circumcised hearts, through the work of the Spirit of Truth, they will be able to answer the question posed in Proverbs 30:4: *"What is His name or His son's name? Surely you know!"*

YAHveh is preparing a remnant that *surely knows* and will not deny His name. They are being called to co-labor with Him in restoring the *name above all names* to its ordained place of prominence within the Scriptures and within the hearts of a "David generation." This remnant understands the awesome responsibility and privilege of being priests made *Holy to YAHveh,* who bring honor to His *memorial-name. While they dwell on this earth, they will rehearse the name that eternally resounds in heaven!*

In his revelation of the Messiah, John was shown a remnant of 144,000 standing on Mount Zion with *YAHshua* at some time during the very last days. Although there is much controversy regarding who will compose this remnant (whether all Jews or both Jews and Gentiles), this scene nevertheless serves as an example to all who wholeheartedly desire *YAHveh* and His righteousness.

> *And I looked, and behold, the Lamb was standing on Mount Zion, and with Him one hundred and forty-four thousand, having HIS NAME and THE NAME OF HIS FATHER written on their foreheads* [like the priestly diadem]. ... *And they sang a new song before the throne ... These are the ones who have not been defiled with women*[1] [or through relationship with the pagan world system], *for they have kept themselves chaste. These are the ones who follow the Lamb wherever He goes. These have been purchased from among men as first fruits to YAHVEH and to the Lamb. And no lie was found in their mouth* [they spoke according to His plumb line of truth]; *they are blameless* [separated from all that is unholy]. (Rev 14:1-5)

The Spirit of Truth is ushering a remnant into His Most Holy Place, where His Shekinah dwells. It is before His throne that a remnant will be transformed from glory to glory, prepared as a spotless bride for her bridegroom's return.

The judgments of the righteous King will soon fall on all who veer from His holy commandments. The *"key of David,"* which includes reverential love for the name of *YAHveh* and *YAHshua,* opens the door for a priesthood to find refuge before the ark of *YAHveh* in His eternal Holy of Holies.

---

[1] *The NIV Study Bible* (Grand Rapids: The Zondervan Corporation, 1985), p.1941. Footnote to Rev 14:4: *"not defile themselves with women.* ... Probably a symbolic description of believers who kept themselves from defiling relationships with the pagan world system."

Whether they are Jews or Gentiles, no one will escape these sovereign judgments except through the blood of the Passover Lamb. *YAHshua's* blood must cover our hearts and separate us from all vestiges of this doomed world, including its man-tainted religious traditions.

Before the dreadful day of judgment, the Almighty is sending the spirit of Elijah as prophesied. Indeed, through the pages of this book, the spirit of *EliYAHu* has cried out to many hearts. He is *"THE VOICE OF ONE CRYING IN THE WILDERNESS, 'MAKE READY THE WAY OF YAHVEH, MAKE HIS PATHS STRAIGHT!'"* (Mt 3:3). *"And the axe is already laid at the root of the trees; every tree therefore that does not bear good fruit is cut down and thrown into the fire"* (Mt 3:10).

The crooked places, especially those made by human religious systems, have been revealed by His plumb line of truth. The high places of pride, arrogance, and compromise are being brought to light by His eternal words. Now the spirit of *EliYAHu* is beseeching a remnant to *"Repent, for the kingdom of heaven is at hand"* (Mt 3:2). Make *AliYAH*; return to the uncompromised worship of *YAHveh.*

As in the days of *EliYAHu, YAHveh* is heralding a remnant who will be as Elisha[2] who was willing to throw everything of earthly value into the fire to receive a double portion of *Elijah's* spirit and anointing (1Ki 19:21; 2Ki 2:9). This remnant is synonymous with true disciples who count the cost, denying themselves, their greeds and lusts to pay a high price as did Elisha. Without reserve they will throw the comforts and securities of their traditional ideals, lifestyles, and familiar religious systems (sometimes even pedestals and pulpits) into *YAHveh's* refiner's fire. This divinely chosen group will separate themselves from the compromises of the "Saul generation" to join the uncompromised ranks of the "David generation." With one voice, united by His truth, they will embrace, proclaim, and honor the holy *memorial-names* of *YAHveh* and *YAHshua.* Like David they will reverence all His name embodies regarding His love and plan for Israel. This generation has heard the resounding heart cry of *YAHveh.* They will readily harken to His words: *"... 'STAND AT THE CROSSROADS and look; ASK FOR THE ANCIENT PATHS, ask where the good way is, AND WALK IN IT, ...'"* (Jer 6:16 NIV)

To those who heed His call, the Almighty says: *"And those*

---

[2] Elisha, in Hebrew, is *Elishua*, which means "my God is salvation."

from among you will REBUILD THE ANCIENT RUINS; *You will raise up the age-old foundations; And you will be called the* REPAIRER OF THE BREACH, *" (Isa 58:12)*

Fervent Prayers for a Righteous Remnant

The desire of David's heart, which was a temple for *YAHveh's* name and presence, will soon be ready for the outpouring of His glory. Won't you yield as a living stone in the Master Builder's hands and allow Him to consecrate you as a priest made *Holy to YAHveh?* May each reader be led by the Spirit of Truth to the appropriate prayers that pertain to his or her specific spiritual needs. May the following prayers be sincerely offered by those who desire to humble themselves before His throne.

I. A Prayer for Eternal Life

Dear *YAHveh*: I haven't known You as my heavenly Father nor have I known Your Son *YAHshua* as my Savior. Until now, I've resisted the call to humble myself before You, a holy God. I've chosen my own ways and desired my own paths; but today, I've heard Your voice speaking deep into the recesses of my stubborn heart. I desire eternal life and not eternal death; I desire eternal blessings and not eternal curses. I desire You, *YAHveh*, to be my God and for *YAHshua* Messiah to be my Savior.

Your Word says if I confess with my mouth that *YAHshua* is *YAHveh* and believe in my heart that *YAHveh* raised Him from the dead, I'll be saved (Ro 10:9). I truly believe in my heart that *YAHveh* came to this earth to dwell in the person of *YAHshua*, and I confess with my mouth that *YAHshua* is my Redeemer and Master. I believe that *YAHshua* died in my place to atone for my sins and that *YAHveh* raised Him from the dead.

It's true I haven't lived honorably before You, the holy God. Please forgive me of my many sins. May the Lamb's blood that covers the heavenly mercy seat become the *Yom Kippur* sacrifice, once and for all, for me this day. May *YAHshua's* blood wash me of every sin and defiling element I've partaken of throughout my life. I give You my life this day; may Your atoning blood purify me. Thank You for giving me your righteousness in place of my unholy flesh and its many desires which destined me for destruction.

Thank You, *YAHshua*, for dying for my sins and giving me your righteousness, for being my *Yom Kippur* sacrifice, and for writing my name in the Lamb's Book of Life. Thank You, *YAHveh*, for loving me so much You allowed Your Son to become my Passover Lamb, and His sacrificial blood applied to my heart will spare me from eternal death. I invite *YAHshua* to dwell in the throne room of my heart and to rule and reign over my life.

Thank You for making me a new creature, cleansed by Your blood, and alive in the Spirit of *YAHshua* who now dwells in the temple of my heart. May I keep this temple clean. I want to be careful not to offend Your Holy Spirit by mixing Your holy things with the common and the profane. From this day on, help me live a life set apart and marked *Holy to YAHveh*—a priestly life, recognizing I have no inheritance in this world, for *YAHveh* is my double portion and my exceedingly great reward.

May I never look back and long for the pleasures of the flesh and its desires for the world. May I never turn my nose up at Your banquet table, calling Your ways of holiness contemptible. May I always with wholehearted devotion seek Your face, Your presence, and Your glory above everything else. May I live a life that brings Your name the praise, honor, and glory it deserves.

I ask You, *YAHshua*, to send Your *Ruach HaKodesh* to empower me with all I need to overcome sin, my flesh, and the pull of this world's system, including Satan's ploys. I've entered the narrow gate today and choose to make my pilgrimage on Your *Highway of Holiness*, making *AliYAH* ascending into Your glorious presence. Praise be to *YAHveh*, who was and is and is to come. Praise be to His glorious name forever and ever. Amen.

II. Prayer for Purification as a Priest
Holy to YAHveh

YAHveh: You've breathed the breath of Your life upon me, raising me up to behold Your glory. Thank You for revealing Your name and Your Son's most holy name to me. I'm grateful for the privilege of knowing You more intimately. I want to love You with all my heart, soul, mind, and strength; and I humbly embrace You and Your righteous ways. I acknowledge with awe all that Your *memorial-name* embodies. You're the great I AM. You are *YAHveh*, the Mighty One of Israel, and *YAHshua* the Messiah who continually sanctifies a priesthood of Jews and Gentiles, drawing them into your presence through Your atoning blood.

Thank You for ushering me out of the world's system and from the outer court of religion closer to Your Shekinah within the Holy of Holies. I'm grateful for Your sharp flint knife of truth, which is circumcising my heart. Even the pain of circumcision is a blessing that I welcome and I give you permission to continue cutting away the foreskin of flesh that separates me from the fuller understanding of Your heart, mind, and eternal purposes.

Surely it's Your mercy to show me the crooked places in my heart and in my own personal relationship with You. Thank You for the plumb line and the bright light of truth. These have exposed many of Satan's schemes which are working through the doctrines and traditions of men. Please forgive me and countless others, for in ignorance we've mixed the holy with the profane by partaking of rituals and traditions that are man-made and rooted in paganism.

Most grievously, Your name has been hidden because of the traditions of men. Until now, I didn't know Your holy *memorial-name* and its eternal importance to You and to me. Oh holy Father, forgive me and the innumerable multitudes who in ignorance have addressed You with common titles and haven't reverenced or proclaimed Your awesome name. I wholeheartedly pray for a remnant to hearken to Your voice, a "David generation" who'll restore Your *memorial-name* to a place of prominence and honor within the holy temples of their hearts.

I count the cost this day to forsake everything hindering me from glorious intimacy with You, my beloved King and Savior. The traditions of men and the doctrines of religion were all I knew. Thank You for the bright light of Your countenance which I choose from this day onward as I forsake all that is compromised, man-tainted, and pagan-rooted. May there be no mixture in me of the holy and the profane. Help me no longer to embrace anything that would defile and desecrate the living temple of my body which You purchased as a dwelling for Your name and glorious presence.

YAHveh, You alone are my heart's desire. I long to worship You in spirit and truth. I've heard the voice of *EliYAHu*. Your holy fire has descended upon my heart. I don't want to waver between two opinions; in my heart I know you are *YAHveh* the Father and that *YAHshua* is Your Son. I've seen the truth of Your oneness as expressed through Your *memorial-names*. I humble myself before You, desiring to see more of Your glory.

I offer You my life as a living sacrifice upon Your holy altar.

Let Your refiner's fire continue to purify me as it burns out every root and vestige of carnality, worldliness, and compromised religious traditions. Purify me as a priest who brings You offerings of righteousness as did Your priests in days of old. Thank You for *YAHshua's* atoning blood which has purchased me and consecrates me as a priest *Holy to YAHveh*. I take seriously this gift of a priest who is called to serve You. I realize I have no inheritance in the world, for You alone are my double portion and utmost blessing. I long to live as a Zadok priest, righteous and faithful in Your sight.

With reverential awe I bow before You, King of Kings, and I ask You to place Your priestly turban upon my head. May the presence of *YAHshua's* mind and thoughts lead and guide me with wisdom from above. Place upon me the gift of Your priestly ephod and breastplate that will keep the memorial of Your people burning within my heart and prayers to You. May Your *Ruach HaKodesh* teach me to distinguish between the holy and the common, that I may learn to direct others on Your *Highway of Holiness*. How gracious You are to draw me, through *YAHshua's* blood, from the distance of the world and the religious court, into the Holy of Holies to have fellowship with You, the King of eternity. Grant me, oh *YAHveh*, the courage and faith to stand with the "David generation." Out of the abundance of my heart, may my lips proclaim Your holy name bringing You praise, honor, and glory which is Your due. In the name of our High Priest *YAHshua*, Amen and Amen.

III. Prayer for Confession and Repentance of Anti-Semitism

YAHveh, God of Abraham, Isaac, and Jacob, You sovereignly promised in Genesis 12:3 to bless any who blesses and to curse any who curses Your people, Israel. I pray You'll have mercy on me, for in ignorance, apathy, and complacency I've allowed the venom of the ancient Serpent to be harbored in my heart and mind. Thank You for shining the bright light of truth on these tainted places.

You're a just King, and You'll act in righteousness. Your blessings and curses will show no favoritism; they'll fall upon the appropriate recipients at the time when You come to judge the world in righteousness. I'm sorry and I repent, for I've grieved

Your Spirit. I've confessed You with my lips but my heart has been far from Your heart for Your people, the Jews. I've called You "Lord and Master" in one breath, yet I've embraced wrong attitudes toward Your people rather than embracing them with a heart filled with love and compassion. *YAHshua* please forgive me; I haven't gathered with You; on the contrary, I've neglected Your Jewish brethren. Please cleanse me with Your blood.

YAHshua, You died and poured out Your blood to tear down the dividing wall between Jews and Gentiles. I confess in some ways I've allowed the ancient Serpent to reconstruct that dividing wall in my own heart, thwarting Your perfect will to reconcile Jews and Gentiles into *one new man.*

Thank You for humbling me and causing me to remember that I was once an alien (Eph 2:19), a Gentile with no place or heritage in Your promised blessings for Your chosen people. Thank You for extending Your mercy to the Gentiles who were *"far away"* (Eph 2:17) by bringing us near You. I'm grateful to be adopted into Your family, sharing with Your Jewish people their promised eternal blessings. I pray that together as *one new man,* reconciled through Your blood, we might become a holy remnant befitting Your *memorial-name* and eternal glory.

YAHveh, You're merciful to have made the two one. This is truly a mystery You've revealed to my once-arrogant heart. With humbled awe, I take seriously the apostle Paul's warning to me, an engrafted Gentile "branch" (Ro 11:17): *"Do not be arrogant... but fear; for if YAHveh did not spare the natural branches, neither will He spare you"* (Ro 11:18-21). The fear of *YAHveh* has given me wisdom and godly sorrow leading me to true repentance.

Thank You for magnifying Romans 11, enabling me to see how far I and corporate Christianity have veered from Your plumb line of truth. I pray You'll have mercy and remove every root and vestige of ancestral curses incurred through anti-Semitism that have found a place in my heart.

May I be an heir to the promised blessings ordained for those who bless Your people (Ge 12:3). Teach me Your ways that I may walk in Your paths. I desire to co-labor with You as You *"... arise and have compassion on Zion; ... to be gracious to her, For the appointed time has come"* (Ps 102:13). May I never in any way scatter those whom You long to gather. I fervently pray the Jewish people will be healed of all wounds inflicted throughout Christian history in the name of Jesus. I pray for a spirit of repentance to fall upon Your true remnant in regard to the deep pain caused to the Jews by corporate Christianity. I pray that in these last days Your blood will no longer be trampled by many who confess You as Lord, yet who are Satan's instruments to rebuild the dividing wall that You died to tear down.

Give me a heart like David's that I might be filled with Your love and purpose for Israel. As an engrafted wild olive branch, may I embrace Your holy Hebrew root, receiving its nourishing sap. I desire to behold and worship You, *YAHshua,* in the full light of Your Jewishness, stripped of all superimposed Gentile trappings and traditions of men.

May I share and express Your infinite lovingkindness to Your people Israel. I pray You would place upon my chest the ephod of a priest that I may always bear the twelve tribes of Israel upon my newly-circumcised heart, carrying them in prayer before You.

At the close of the Gentile age, as anti-Semitism flares one final time in the nostrils of the ancient Serpent, may I never again fall prey to his tactics. Help me to become a watchman on the wall for Israel, guarding my own heart and teaching others to recognize and resist his anti-Semitic venom. I wholeheartedly thank You for Your great mercy extended to me so that I might extend Your mercy to Your people the Jews.

YAHshua, as You're drawing Your Jewish brethren, may I co-labor with You. I choose to obey Your compelling words beseeching me to *"Build up, build up, prepare the road! Remove the obstacles out of the way of my people"* (Isa 57:14 NIV). May it be so, in the name of *YAHveh* and *YAHshua* by the power of Your Spirit. Amen and Amen.

IV. A Prayer to Heal the Anti-Semitic Wounds on Jewish Hearts

YAHveh: You love Your people Israel as a Father loves His firstborn son. *YAHshua,* You've never ceased to weep over Your brethren, longing to gather them as a mother hen gathers her chicks (Mt 23:37). Father in heaven, the Gentiles have received infinite mercy and blessings that were ordained to go to the Jews first. This same love and mercy has rarely been given from the Gentiles back to the Jewish people. I pray that You'll make streams in the desert of men's repentant hearts. May Your infinite love, Your river of life, find tributaries through these humbled hearts who bring Your love to Your beloved brethren. May a remnant hearken to Your cry to carry Your sons and daughters in their arms and on their shoulders back to You (Isa 49:22).

I grieve with You over the atrocities and damage that have been done in the name of Jesus Christ, causing Jews around the world to detest and run from any association with that name. *YAHveh,* forgive me and much of historical Christianity for falling prey to Satan's schemes through the doctrines and traditions of Gentile men. Forgive us for allowing anti-Semitism to breed within the body of the corporate church system. Have mercy and raise up a remnant of Gentiles who'll stand in the gap and repent for the stain of guilt resulting from Christian anti-Semitism. I pray You'll wash me and this remnant with Your blood, removing the resulting curses and spiritual sickness incurred by anti-Semitism. Please replace it with Your blessings of spiritual health and revival, raising up a holy priesthood for Your glory.

YAHveh Rapha, the Great Physician, pour out Your healing balm upon the Jewish people. May Your great love flow through the hearts of a humble remnant upon the deep wounds in individual Jewish hearts.

Thank You for Your Spirit of Truth, Who has opened my eyes, heart, and mind. I'm beginning to see my Savior and my faith in the light of the holy Hebrew root. May I and a righteous remnant bring the Jews a vivid portrait of *YAHshua* the Messiah, rightly conveying His Jewish nature and love to their hearts. I understand it's the *"set time to favor Zion"* (Ps 102:13). *YAHveh,* may I along with other Gentiles, help rebuild the ancient ruins of Your truths that have been distorted through the traditions and doctrines of men. May we uphold Your biblical mandates reflecting them in word and deed to Your chosen people. Please reveal to me the many ways I can personally bless Your Jewish people.

May our continual prayers on behalf of Israel be a major support in building up a spiritually healthy body filled with the glory of *YAHveh* almighty, the Holy One of Israel. May our hearts be so contrite and humbled that we hearken to the words of Isaiah to *comfort* Your people and to *speak tenderly* to them.

May I personally, as a Gentile believer in the Messiah, hearken to these mandates spoken by the prophets and the apostle Paul in regard to Your people. Please strengthen me by Your Spirit to heed this divine call to bring them the knowledge of *YAHveh* their God and *YAHshua* their Messiah. As part of the

"David generation," may I join in David's "Song of Accents," proclaiming:

Pray for the peace of Jerusalem [YAHrushalayim]: "May they prosper who love you. May peace [shalom] be within your walls, And prosperity within your palaces." For the sake of my brothers and my friends, I will now say, "May peace [shalom] be within you." For the sake of the house of YAHveh our God I will seek your good. (Ps 122:6-9)

In the name of *YAHveh* the Holy One of Israel and *YAHshua* the Messiah, Amen.

V. A Prayer to Be Prayed Specifically by Jewish People Who Desire to Embrace *YAHshua* the Messiah

Dear YAHveh—God of my forefathers, Abraham, Isaac, and Jacob—I acknowledge You, *YAHveh*, as my heavenly Father and Your Son *YAHshua* as my Messiah. Until now, I didn't reverence Your holy *memorial name* or know of its glory and importance to You. Surely I now know Your name is *YAHveh* and Your Son's name is *YAHshua*, and You are inseparably One.

YAHshua, I embrace You with all my heart, mind, soul, and strength. I love You; truly You're the promised Messiah whom I and my people Israel have long awaited. I sense You're standing and knocking at the door of my heart and I welcome You to enter and dwell within me. I want to be one with You as You and *YAHveh* are One. I acknowledge I've sinned; please forgive me for falling short of Your glory. Please cleanse me with Your atoning blood; I accept You as my *Yom Kippur* sacrifice. Make my heart as the Holy of Holies in which Your Shekinah dwells. Thank You for becoming the Passover Lamb whose blood saves me from eternal death and delivers me into eternal life. You are most worthy to be praised.

Please forgive me for my past rejections of You, for truly *YAHshua*, You gave Your life as a ransom for the Jew first. Thank You for Your infinite love and grace. I humbly receive You by faith with reverential awe, for You're the Holy One of Israel who came to dwell on earth in the person of *YAHshua* Messiah. Thank You for sacrificing Your life, making a way through Your blood to dwell by Your Spirit in my heart.

I'm sorry for the ways I've grieved Your *Ruach HaKodesh* by living apart from Your righteous decrees. I repent; please forgive me for pride, stubbornness, rebellion, lusts for this world, and all the sins that so easily beset me. I want to be part of Your eternal *one new man* (Eph 2:15) remnant whom You died to purchase. I welcome the heavenly *mohel*[3] to circumcise my heart. I pray *YAHshua*, You'll purify and consecrate me by the power of Your atoning blood and make me, like the Levites of old, a priest that is *Holy to YAHveh*. Teach me to live a life that will bring You the praise and honor due Your holy name.

Thank You for opening Your Scriptures to my understanding. You're the One of whom our prophets spoke and wrote. Thank You for lighting my path with Your truth. I desire to make spiritual *AliYAH* to ascend upward on Your *Highway of Holiness*, returning to the pure worship of *YAHveh*. I'm grateful I'm not required to become as a Gentile, forsaking my Jewish heritage. You've redeemed me to become a completed Jew to worship You in the spirit and truth of the holy Hebraic root.

Please forgive and cleanse me of negative attitudes. I pray for a heart of mercy and forgiveness for those who have wronged me and my Jewish people. I understand I can't blame the Gentiles for persecuting the Jews any more than the Gentiles can blame the Jews for killing the Messiah.

Thank you for showing me Satan's schemes; I understand more clearly that the continual hostility and persecution of the Jews stems from the ancient Serpent's venom and his diabolical strategies. Until now, I like many of my people, have been leery of many Gentiles and Christians and have viewed them as enemies.

I'm sorry for the anti-Christian and anti-Gentile attitudes I've harbored. May these attitudes, like the dividing wall, be torn down in my heart. I choose to forgive Christendom for their historical persecution of our people in the name of Jesus Christ.

I behold You as the King of Kings and desire for You to reign over my life from this day on. I thank You *YAHveh* for your infinite love in sending Your only begotten Son as the Passover Lamb and the *Yom Kippur* sacrifice for the world. I believe, *YAHshua*, You're the "firstfruit" of those to rise from the dead. I'm grateful for Your promise that all who believe in You and appropriate Your atoning blood won't see eternal death but will rise to eternal life.

---

[3] Pronounced *moy-l*. The Hebrew term for "the one who performs the circumcision."

May Your *Ruach HaKodesh* separate me from everything that hinders and defiles. May I wholeheartedly proclaim: "... *'BLESSED IS HE [YAHSHUA] WHO COMES IN THE NAME OF YAHVEH!'"* (Mt 23:39); *"SHEMA, ISRAEL! YAHVEH, ELOHEINU, YAHVEH 'ECHAD!"* — *"Hear, O Israel! YAHveh is our God, YAHveh is one!"* (Dt 6:4).

In the name of *YAHshua* my Messiah, Amen and Amen.

A Pastor and a Rabbi — A Heartwarming Story

This true story is a glowing example of *YAHveh* at work bringing peace and reconciliation between the Jews and Gentiles.

In 1992, the author was teaching on circumcision of the heart in a prominent church. At the close of the service, it was obvious the pastor had been sincerely humbled as *YAHveh* had spoken to his heart concerning His chosen people. Out of the overflow of his freshly circumcised heart, the pastor began to weep as he called for the congregation to join him in prayer. He asked that all the Jews present to come to the front that he might pray for them.

As his godly sorrow engulfed him and his eyes filled with tears, he repented asking for forgiveness from the God of Israel and from all of the Jews in attendance. With humble abandon, he began confessing his sins regarding the Jews, praying also for forgiveness for all anti-Semitic acts that had been committed through corporate Christianity in the name of Jesus Christ.

After this, the pastor asked me to go with him to visit the rabbi. Immersed in prayer and with contriteness of heart, the pastor and I met with the rabbi at the synagogue. It soon became obvious this was going to be an unusual interlude. The pastor expressed to the rabbi his new found love for Jewish people, then he took out a letter. With unceasing tears, he bathed the rabbi's anti Semitic wounds in a healing balm expressed through the sincerity of his words:

Dear Rabbi:

Several years ago, while living in Oregon, I had the opportunity to meet the local rabbi. During a brief conversation, I asked him a loaded question: "What do you think of Jesus Christ?" I wasn't being antagonistic; as a Christian, I really wanted to know. His response was candid. He told me that he thought Jesus was a good man and a good teacher, and that his problem really wasn't with Jesus at all; it was with Jesus's followers. He shared how it seemed wrong to him that those who claim to serve a man who taught love, acceptance, and forgiveness could treat others with such hatred. To the rabbi, it seemed that the attitudes and actions of Christians betrayed those of their master.

I thanked my new friend for his honesty, and promptly went on with my life, unchanged and unchallenged by his remarks.

Recently my mind has taken me back to that conversation of nearly ten years ago. I have begun to realize that the rabbi wasn't talking about some nebulous group of people somewhere "out there"; he was taking about me. My people, the Christians, had deeply hurt his people, the Jews. While I have never considered myself to be anti-Semitic, God has shown me that I have played a part in the pain of His people Israel, if not by sins of commission then by sins of omission, namely apathy and indifference. I have looked the other way concerning the horrible mistreatment of the Jews at the hands of the nations and the Church. I have neglected to pray for the Jews; I have failed to sense God's heart of love and care for His chosen people.

My greatest offense, however, has been to blame the Jews for the horrible crime of crucifying the one I call Savior. How easily my self-righteousness has prompted me to invoke the words of John: "He came to that which was His own, but His own did not receive Him." In reality, it was not a nation that was responsible for the crucifixion of Messiah, it was a person—me. It was not the collective sins of Israel that put Him on the cross, it was my sin that put Him there. How utterly deceived can a man be as to blame others for his own transgressions?

Rabbi, I come to you today to share the burden on my heart. On behalf of the Gentiles and especially on behalf of my fellow Christians, I acknowledge that we have sinned a great sin against you and your people ... we have sinned mightily against a holy God who calls Israel the apple of His eye ... and we have sinned tragically against Messiah who from His own lips, declared that *salvation is from the Jews. Please forgive us—please forgive me.*

I can only hope and pray that as God continues to reveal His heart concerning His chosen people, I will have the courage and commitment necessary to bring forth fruit in keeping with repentance. My desire is to become a true friend of Israel and to bear accurate testimony to the nature and character of the One about whom the angel said to Joseph, "You shall call His name YAHshua, for He shall save His people from their sins."

In YAHshua's name,
Pastor _____

Stunned and awestruck the rabbi responded, "It seems that at best we Jews have been tolerated by the Christians; this most humble display of grief and repentance is beyond what we could ever imagine." He then looked at me and said: "Truly your work and message help to bring reconciliation."

May this account serve as an example for Gentiles circumcised in heart who are prompted to obedience in blessing the Jews. This profound display of godly sorrow over the sins of Christendom will bypass the natural defense system of most Jewish people, allowing the love, mercy, and comfort of *YAHshua* to be deposited within their hearts. Fervent prayer and repentance are the first steps in reconciling Jews and Gentiles to one another and to the Holy One of Israel.

A Fitting Finale of *HalleluYAHs*

The concluding words of David in the book of Psalms are also a fitting conclusion for this book, which was written to bring forth a "David generation" and a "holy priesthood." May a remnant of redeemed Jews and Gentiles, together as *one new man,* wholeheartedly embrace, reverence, honor, and praise the *memorial-name* of *YAHveh.* "I will extol Thee, my God, O King; AND I WILL BLESS THY NAME FOREVER AND EVER. Every day I will bless Thee, AND I WILL PRAISE THY NAME FOREVER AND EVER" (Ps 145:1-2).

Great is YAHveh, and highly to be praised;
And His greatness is unsearchable... .
YAHveh is righteous in all His ways ...
YAHveh is near to all who call upon Him,
To all who CALL UPON HIM IN TRUTH.
He will fulfill the desire of those who fear Him;
He will also hear their cry and WILL SAVE THEM.
YAHveh keeps all who love Him ...
My mouth will speak the praise of YAHveh;
AND ALL FLESH WILL BLESS HIS HOLY NAME FOREVER AND EVER.
(Ps 145:3, 17-21)

YAHveh will reign forever,
Thy God, O Zion, to all generations... .
Praise YAHveh [HalleluYAH], O Jerusalem!
Praise your God, O Zion!
(Ps 146:10; 147:12)

HalleluYAH

Praise YAHveh!
Praise YAHveh [HalleluYAH] from the heavens;
Praise Him in the heights! Praise Him, all His angels;
Praise Him, all His hosts! Praise Him, sun and moon;
Praise Him, all stars of light! Praise Him, highest heavens ...
LET THEM PRAISE THE NAME OF YAHVEH ...
Praise YAHveh [HalleluYAH] from the earth ...
Kings of the earth and all peoples ...
Both young men and virgins; Old men and children.
LET THEM PRAISE THE NAME OF YAHVEH,
FOR HIS NAME ALONE IS EXALTED ...
And He has lifted up a horn for His people,
Praise for all His godly ones;
Even for the sons of Israel, a people near to Him.
Praise YAHveh [HalleluYAH]!
(Ps 148:1-14)

Let everything that has breath praise YAHveh. ...

HalleluYAH!
(Ps 150:6)

Dear *YAHveh*, in humility and awe I, Terrye Goldblum Seedman, thank You for Your utmost faithfulness: by Your Spirit You began this work and in mercy You have completed it. I thank You for the many hearts that You are circumcising with the flint knife of Your immutable truths. I am grateful for a remnant that has witnessed the opening of Your ancient scroll, seeing the magnification of Your eternal words and the glorification of Your holy *memorial-name.*

    I rejoice with You, *YAHshua*, my precious Messiah, for You are accomplishing the desire of Your heart, to prepare a priesthood who will truly be *Holy to YAHveh.* With deepest gratitude,

I will bow down ...

and will praise your name

for your love and your faithfulness,

FOR YOU HAVE EXALTED ABOVE ALL THINGS

YOUR NAME AND YOUR WORD.

(Ps 138:2 NIV — emphasis added)

Supplementary Items
Related to *Holy to YAHveh*

The two exclusive designs shown on the back cover have been fashioned into fine-quality jewelry. These service marked designs of the integrated star and cross, and the symbol depicting the oneness of *YAHveh's* and *YAHshua's* names are captured in several variations of men's and women's jewelry and are created in 14-karat yellow gold.

The sole purpose in producing these attractive and unique symbols into wearable items is to advance two of the vital scriptural truths contained in *Holy to YAHveh*. The first is a symbol of *reconciliation of Jews and Gentiles* through Messiah, and the second is the *oneness of the Father and Son* as conveyed through the sharing of their holy Hebrew *memorial-names*. These symbols are valuable witnessing tools in expressing their embodied truths for they will attract the attention of many who will inquire as to their meanings.

These original and exclusive designs are the property of the author and are solely authorized to be used by the Goldblum Seedman Corporation and may not be duplicated or reproduced in any manner.

A dynamic workbook accompanies *Holy to YAHveh*. This supplementary study guide will be most challenging and effective for individuals and groups who desire to grasp the depths of Scriptural truths revealed and magnified throughout *Holy to YAHveh*.

Reproductions of the front cover design are available in captivating 18 x 24 inch frameable posters. The symbols composing this glorious design are powerful teaching elements in visually conveying the message of *YAHveh* the holy God, His salvation through the blood of *YAHshua* the Lamb, and the high call for a priesthood to be *Holy to YAHveh*.

Proceeds from the sale of all items related to this book will be for the perpetuation of the life-changing and vital scriptural truths revealed and magnified through **Holy to YAHveh**. *Our hope is to facilitate the continual production and distribution of this book and others commissioned by* **YAHveh**.

The Goldblum Seedman Corporation is dedicated to reconciling both Jewish and Gentile people through *YAHshua* Messiah, for the glory of *YAHveh's memorial-name*, and for the advancement of His holy eternal kingdom.

For further information:

Phone (toll free)	—	1-888/"AWE NAME" (293-6263); ask for Operator 7
FAX	—	408/753-9432
Internet Access	—	http://www.yahveh.com and http://www.yhvh.com
Mailing address	—	The Goldblum Seedman Corporation P.O. Box 1371 Salinas, CA 93902

Scripture Index

Listing of all Scriptures quoted or referenced in this book—footnote references are also included. Number in parentheses indicates chapter.